C000156091

DREAMS
&
GHOSTS

ANDREW LANG

DOVER PUBLICATIONS, INC.
Mineola, New York

Bibliographical Note

This Dover edition, first published in 2020, is an unabridged republication of *The Book of Dreams and Ghosts,* originally published in 1897 by Longmans, Green, and Company, London.

Library of Congress Cataloging-in-Publication Data

Names: Lang, Andrew, 1844-1912, author.
Title: Dreams and ghosts / Andrew Lang.
Other titles: Book of dreams and ghosts
Description: Mineola, New York : Dover Publications, Inc., 2020. | "An unabridged republication of The Book of Dreams and Ghosts, originally published in 1897 by Longmans, Green, and Company, London." | Summary:
    "A pioneering anthropologist and folklorist, Andrew Lang was the first to compile a serious, critical survey of ghost stories. This volume presents scores of well-attested tales from civilizations around the world about visitations from spirits. Supernatural guests include the naked ghost, the wraith of the czarina, the dancing devil, and other apparitions from both the remote past and modern times"— Provided by publisher.
Identifiers: LCCN 2019035474 | ISBN 9780486841878 (trade paperback)
Subjects: LCSH: Ghosts. | Dreams.
Classification: LCC BF1461 .L22 2020 | DDC 133.1—dc23
LC record available at https://lccn.loc.gov/2019035474

Manufactured in the United States by LSC Communications
84187101
www.doverpublications.com

2 4 6 8 10 9 7 5 3 1

2019

PREFACE.

THE chief purpose of this book is, if fortune helps, to entertain people interested in the kind of narratives here collected. For the sake of orderly arrangement, the stories are classed in different grades, as they advance from the normal and familiar to the undeniably startling. At the same time an account of the current theories of Apparitions is offered, in language as free from technicalities as possible. According to modern opinion every "ghost" is a "hallucination," a false perception, the perception of something which is not present.

It has not been thought necessary to discuss the psychological and physiological processes involved in perception, real or false. Every "hallucination" is a perception, "as good and true a sensation as if there were a real object there. The object happens *not* to be there, that is all." [1] We are not here concerned with

---

[1] *Principles of Psychology*, vol. ii., p. 115. By Professor William James, Harvard College, Macmillan's, London, 1890. The physical processes believed to be involved, are described on pp. 123, 124 of the same work.

the visions of insanity, delirium, drugs, drink,
remorse, or anxiety, but with "sporadic cases
of hallucination, visiting people only once in a
lifetime, which seems to be by far the most
frequent type". "These," says Mr. James, "are
on any theory hard to understand in detail.
They are often extraordinarily complete; and
the fact that many of them are reported as
veridical, that is, as coinciding with real events,
such as accidents, deaths, etc., of the persons
seen, is an additional complication of the phenomenon."[1] A ghost, if seen, is undeniably so far a
"hallucination" that it gives the impression of
the presence of a real person, in flesh, blood,
and usually clothes. No such person in flesh,
blood, and clothes, is actually there. So far, at
least, every ghost is a hallucination, "*that*," in
the language of Captain Cuttle, "you may lay
to," without offending science, religion, or
common-sense. And that, in brief, is the
modern doctrine of ghosts.

The old doctrine of "ghosts" regarded them
as actual "spirits" of the living or the dead,
freed from the flesh or from the grave. This
view, whatever else may be said for it, represents
the simple philosophy of the savage, which may
be correct or erroneous. About the time of

[1] *Op. cit.*, ii., 130.

the Reformation, writers, especially Protestant writers, preferred to look on apparitions as the work of deceitful devils, who masqueraded in the aspect of the dead or living, or made up phantasms out of "compressed air". The common-sense of the eighteenth century dismissed all apparitions as "dreams" or hoaxes, or illusions caused by real objects misinterpreted, such as rats, cats, white posts, maniacs at large, sleep-walkers, thieves, and so forth. Modern science, when it admits the possibility of occasional hallucinations in the sane and healthy, also admits, of course, the existence of apparitions. These, for our purposes, are hallucinatory appearances occurring in the experience of people healthy and sane. The difficulty begins when we ask whether these appearances ever have any provoking mental cause outside the minds of the people who experience them— any cause arising in the minds of others, alive or dead. This is a question which orthodox psychology does not approach, standing aside from any evidence which may be produced.

This book does not pretend to be a convincing, but merely an illustrative collection of evidence. It may, or may not, suggest to some readers the desirableness of further inquiry; the author certainly does not hope to do more, if as much.

It may be urged that many of the stories here narrated come from remote times, and, as the testimony for these cannot be rigidly studied, that the old unauthenticated stories clash with the analogous tales current on better authority in our own day.   But these ancient legends are given, not as evidence, but for three reasons : first, because of their merit as mere stories ; next, because several of them are now perhaps for the first time offered with a critical discussion of their historical sources ; lastly, because the old legends seem to show how the fancy of periods less critical than ours dealt with such facts as are now reported in a dull un-dramatic manner.   Thus (1) the Icelandic ghost stories have peculiar literary merit as simple dramatic narratives.   (2) Every one has heard of the Wesley ghost, Sir George Villiers's spectre, Lord Lyttelton's ghost, the Beresford ghost, Mr. Williams's dream of Mr. Perceval's murder, and so forth.   But the original sources have not, as a rule, been examined in the ordinary spirit of calm historical criticism, by aid of a comparison of the earliest versions in print or manuscript.   (3) Even ghost stories, as a rule, have some basis of fact, whether fact of hallucination, or illusion, or imposture. They are, at lowest, "human documents".

Now, granting such facts (of imposture, hallucination, or what you will), as our dull, modern
narratives contain, we can regard these facts,
or things like these, as the *nuclei* which our less
critical ancestors elaborated into their extraordinary romances. In this way the belief in
demoniacal possession (distinguished, as such,
from madness and epilepsy) has its nucleus,
some contend, in the phenomena of alternating
personalities in certain patients. Their characters, ideas, habits, and even voices change, and
the most obvious solution of the problem, in the
past, was to suppose that a new alien personality
—a " devil "—had entered into the sufferer.

Again, the phenomena occurring in " haunted
houses " (whether caused, or not, by imposture
or hallucination, or both) were easily magnified
into such legends as that of Grettir and Glam,
and into the monstrosities of the witch trials.
Once more the simple hallucination of a dead
person's appearance in his house demanded an
explanation. This was easily given by evolving
a legend that he was a spirit, escaped from pur-
gatory or the grave, to fulfil a definite purpose.
The rarity of such purposeful ghosts in an age
like ours, so rich in ghost stories, must have a
cause. That cause is, probably, a dwindling of
the myth-making faculty.

Any one who takes these matters seriously, as facts in human nature, must have discovered the difficulty of getting evidence at first hand. This arises from several causes. First, the cock-sure common-sense of the years from 1660 to 1850, or so, regarded every one who had experience of a hallucination as a dupe, a lunatic, or a liar. In this healthy state of opinion, eminent people like Lord Brougham kept their experience to themselves, or, at most, nervously protested that they " were sure it was only a dream ". Next, to tell the story was, often, to enter on a narrative of intimate, perhaps painful, domestic circumstances. Thirdly, many persons now refuse information as a matter of "principle," or of "religious principle," though it is difficult to see where either principle or religion is concerned, if the witness is telling what he believes to be true. Next, some devotees of science aver that these studies may bring back faith by a side wind, and, with faith, the fires of Smithfield and the torturing of witches. These opponents are what Professor Huxley called "dreadful consequences argufiers," when similar reasons were urged against the doctrine of evolution. Their position is strongest when they maintain that these topics have a tendency to befog the intellect. A desire to prove the existence of "new forces" may beget indifference to logic and to the laws of evidence. This is true, and we have several dreadful examples among men otherwise scientific. But all studies have their temptations. Many a historian, to prove the guilt or innocence of Queen Mary, has put evidence, and logic, and common honesty far from him. Yet this is no reason for abandoning the study of history.

There is another class of difficulties. As anthropology becomes popular, every inquirer knows what customs he *ought* to find among savages, so, of course, he finds them. In the same way, people may now know what customs it is orthodox to find among ghosts, and may pretend to find them, or may simulate them by imposture. The white sheet and clanking chains are forsaken for a more realistic rendering of the ghostly part. The desire of social notoriety may beget wanton fabrications. In short, all studies have their perils, and these are among the dangers which beset the path of the inquirer into things ghostly. He must adopt the stoical maxim : " Be sober and do not believe "—in a hurry.

If there be truth in even one case of "telepathy," it will follow that the human soul is a thing endowed with attributes not yet recognised by science. It cannot be denied that this is a serious consideration, and that very startling consequences might be deduced from it; such beliefs, indeed, as were generally entertained in the ages of Christian darkness which preceded the present era of enlightenment. But our business in studies of any kind is, of course, with truth, as we are often told, not with the consequences, however ruinous to our most settled convictions, or however pernicious to society.

The very opposite objection comes from the side of religion. These things we learn, are spiritual mysteries into which men must not inquire. This is only a relic of the ancient opinion that he was an impious character who first launched a boat, God having made man a terrestrial animal. Assuredly God put us into a world of phenomena, and gave us inquiring minds. We have as much right to explore the phenomena of these minds as to explore the ocean. Again, if it be said that our inquiries may lead to an undignified theory of the future life (so far they have not led to any theory at all), that, also, is the position of the Dreadful Consequences Argufier. Lastly, "the stories may frighten children". For children the book is not written, any more than if it were a treatise on comparative anatomy.

The author has frequently been asked, both publicly and privately : " Do you believe in ghosts ? " One can only answer : " How do you define a ghost ? " I do believe, with all students of human nature, in hallucinations of one, or of several, or even of all the senses. But as to whether such hallucinations, among the sane, are ever caused by psychical influences from the minds of others, alive or dead, not communicated through the ordinary channels of sense, my mind is in a balance of doubt. It is a question of evidence.

In this collection many stories are given without the real names of the witnesses. In most of the cases the real names, and their owners, are well known to myself. In not publishing the names I only take the common privilege of writers on medicine and psychology. In other instances the names are known to the managers of the Society for Psychical Research, who have kindly permitted me to borrow from their collections.

While this book passed through the press, a long correspondence called " On the Trail of a Ghost " appeared in *The Times*. It illustrated the copious fallacies which haunt the human intellect. Thus it was maintained by some persons, and denied by others, that sounds of

unknown origin were occasionally heard in a
certain house. These, it was suggested, might
(if really heard) be caused by slight seismic
disturbances. Now many people argue,
"Blunderstone House is not haunted, for I
passed a night there, and nothing unusual
occurred". Apply this to a house where noises
are actually caused by young earthquakes.
Would anybody say: "There are no seismic
disturbances near Blunderstone House, for I
passed a night there, and none occurred"?
Why should a noisy ghost (if there is such a
thing) or a hallucinatory sound (if there is such
a thing), be expected to be more punctual and
pertinacious than a seismic disturbance? Again,
the gentleman who opened the correspondence
with a long statement on the negative side,
cried out, like others, for scientific publicity, for
names of people and places. But neither he
nor his allies gave their own names. He did
not precisely establish his claim to confidence by
publishing his version of private conversations.
Yet he expected science and the public to
believe his anonymous account of a conversation, with an unnamed person, at which he
did not and could not pretend to have been
present. He had a theory of sounds heard by
himself which could have been proved, or

disproved, in five minutes, by a simple experiment. But that experiment he does not say that he made.

This kind of evidence is thought good enough on the negative side. It certainly would not be accepted by any sane person for the affirmative side. If what is called psychical research has no other results, at least it enables us to perceive the fallacies which can impose on the credulity of common-sense.

In preparing this collection of tales, I owe much to Mr. W. A. Craigie, who translated the stories from the Gaelic and the Icelandic; to Miss Elspeth Campbell, who gives a version of the curious Argyll tradition of Ticonderoga (rhymed by Mr. Robert Louis Stevenson, who put a Cameron where a Campbell should be); to Miss Violet Simpson, who found the Windham MS. about the Duke of Buckingham's story, and made other researches; and to Miss Goodrich Freer, who pointed out the family version of " The Tyrone Ghost ".

CONTENTS.

CHAPTER I.

ARBUTHNOT, in his humorous work on *Political Lying*, commends the Whigs for occasionally trying the people with "great swingeing falsehoods". When these are once got down by the populace, anything may follow without difficulty. Excellently as this practice has worked in politics (compare the warming-pan lie of 1688), in the telling of ghost stories a different plan has its merits. Beginning with the common-place and familiar, and therefore credible, with the thin end of the wedge, in fact, a wise narrator will advance to the rather unusual, the extremely rare, the undeniably startling, and so arrive at statements which, without this discreet and gradual initiation, a hasty reader might, justly or unjustly, dismiss as " great swingeing falsehoods ".

The nature of things and of men has fortunately made this method at once easy, obvious, and scientific. Even in the rather fantastic realm of ghosts, the stories fall into regular groups, advancing in difficulty, like exercises in music or in a foreign language. We therefore start from the easiest Exercises in Belief, or even from those which present no difficulty at all. The defect of the method is that easy stories are dull reading. But the student can " skip ". We begin with common every-night dreams.

Sleeping is as natural as waking ; dreams are nearly as frequent as every-day sensations, thoughts, and emotions. But dreams, being familiar, are credible ; it is admitted that people do dream ; we reach the less credible as we advance to the less familiar. For, if we think for a moment, the alleged events of ghostdom—apparitions of all sorts—are precisely identical with the every-night phenomena of dreaming, except for the avowed element of sleep in dreams.

In dreams, time and space are annihilated, and two severed lovers may be made happy. In dreams, amidst a grotesque confusion of things remembered and things forgot, we *see* the events of the past (I have been at Culloden fight and at the siege of Troy); we are present in places remote; we behold the absent; we converse with the dead, and we may even (let us say by chance coincidence) forecast the future. All these things, except the last, are familiar to everybody who dreams. It is also certain that similar, but yet more vivid, false experiences may be produced, at the word of the hypnotiser, in persons under the hypnotic sleep. A hypnotised man will take water for wine, and get drunk on it.

Now, the ghostly is nothing but the experience, when men are awake, or *apparently* awake, of the every-night phenomena of dreaming. The vision of the absent seen by a waking, or apparently waking, man is called " a wraith "; the waking, or apparently waking, vision of the dead is called " a ghost ". Yet, as St. Augustine says, the absent man, or the dead man, may know no more of the vision, and may have no more to do with causing it, than have the absent or the dead whom we are perfectly accustomed to see in our dreams. Moreover, the comparatively rare cases in which two or more waking people are alleged to have seen the same " ghost," simultaneously or in succession, have *their* parallel in sleep, where two or more persons simultaneously dream the same dream. Of this curious fact let us give one example : the names only are altered.

THE DOG FANTI.

Mrs. Ogilvie of Drumquaigh had a poodle named Fanti. Her family, or at least those who lived with her, were her son, the laird, and three daughters. Of these the two younger, at a certain recent date, were paying a short visit to a neighbouring country house. Mrs. Ogilvie was accustomed to breakfast in her bedroom, not being in the best of health. One morning Miss Ogilvie came down to breakfast and said to her brother, " I had an odd dream; I dreamed Fanti went mad ".

" Well, that *is* odd," said her brother. " So did I. We had better not tell mother; it might make her nervous."

Miss Ogilvie went up after breakfast to see the elder lady, who said, " Do turn out Fanti; I dreamed last night that he went mad and bit ".

In the afternoon the two younger sisters came home.

" How did you enjoy yourselves ? " one of the others asked.

" We didn't sleep well. I was dreaming that Fanti went mad when Mary wakened me, and said she had dreamed Fanti went mad, and turned into a cat, and we threw him into the fire."

Thus, as several people may see the same ghost at once, several people may dream the same dream at once. As a matter of fact, Fanti lived, sane and harmless, " all the length of all his years ".[1]

[1] Story received from Miss ——; confirmed on inquiry by Drumquaigh.

Now, this anecdote is credible, certainly is credible by people who know the dreaming family. It is nothing more than a curiosity of coincidences ; and, as Fanti remained a sober, peaceful hound, in face of five dreamers, the absence of fulfilment increases the readiness of belief. But compare the case of the Swithinbanks. Mr. Swithinbank, on 20th May, 1883, signed for publication a statement to this effect :—

During the Peninsular war his father and his two brothers were quartered at Dover. Their family were at Bradford. The brothers slept in various quarters of Dover camp. One morning they met after parade. "O William, I have had a queer dream," said Mr. Swithinbank's father. "So have I," replied the brother, when, to the astonishment of both, the other brother, John, said, "I have had a queer dream as well. I dreamt that mother was dead." "So did I," said each of the other brothers. And the mother had died on the night of this dreaming. Mrs. Hudson, daughter of one of the brothers, heard the story from all three.[1]

The distribution of the fulfilled is less than that of the unfulfilled dream by three to five. It has the extra coincidence of the death. But as it is very common to dream of deaths, some such dreams must occasionally hit the target.

Other examples might be given of shared dreams :[2] they are only mentioned here to prove that all the *waking* experiences of things ghostly, such as visions

[1] *Phantasms of the Living*, ii., 382.
[2] To "send" a dream the old Egyptians wrote it out and made a cat swallow it !

of the absent and of the dead, and of the non-existent,
are familiar, and may even be common simultaneously
to several persons, in *sleep*. That men may sleep
without being aware of it, even while walking abroad;
that we may drift, while we think ourselves awake,
into a semi-somnolent state for a period of time perhaps almost imperceptible is certain enough. Now,
the peculiarity of sleep is to expand or contract time,
as we may choose to put the case. Alfred Maury,
the well-known writer on Greek religion, dreamed a
long, vivid dream of the Reign of Terror, of his own
trial before a Revolutionary Tribunal, and of his execution, in the moment of time during which he was
awakened by the accidental fall of a rod in the canopy
of his bed, which touched him on the neck. Thus
even a prolonged interview with a ghost may *conceivably* be, in real time, a less than momentary
dream occupying an imperceptible tenth of a second
of somnolence, the sleeper not realising that he has
been asleep.

Mark Twain, who is seriously interested in these
subjects, has published an experience illustrative of
such possibilities. He tells his tale at considerable
length, but it amounts to this:—

MARK TWAIN'S STORY.

Mark was smoking his cigar outside the door of
his house when he saw a man, a stranger, approaching him. Suddenly he ceased to be visible! Mark,
who had long desired to see a ghost, rushed into his
house to record the phenomenon. There, seated on

a chair in the hall, was the very man, who had come on some business. As Mark's negro footman acts, when the bell is rung, on the principle, "Perhaps they won't persevere," his master is wholly unable to account for the disappearance of the visitor, whom he never saw passing him or waiting at his door— except on the theory of an unconscious nap. Now, a disappearance is quite as mystical as an appearance, and much less common.

This theory, that apparitions come in an infinitesimal moment of sleep, while a man is conscious of his surroundings and believes himself to be awake was the current explanation of ghosts in the eighteenth century. Any educated man who "saw a ghost" or "had a hallucination" called it a "dream," as Lord Brougham and Lord Lyttelton did. But, if the death of the person seen coincided with his appearance to them, they illogically argued that, out of the innumerable multitude of dreams, some *must* coincide, accidentally, with facts. They strove to forget that though dreams in sleep are universal and countless, " dreams " in waking hours are extremely rare — unique, for instance, in Lord Brougham's own experience. Therefore, the odds against chance coincidence are very great.

Dreams only form subjects of good dream-stories when the vision coincides with and adequately represents an *unknown* event in the past, the present, or the future. We dream, however vividly, of the murder of Rizzio. Nobody is surprised at that, the incident being familiar to most people, in history and art. But, if we dreamed of being present at an unchronicled scene

in Queen Mary's life, and if, *after* the dream was recorded, a document proving its accuracy should be
for the first time recovered, then there is matter for
a good dream-story.[1] Again, we dream of an event
not to be naturally guessed or known by us, and our
dream (which should be recorded before tidings of
the fact arrive) tallies with the news of the event
when it comes. Or, finally, we dream of an event
(recording the dream), and that event occurs in the
future. In all these cases the actual occurrence of
the unknown event is the only addition to the dream's
usual power of crumpling up time and space.

As a rule such dreams are only mentioned *after*
the event, and so are not worth noticing. Very
often the dream is forgotten by the dreamer till he
hears of or sees the event. He is then either re-
minded of his dream by association of ideas or *he
has never dreamed at all*, and his belief that he has
dreamed is only a form of false memory, of the
common sensation of "having been here before,"
which he attributes to an awakened memory of a
real dream. Still more often the dream is unconsciously cooked by the narrator into harmony with
facts.

As a rule fulfilled dreams deal with the most
trivial affairs, and such as, being usual, may readily
occur by chance coincidence. Indeed it is impossible
to set limits to such coincidence, for it would indeed
be extraordinary if extraordinary coincidences never
occurred.

To take examples :—

[1] See "Queen Mary's Jewels" in chapter ii.

THE PIG IN THE DINING-ROOM.

Mrs. Atlay, wife of a late Bishop of Hereford, dreamed one night that there was a pig in the dining-room of the palace. She came downstairs, and in the hall told her governess and children of the dream, before family prayers. When these were over, nobody who was told the story having left the hall in the interval, she went into the dining-room and there was the pig. It was proved to have escaped from the sty after Mrs. Atlay got up. Here the dream is of the common grotesque type; millions of such things are dreamed. The event, the pig in the palace, is unusual, and the coincidence of pig and dream is still more so. But unusual events must occur, and each has millions of dreams as targets to aim at, so to speak. It would be surprising if no such target were ever hit.

Here is another case—curious because the dream was forgotten till the corresponding event occurred, but there was a slight discrepancy between event and dream.

THE MIGNONETTE.

Mrs. Herbert returned with her husband from London to their country home on the Border. They arrived rather late in the day, prepared to visit the garden, and decided to put off the visit till the morrow. At night Mrs. Herbert dreamed that they went into the garden, down a long walk to a mignonette bed near the vinery. The mignonette was black with innumerable bees, and Wilburd, the gardener, came up and advised Mr. and Mrs. Herbert not to go nearer. Next morning the pair went to the garden. The air round the mignonette was dark with *wasps*. Mrs. Herbert now first remembered and told her dream, adding, " but in the dream they were *bees* ". Wilburd now came up and advised them not to go nearer, as a wasps' nest had been injured and the wasps were on the warpath.

Here accidental coincidence is probable enough.[1]

There is another class of dreams very useful, and apparently not so very uncommon, that are veracious and communicate correct information, which the dreamer did not know that he knew and was very anxious to know. These are rare enough to be rather difficult to believe.

Thus :—

THE LOST CHEQUE.

Mr. A., a barrister, sat up one night to write letters, and about half-past twelve went out to put them in the post. On undressing he missed a cheque for a large sum, which he had received during the day. He hunted everywhere in vain, went to bed, slept, and dreamed that he saw the cheque curled round an area railing not far from his own door. He woke, got up, dressed, walked down the street and found his cheque in the place he had dreamed of. In his opinion he had noticed it fall from his pocket as he walked to the letter-box, without con-

---

[1] Narrated by Mrs. Herbert.

sciously remarking it, and his deeper memory awoke in slumber.[1]

THE DUCKS' EGGS.

A little girl of the author's family kept ducks and was anxious to sell the eggs to her mother. But the eggs could not be found by eager search. On going to bed she said, " Perhaps I shall dream of them ". Next morning she exclaimed, " I *did* dream of them, they are in a place between grey rock, broom, and mallow; that must be ' The Poney's Field' ! " And there the eggs were found.[2]

THE LOST KEY.

Lady X., after walking in a wood near her house in Ireland, found that she had lost an important key. She dreamed that it was lying at the root of a certain tree, where she found it next day, and her theory is the same as that of Mr. A., the owner of the lost cheque.[3]

[1] Story confirmed by Mr. A.

[2] This child had a more curious experience. Her nurse was very ill, and of course did not sleep in the nursery. One morning the little girl said, " Macpherson is better, I saw her come in last night with a candle in her hand. She just stooped over me and then went to Tom " (a younger brother) " and kissed him in his sleep." Macpherson had died in the night, and her attendants, of course, protested ignorance of her having left her deathbed.

[3] Story received from Lady X. See another good case in *Proceedings of the Psychical Society*, vol. xi., 1895, p. 397. In this case, however, the finder was not nearer than forty rods to the person who lost a watch in long grass. He assisted in the search, however, and may have seen the watch unconsciously, in a moment of absence of mind. Many other cases in *Proceedings of S.P.R.*

As a rule dreams throw everything into a dramatic form. Some one knocks at our door, and the dream bases a little drama on the noise; it constructs an explanatory myth, a myth to account for the noise, which is acted out in the theatre of the brain.

To take an instance, a disappointing one :—

THE LOST SECURITIES.

A lady dreamed that she was sitting at a window, watching the end of an autumn sunset. There came a knock at the front door and a gentleman and lady were ushered in. The gentleman wore an old-fashioned snuff-coloured suit, of the beginning of the century; he was, in fact, an aged uncle, who, during the Napoleonic wars, had been one of the English *détenus* in France. The lady was very beautiful and wore something like a black Spanish mantilla. The pair carried with them a curiously wrought steel box. Before conversation was begun, the maid (still in the dream) brought in the lady's chocolate and the figures vanished. When the maid withdrew, the figures reappeared standing by the table. The box was now open, and the old gentleman drew forth some yellow papers, written on in faded ink. These, he said, were lists of securities, which had been in his possession, when he went abroad in 18—, and in France became engaged to his beautiful companion.

"The securities," he said, "are now in the strong box of Messrs. —— ;" another rap at the door, and the actual maid entered with real hot water. It was

time to get up. The whole dream had its origin in
the first rap, heard by the dreamer and dramatised
into the arrival of visitors. Probably it did not last
for more than two or three seconds of real time. The
maid's second knock just prevented the revelation of
the name of " Messrs. ——," who, like the lady in the
mantilla, were probably non-existent people.[1]

Thus dream dramatises on the impulse of some
faint, hardly perceived real sensation. And thus
either mere empty fancies (as in the case of the lost
securities) or actual knowledge which we may have
once possessed but have totally forgotten, or conclusions which have passed through our brains as un-
heeded guesses, may in a dream be, as it were,
" revealed " through the lips of a character in the
brain's theatre—that character may, in fact, be alive,
or dead, or merely fantastical. A very good case is
given with this explanation (lost knowledge revived
in a dramatic dream about a dead man) by Sir
Walter Scott in a note to *The Antiquary*. Familiar
as the story is it may be offered here, for a reason
which will presently be obvious.

THE ARREARS OF TEIND.

" Mr. Rutherford, of Bowland, a gentleman of
landed property in the Vale of Gala, was prosecuted for a very considerable sum, the accumulated
arrears of teind (or tithe) for which he was said to
be indebted to a noble family, the titulars (lay im-
propriators of the tithes). Mr. Rutherford was

[1] Story received in a letter from the dreamer.

strongly impressed with the belief that his father
had, by a form of process peculiar to the law of
Scotland, purchased these teinds from the titular,
and, therefore, that the present prosecution was
groundless. But, after an industrious search among
his father's papers, an investigation among the public records and a careful inquiry among all persons
who had transacted law business for his father, no
evidence could be recovered to support his defence.
The period was now near at hand, when he conceived
the loss of his law-suit to be inevitable ; and he had
formed the determination to ride to Edinburgh next
day and make the best bargain he could in the way
of compromise. He went to bed with this resolution,
and, with all the circumstances of the case floating
upon his mind, had a dream to the following purpose.
His father, who had been many years dead, appeared
to him, he thought, and asked him why he was disturbed in his mind. In dreams men were not surprised at such apparitions. Mr. Rutherford thought
that he informed his father of the cause of his distress, adding that the payment of a considerable
sum of money was the more unpleasant to him
because he had a strong consciousness that it was
not due, though he was unable to recover any
evidence in support of his belief. 'You are right,
my son,' replied the paternal shade. ' I did ac-
quire right to these teinds for payment of which
you are now prosecuted. The papers relating to
the transaction are in the hands of Mr. ——, a
writer (or attorney), who is now retired from pro-
fessional business and resides at Inveresk, near

Edinburgh. He was a person whom I employed on that occasion for a particular reason, but who never on any other occasion transacted business on my account. It is very possible,' pursued the vision, 'that Mr. —— may have forgotten a matter which is now of a very old date; but you may call it to his recollection by this token, that when I came to pay his account there was difficulty in getting change for a Portugal piece of gold and we were forced to drink out the balance at a tavern.'

"Mr. Rutherford awoke in the morning with all the words of the vision imprinted on his mind, and thought it worth while to walk across the country to Inveresk instead of going straight to Edinburgh. When he came there he waited on the gentleman mentioned in the dream—a very old man. Without saying anything of the vision he inquired whether he ever remembered having conducted such a matter for his deceased father. The old gentleman could not at first bring the circumstance to his recollection, but on mention of the Portugal piece of gold the whole returned upon his memory. He made an immediate search for the papers and recovered them, so that Mr. Rutherford carried to Edinburgh the documents necessary to gain the cause which he was on the verge of losing."

The story is reproduced because it is clearly one of the tales which come round in cycles, either because events repeat themselves or because people will unconsciously localise old legends in new places and assign old occurrences or fables to new

persons. Thus every one has heard how Lord Westbury called a certain man in the Herald's office " a
foolish old fellow who did not even know his own
foolish old business ". Lord Westbury may very
well have said this, but long before his time the
remark was attributed to the famous Lord Chesterfield. Lord Westbury may have quoted it from
Chesterfield or hit on it by accident, or the old
story may have been assigned to him. In the
same way Mr. Rutherford may have had his dream
or the following tale of St. Augustine's (also cited
by Scott) may have been attributed to him, with the
picturesque addition about the piece of Portuguese
gold. Except for the piece of Portuguese gold St.
Augustine practically tells the anecdote in his *De
Cura pro Mortuis Habenda*, adding the acute reflection
which follows.[1]

" Of a surety, when we were at Milan, we heard
tell of a certain person of whom was demanded
payment of a debt, with production of his deceased
father's acknowledgment, which debt, unknown to
the son, the father had paid, whereupon the man
began to be very sorrowful, and to marvel that his
father while dying did not tell him what he owed
when he also made his will. Then in this exceeding
anxiousness of his, his said father appeared to him
in a dream, and made known to him where was
the counter acknowledgment by which that acknowledgment was cancelled. Which when the young
man had found and showed, he not only rebutted

---

[1] Augustine. In Library of the Fathers, *XVII. Short Treatises*,
pp. 530-531.

the wrongful claim of a false debt, but also got back his father's note of hand, which the father had not got back when the money was paid.

"Here then the soul of a man is supposed to have had care for his son, and to have come to him in his sleep, that, teaching him what he did not know, he might relieve him of a great trouble. But about the very same time as we heard this, it chanced at Carthage that the rhetorician Eulogius, who had been my disciple in that art, being (as he himself, after our return to Africa, told us the story) in course of lecturing to his disciples on Cicero's rhetorical books, as he looked over the portion of reading which he was to deliver on the following day, fell upon a certain passage, and not being able to understand it, was scarce able to sleep for the trouble of his mind : in which night, as he dreamed, I expounded to him that which he did not understand ; nay, not I, but my likeness, while I was unconscious of the thing and far away beyond sea, it might be doing, or it might be dreaming, some other thing, and not in the least caring for his cares. In what way these things come about I know not ; but in what way soever they come, why do we not believe it comes in the same way for a person in a dream to see a dead man, as it comes that he sees a living man ? both, no doubt, neither knowing nor caring who dreams of their images, or where or when.

"Like dreams, moreover, are some visions of persons awake, who have had their senses troubled, such as phrenetic persons, or those who are mad in any way, for they, too, talk to themselves just as though they were speaking to people verily present, and as well with absent men as with present, whose images they perceive whether persons living or dead. But just as they who live are unconscious that they are seen of them and talk with them (for indeed they are not really themselves present, or themselves make speeches, but through troubled senses these persons are wrought upon by such like imaginary visions), just so they also who have departed this life, to persons thus affected appear as present while they be absent, and are themselves utterly unconscious whether any man sees them in regard of their image."[1]

St. Augustine adds a similar story of a trance.

THE TWO CURMAS.

A rustic named Curma, of Tullium, near Hippo, Augustine's town, fell into a catalepsy. On reviving he said: " Run to the house of Curma the smith and see what is going on ". Curma the smith was found to have died just when the other Curma awoke. " I knew it," said the invalid, "for I heard it said in that place whence I have returned that not I, Curma of the Curia, but Curma the smith, was wanted." But Curma of the Curia saw living as well as dead people, among others Augustine, who, in his vision, baptised him at Hippo. Curma then, in the vision, went to Paradise, where he was told to go and be baptised. He said it had

[1] St. Augustine, *De Cura pro Mortuis.*

been done already, and was answered, " Go and be truly baptised, for *that* thou didst but see in vision". So Augustine christened him, and later, hearing of the trance, asked him about it, when he repeated the tale already familiar to his neighbours. Augustine thinks it a mere dream, and apparently regards the death of Curma the smith as a casual coincidence. *Un esprit fort, le Saint Augustin !*

" If the dead could come in dreams," he says, " my pious mother would no night fail to visit me. Far be the thought that she should, by a happier life, have been made so cruel that, when aught vexes my heart, she should not even console in a dream the son whom she loved with an only love."

Not only things once probably known, yet forgotten, but knowledge never *consciously* thought out, may be revealed in a dramatic dream, apparently through the lips of the dead or the never existent. The books of psychology are rich in examples of problems worked out, or music or poetry composed in sleep. The following is a more recent and very striking example :—

THE ASSYRIAN PRIEST

Herr H. V. Hilprecht is Professor of Assyriology in the University of Pennsylvania. That university had despatched an expedition to explore the ruins of Babylon, and sketches of the objects discovered had been sent home. Among these were drawings of two small fragments of agate, inscribed with characters. One Saturday night in March, 1893, Professor Hilprecht had wearied himself with puzzling over these two fragments, which were supposed to be broken pieces of finger-rings. He was inclined, from the nature of the characters, to date them about 1700-1140 B.C.; and as the first character of the third line of the first fragment seemed to read KU, he guessed that it might stand for Kurigalzu, a king of that name.

About midnight the professor went, weary and perplexed, to bed.

"Then I dreamed the following remarkable dream. A tall thin priest of the old pre-Christian Nippur, about forty years of age, and clad in a simple *abba*, led me to the treasure-chamber of the temple, on its south-east side. He went with me into a small low-ceiled room without windows, in which there was a large wooden chest, while scraps of agate and *lapis lazuli* lay scattered on the floor. Here he addressed me as follows :—

" ' The two fragments, which you have published separately upon pages 22 and 26, *belong together*' " (this amazing Assyrian priest spoke American !).[1] " ' They are not finger-rings, and their history is as follows :—

" ' King Kurigalzu (about 1300 B.C.) once sent to the temple of Bel, among other articles of agate and *lapis lazuli*, an inscribed votive cylinder of agate. Then the priests suddenly received the command to make for the statue of the god Nibib a pair of ear-rings of agate. We were in great dismay, since there was no agate as raw material at hand. In order to execute the command there was nothing

---

[1] The professor is not sure whether he spoke English or German.

for us to do but cut the votive cylinder in three parts, thus making three rings, each of which contained a portion of the original inscription. The first two rings served as ear-rings for the statue of the god; the two fragments which have given you so much trouble are parts of them. If you will put the two together, you will have confirmation of my words. But the third ring you have not found yet, and you never will find it.'"

The professor awoke, bounded out of bed, as Mrs. Hilprecht testifies, and was heard crying from his study, "It is so, it is so!" Mrs. Hilprecht followed her lord, "and satisfied myself in the midnight hour as to the outcome of his most interesting dream".

The professor, however, says that he awoke, told his wife the dream, and verified it next day. Both statements are correct. There were two sets of drawings, one in the study (used that night) one used next day in the University Library.

The inscription ran thus, the missing fragment being restored, "by analogy from many similar inscriptions" :—

> To the god Nibib, child
> of the god Bel,
> his Lord
> Kurigalzu,
> Pontifex of the god Bel
> has presented it.

But, in the drawings, the fragments were of different colours, so that a student working on the drawings would not guess them to be parts of one cylinder. Professor Hilprecht, however, examined the two actual fragments in the Imperial Museum at Constantinople. They lay in two distinct cases, but, when put together, fitted. When cut asunder of old, in Babylon, the white vein of the stone showed on one fragment, the grey surface on the other.

Professor Romaine Newbold, who publishes this dream, explains that the professor had unconsciously reasoned out his facts, the difference of colour in the two pieces of agate disappearing in the dream. The professor had heard from Dr. Peters of the expedition, that a room had been discovered with fragments of a wooden box and chips of agate and *lapis lazuli*. The sleeping mind " combined its information," reasoned rightly from it, and threw its own conclusions into a dramatic form, receiving the information from the lips of a priest of Nippur.

Probably we do a good deal of reasoning in sleep. Professor Hilprecht, in 1882-83, was working at a translation of an inscription wherein came *Nabû—Kudûrru—usur*, rendered by Professor Delitzsch "Nebo protect my mortar-board". Professor Hilprecht accepted this, but woke one morning with his mind full of the thought that the words should be rendered " Nebo protect my boundary," which " sounds a deal likelier," and is now accepted. I myself, when working out the MSS. of the exiled Stuarts, was puzzled by the scorched appearance of the paper on which Prince Charlie's and the king's letters were

often written and by the peculiarities of the ink. I
woke one morning with a sudden flash of common-
sense. Sympathetic ink had been used, and the
papers had been toasted or treated with acids. This
I had probably reasoned out in sleep, and, had I
dreamed, my mind might have dramatised the idea.
Old Mr. Edgar, the king's secretary, might have appeared and given me the explanation. Maury publishes tales in which a forgotten fact was revealed to
him in a dream from the lips of a dream-character
(*Le Sommeil et les Rêves*, pp. 142-143. The curious
may also consult, on all these things, *The Philosophy
of Mysticism*, by Karl du Prel, translated by Mr.
Massey. The Assyrian Priest is in *Proceedings*,
S.P.R., vol. xii., p. 14).

On the same plane as the dreams which we have
been examining is the waking sensation of the
déjà vu.

> " I have been here before,
> But when or how I cannot tell."

Most of us know this feeling, all the circumstances
in which we find ourselves have already occurred, we
have a prophecy of what will happen next " on the
tip of our tongues " (like a half-remembered name),
and then the impression vanishes. Scott complains
of suffering through a whole dinner-party from this
sensation, but he had written " copy " for fifty printed
pages on that day, and his brain was breaking down.

Of course psychology has explanations. The scene
may have really occurred before, or may be the result
of a malady of perception, or one hemisphere of the
brain not working in absolute simultaneousness with

the other may produce a double impression, the first being followed by the second, so that we really have had two successive impressions, of which one seems much more remote in time than it really was. Or we may have dreamed something like the scene and forgotten the dream, or we may actually, in some not understood manner, have had a "prevision" of what is now actual, as when Shelley almost fainted on coming to a place near Oxford which he had beheld in a dream.

Of course, if this "prevision" could be verified in detail, we should come very near to dreams of the future fulfilled. Such a thing—verification of a detail—led to the conversion of William Hone, the free-thinker and Radical of the early century, who consequently became a Christian and a pessimistic, clear-sighted Tory. This tale of the *déjà vu*, therefore, leads up to the marvellous narratives of dreams simultaneous with, or prophetic of, events not capable of being guessed or inferred, or of events lost in the historical past, but, later, recovered from documents.

Of Hone's affair there are two versions. Both may be given, as they are short. If they illustrate the *déjà vu*, they also illustrate the fond discrepancies of all such narratives.[1]

THE KNOT IN THE SHUTTER.

"It is said that a dream produced a powerful effect on Hone's mind. He dreamt that he was intro-

---

[1] From *Some Account of the Conversion of the late William Hone,* supplied by some friend of W. H. to compiler. Name not given.

duced into a room where he was an entire stranger, and saw himself seated at a table, and on going towards the window his attention was somehow or other attracted to the window-shutter, and particularly to a knot in the wood, which was of singular appearance; and on waking the whole scene, and especially the knot in the shutter, left a most vivid impression on his mind. Some time afterwards, on going, I think, into the country, he was at some house shown into a chamber where he had never been before, and which instantly struck him as being the identical chamber of his dream. He turned directly to the window, where the same knot in the shutter caught his eye. This incident, to his investigating spirit, induced a train of reflection which overthrew his cherished theories of materialism, and resulted in conviction that there were spiritual agencies as susceptible of proof as any facts of physical science; and this appears to have been one of the links in that mysterious chain of events by which, according to the inscrutable purposes of the Divine will, man is sometimes compelled to bow to an unseen and divine power, and ultimately to believe and live."

"Another of the Christian friends from whom, in his later years, William Hone received so much kindness, has also furnished recollections of him.

". . . Two or three anecdotes which he related are all I can contribute towards a piece of mental history which, if preserved, would have been highly interesting. The first in point of time as to his taste of mind, was a circumstance which shook his confidence in *materialism*, though it did not lead to his conversion. It was one of those mental phenomena which he saw to be *inexplicable* by the doctrines he then held.

"It was as follows: He was called in the course of business into a part of London quite new to him, and as he walked along the street he noticed to himself that he had never been there; but on being shown into a room in a house where he had to wait some time, he immediately fancied that it was all familiar, that he had seen it before, 'and if so,' said he to himself, 'there is a very peculiar knot in this shutter'. He opened the shutter and found the knot. 'Now then,' thought he, 'here is something I cannot explain on my principles!'"

Indeed the occurrence is not very explicable on any principles, as a detail not visible without search was sought and verified, and that by a habitual mocker at anything out of the common way. For example, Hone published a comic explanation, correct or not, of the famous Stockwell mystery.

Supposing Hone's story to be true, it naturally conducts us to yet more unfamiliar, and therefore less credible dreams, in which the unknown past, present, or future is correctly revealed.

CHAPTER II.

PERHAPS nothing, not even a ghost, is so staggering to the powers of belief as a well-authenticated dream which strikes the bull's eye of facts not known to the dreamer nor capable of being guessed by him. If the events beheld in the dream are far away in space, or are remote in time past, the puzzle is difficult enough. But if the events are still in the future, perhaps no kind of explanation except a mere "fluke" can even be suggested. Say that I dream of an event occurring at a distance, and that I record or act on my dream before it is corroborated. Suppose, too, that the event is not one which could be guessed, like the death of an invalid or the result of a race or of an election. This would be odd enough, but the facts of which I dreamed must have been present in the minds of living people. Now, if there is such a thing as "mental telegraphy" or "telepathy,"[1] my mind, in dream, may have "tapped" the minds of the people who knew the facts. We may not believe in "mental telegraphy," but we can *imagine* it as one of the unknown possibilities of nature. Again, if I

[1] What is now called "mental telegraphy" or "telepathy" is quite an old idea. Bacon calls it "sympathy" between two distant minds, sympathy so strong that one communicates with the other without using the recognised channels of the senses. Izaak Walton explains in the same way Dr. Donne's vision, in Paris, of his wife and dead child. "If two lutes are strung to an exact harmony, and one is struck, the other sounds," argues Walton. Two minds may be as harmoniously attuned and communicate each with each. Of course, in the case of the lutes there are actual vibrations, physical facts. But we know nothing of vibrations in the brain which can traverse space to another brain.

Many experiments have been made in consciously transferring thoughts or emotions from one mind to another. These are very liable to be vitiated by bad observation, collusion and other causes. Meanwhile, intercommunication between mind and mind without the aid of the recognised senses—a supposed process of "telepathy"—is a current explanation of the dreams in which knowledge is obtained that exists in the mind of another person, and of the delusion by virtue of which one person sees another who is perhaps dying, or in some other crisis, at a distance. The idea is popular. A poor Highland woman wrote to her son in Glasgow: "Don't be thinking too much of us, or I shall be seeing you some evening in the byre". This is a simple expression of the hypothesis of "telepathy" or "mental telegraphy".

dream of an unchronicled event in the past, and if a letter of some historical person is later discovered which confirms the accuracy of my dream, we can at least *conceive* (though we need not believe) that the intelligence was telegraphed to my dreaming mind from the mind of a *dead* actor in, or witness of the historical scene, for the facts are unknown to living man. But even these wild guesses cannot cover a dream which correctly reveals events of the future ; events necessarily not known to any finite mind of the living or of the dead, and too full of detail for an explanation by aid of chance coincidence.

In face of these difficulties mankind has gone on believing in dreams of all three classes : dreams revealing the unknown present, the unknown past, and the unknown future. The judicious reasonably set them all aside as the results of fortuitous coincidence, or revived recollection, or of the illusions of a false memory, or of imposture, conscious or unconscious. However, the stories continue to be told, and our business is with the stories.

Taking, first, dreams of the unknown past, we find a large modern collection of these attributed to a lady named " Miss A——". They were waking dreams representing obscure incidents of the past, and were later corroborated by records in books, newspapers and manuscripts. But as these books and papers existed, and were known to exist, before the occurrence of the visions, it is obvious that the matter of the visions *may* have been derived from the books and so forth, or at least, a sceptic will vastly prefer this explanation. What we need is a dream or vision of the unknown past, corroborated by a document *not known to exist* at the time when the vision took place and was recorded. Probably there is no such instance, but the following tale, picturesque in itself, has a kind of shadow of the only satisfactory sort of corroboration.

The author responsible for this yarn is Dr. Gregory, F.R.S., Professor of Chemistry in the University of Edinburgh. After studying for many years the real or alleged phenomena of what has been called mesmerism, or electro-biology, or hypnotism, Dr. Gregory published in 1851 his *Letters to a Candid Inquirer on Animal Magnetism.*

Though a F.R.S. and a Professor of Chemistry, the Doctor had no more idea of what constitutes evidence than a baby. He actually mixed up the Tyrone with the Lyttelton ghost story! His legend of Queen Mary's jewels is derived from (1) the notebook, *or* (2) a letter containing, or professing to contain, extracts from the note-book, of a Major Buckley, an Anglo-Indian officer. This gentleman used to "magnetise" or hypnotise people, some of whom became clairvoyant, as if possessed of eyes acting as "double-patent-million magnifiers," permeated by X rays.

"What follows is transcribed," says the Doctor, "from Major Buckley's note-book." We abridge the narrative. Major Buckley hypnotised a young officer, who, on November 15, 1845, fell into "a deeper state" of trance. Thence he awoke into a "clairvoyant" condition and said:—

QUEEN MARY'S JEWELS.

" I have had a strange dream about your ring "
(a " medallion " of Anthony and Cleopatra) ; " it
is very valuable."

Major Buckley said it was worth £60, and put
the ring into his friend's hand.

" It belonged to royalty."

" In what country ? "

" I see Mary, Queen of Scots. It was given to
her by a man, a foreigner, with other things from
Italy. It came from Naples. It is not in the old
setting. She wore it only once. The person who
gave it to her was a musician."

The seer then " saw " the donor's signature,
" Rizzio". But Rizzio spelled his name Riccio!
The seer now copied on paper a writing which in
his trance he saw on vellum. The design here en-
graved (p. 32) is only from a rough copy of the seer's
original drawing, which was made by Major Buckley.

" Here " (pointing to the middle) " I see a
diamond cross." The smallest stone was above
the size of one of four carats. " It " (the cross)
" was worn out of sight by Mary. The vellum has
been shown in the House of Lords." [1]

" . . . The ring was taken off Mary's finger by
a man in anger and jealousy : he threw it into
the water. When he took it off, she was being
carried in a kind of bed with curtains " (a litter).

[1] Perhaps among such papers as the *Casket Letters*, exhibited to
the Commission at Westminster, and " tabled " before the Scotch
Privy Council.

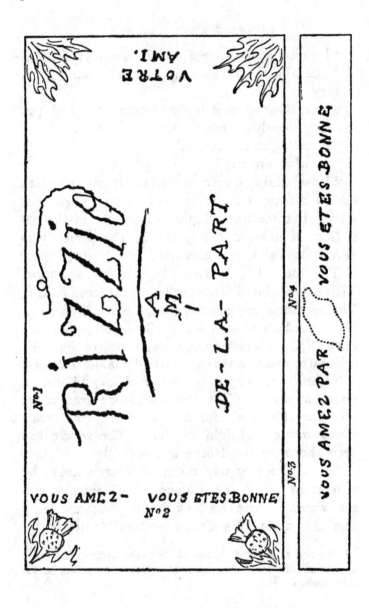

Just before Rizzio's murder Mary was *enceinte*, and might well be carried in a litter, though she usually rode.

The seer then had a view of Rizzio's murder, which he had probably read about.

Three weeks later, in another trance, the seer finished his design of the vellum. The words

A

M

De la Part

probably stand for *à Marie, de la part de* ——
The thistle heads and leaves in gold at the corners were a usual decoration of the period ; compare the ceiling of the room in Edinburgh Castle where James VI. was born, four months after Rizzio's murder. They also occur in documents. Dr. Gregory conjectures that so valuable a present as a diamond cross may have been made not by Rizzio, but through Rizzio by the Pope.

It did not seem good to the doctor to consult Mary's lists of jewels, nor, if he had done so, would he have been any the wiser. In 1566, just before the birth of James VI., Mary had an inventory drawn up, and added the names of the persons to whom she bequeathed her treasures in case she died in child-bed. But this inventory, hidden among a mass of law-papers in the Record Office, was not discovered till 1854, nine years after the vision of 1845, and three after its publication by Dr. Gregory in 1851. Not till 1863 was the inventory of 1566, discovered in 1854, published for the Bannatyne Club by Dr. Joseph Robertson.

Turning to the inventory we read of a valuable present made by David Rizzio to Mary, a tortoise of rubies, which she kept till her death, for it appears in a list made after her execution at Fotheringay. The murdered David Rizzio left a brother Joseph. Him the queen made her secretary, and in her will of 1566 mentions him thus:—

"*A Josef, pour porter à celui qui je luy ay dit,* une emeraude emaille de blanc.

"*A Josef, pour porter à celui qui je luy ai dit, dont il ranvoir quittance.*

"Une bague garnye de vingt cinq diamens tant grands que petis."

Now the diamond cross seen by the young officer in 1845 was set with diamonds great and small, and was, in his opinion, a gift from or through Rizzio. "The queen wore it out of sight." Here in the inventory we have a *bague* (which may be a cross) of diamonds small and great, connected with a secret only known to Rizzio's brother and to the queen. It is "to be carried to one whose name the queen has spoken in her new secretary's ear" (Joseph's), "but dare not trust herself to write". "It would be idle now to seek to pry into the mystery which was thus anxiously guarded," says Dr. Robertson, editor of the queen's inventories. The doctor knew nothing of the vision which, perhaps, so nearly pried into the mystery.

There is nothing like proof here, but there is just a presumption that the diamonds connected with Rizzio, and secretly worn by the queen, seen in the vision of 1845, are possibly the diamonds which, had Mary died in 1566, were to be carried by Joseph Rizzio to a person whose name might not safely be written.[1]

We now take a dream which apparently reveals a real fact occurring at a distance. It is translated from Brierre de Boismont's book, *Des Hallucinations*[2] (Paris, 1845). "There are," says the learned author, "authentic dreams which have revealed an event occurring at the moment, or later." These he explains by accidental coincidence, and then gives the following anecdote, as within his own intimate knowledge :—

THE DEATHBED.

Miss C., a lady of excellent sense, religious but not bigoted, lived before her marriage in the house of her uncle D., a celebrated physician, and member of the Institute. Her mother at this time was seriously ill in the country. One night the girl dreamed that she saw her mother, pale and dying, and especially grieved at the absence of two of her children : one a *curé* in Spain, the other—herself—in Paris. Next she heard her own Christian name called, " Charlotte ! " and, in her dream, saw

---

[1] To Joseph himself she bequeathed the ruby tortoise given to her by his brother. Probably the diamonds were not Rizzio's gift.

[2] Boismont was a distinguished physician and " Mad Doctor," or "Alienist ". He was also a Christian, and opposed a tendency, not uncommon in his time, as in ours, to regard all " hallucinations " as a proof of mental disease in the " hallucinated ".

the people about her mother bring in her own little niece and god-child Charlotte from the next room. The patient intimated by a sign that she did not want *this* Charlotte, but her daughter in Paris. She displayed the deepest regret ; her countenance changed, she fell back, and died.

Next day the melancholy of Mademoiselle C. attracted the attention of her uncle. She told him her dream ; he pressed her to his heart, and admitted that her mother was dead.

Some months later Mademoiselle C., when her uncle was absent, arranged his papers, which he did not like any one to touch. Among these was a letter containing the story of her mother's death, with all the details of her own dream, which D. had kept concealed lest they should impress her too painfully.

Boismont is staggered by this circumstance, and inclined to account for it by " still unknown relations in the moral and physical world ". " Mental tele-graphy," of course, would explain all, and even chance coincidence is perfectly conceivable.

The most commonly known of dreams prior to, or simultaneous with an historical occurrence repre-sented in the vision, is Mr. Williams's dream of the murder of Mr. Perceval in the lobby of the House of Commons, May 11, 1812. Mr. Williams, of Scorrier House, near Redruth, in Cornwall, lived till 1841. He was interested in mines, and a man of substance. Unluckily the versions of his dream are full of discrepancies. It was first published, apparently, in *The Times* during the " silly season " of 1828 (August 28). According to *The Times*, whose account is very minute, Mr. Williams dreamed of the murder thrice before 2 A.M. on the night of May 11. He told Mrs. Williams, and was so disturbed that he rose and dressed at two in the morning. He went to Falmouth next day (May 12), and told the tale to every one he knew. On the evening of the 13th he told it to Mr. and Mrs. Tucker (his married daughter) of Tremanton Castle. Mr. Williams only knew that the *chancellor* was shot; Mr. Tucker said it must be the Chancellor of the Exchequer. From the description he recog·nised Mr. Perceval, with whom he was at enmity. Mr. Williams had never been inside the House of Commons. As they talked, Mr. William's son galloped up from Truro with news of the murder, got from a traveller by coach. Six weeks later, Mr. Williams went to town, and in the House of Commons walked up to and recognised the scene of the various incidents in the murder.

So far *The Times*, in 1828. But two forms of a version of 1832 exist, one in a note to Mr. Walpole's *Life of Perceval* (1874), "an attested statement, drawn up and signed by Mr. Williams in the presence of the Rev. Thomas Fisher and Mr. Charles Prideaux Brune". Mr. Brune gave it to Mr. Walpole. With only verbal differences this variant corresponds to another signed by Mr. Williams and given by him to his grandson, who gave it to Mr. Perceval's great-niece, by whom it was lent to the Society for Psychical Research.

These accounts differ *toto cælo* from that in *The*

Times of 1828. The dream is *not* of May 11, but "about" May 2 or 3. Mr. Williams is *not* a stranger to the House of Commons; it is "a place well known to me". He is *not* ignorant of the name of the victim, but "understood that it was Mr. Perceval". He thinks of going to town to give warning. We hear nothing of Mr. Tucker. Mr. Williams does *not* verify his dream in the House, but from a drawing. A Mr. C. R. Fox, son of one to whom the dream was told *before* the event, was then a boy of fourteen, and sixty-one years later was sure that he himself heard of Mr. Williams's dream *before* the news of the murder arrived. After sixty years, however, the memory cannot be relied upon.

One very curious circumstance in connection with the assassination of Mr. Perceval has never been noticed. A rumour or report of the deed reached Bude Kirk, a village near Annan, on the night of Sunday, May 10, a day before the crime was committed! This was stated in the *Dumfries and Galloway Courier*, and copied in *The Times* of May 25. On May 28, the *Perth Courier* quotes the Dumfries paper, and adds that "the Rev. Mr. Yorstoun, minister of Hoddam (*ob.* 1833), has visited Bude Kirk and has obtained the most satisfactory proof of the rumour having existed" on May 10, but the rumour cannot be traced to its source. Mr. Yorstoun authorises the mention of his name. *The Times* of June 2 says that "the report is without foundation".

If Williams talked everywhere of his dream, on May 3, some garbled shape of it may conceivably

have floated to Bude Kirk by May 10, and originated
the rumour. Whoever started it would keep quiet
when the real news arrived for fear of being implicated in a conspiracy as accessory before the
fact. No trace of Mr. Williams's dream occurs in
the contemporary London papers.

The best version of the dream to follow is probably that signed by Mr. Williams himself in 1832.[1]

It may, of course, be argued by people who accept
Mr. Williams's dream as a revelation of the future
that it reached his mind from the *purpose* conceived
in Bellingham's mind, by way of "mental telegraphy".[2]

DREAM OF MR. PERCEVAL'S MURDER.

" SUNDHILL, *December*, 1832.

"[Some account of a dream which occurred to John
Williams, Esq., of Scorrier House, in the county
of Cornwall, in the year 1812. Taken from his
own mouth, and narrated by him at various times
to several of his friends.]

" Being desired to write out the particulars of
a remarkable dream which I had in the year 1812,
before I do so I think it may be proper for me to
say that at that time my attention was fully occupied with affairs of my own—the superintendence
of some very extensive mines in Cornwall being
entrusted to me. Thus I had no leisure to pay
any attention to political matters, and hardly knew
at that time who formed the administration of the

[1] *S.P.R.*, v., 324.　　　　[2] *Ibid.*, 324.

country. It was, therefore, scarcely possible that my own interest in the subject should have had any share in suggesting the circumstances which presented themselves to my imagination. It was, in truth, a subject which never occurred to my waking thoughts.

"My dream was as follows :—

"About the second or third day of May, 1812, I dreamed that I was in the lobby of the House of Commons (a place well known to me). A small man, dressed in a blue coat and a white waistcoat, entered, and immediately I saw a person whom I had observed on my first entrance, dressed in a snuff-coloured coat with metal buttons, take a pistol from under his coat and present it at the little man above-mentioned. The pistol was discharged, and the ball entered under the left breast of the person at whom it was directed. I saw the blood issue from the place where the ball had struck him, his countenance instantly altered, and he fell to the ground. Upon inquiry who the sufferer might be, I was informed that he was the chancellor. I understood him to be Mr. Perceval, who was Chancellor of the Exchequer. I further saw the murderer laid hold of by several of the gentlemen in the room. Upon waking I told the particulars above related to my wife; she treated the matter lightly, and desired me to go to sleep, saying it was only a dream. I soon fell asleep again, and again the dream presented itself with precisely the same circumstances. After waking a second time and stating the matter again to my wife, she only repeated her request that I would compose myself and dismiss the subject from my mind. Upon my falling asleep the third time, the same dream without any alteration was repeated, and I awoke, as on the former occasions, in great agitation. So much alarmed and impressed was I with the circumstances above related, that I felt much doubt whether it was not my duty to take a journey to London and communicate upon the subject with the party principally concerned. Upon this point I consulted with some friends whom I met on business at the Godolphin mine on the following day. After having stated to them the particulars of the dream itself and what were my own feelings in relation to it, they dissuaded me from my purpose, saying I might expose myself to contempt and vexation, or be taken up as a fanatic. Upon this I said no more, but anxiously watched the newspapers every evening as the post arrived.

"On the evening of the 13th of May (as far as I recollect) no account of Mr. Perceval's death was in the newspapers, but my second son, returning from Truro, came in a hurried manner into the room where I was sitting and exclaimed: 'O father, your dream has come true! Mr. Perceval has been shot in the lobby of the House of Commons; there is an account come from London to Truro written after the newspapers were printed.'

"The fact was Mr. Percival was assassinated on the evening of the 11th.

"Some business soon after called me to London, and in one of the print-shops I saw a drawing for sale, representing the place and the circumstances which attended Mr. Perceval's death. I purchased it, and upon a careful examination I found it to coincide in all respects with the scene which had passed through my imagination in the dream. The colours of the dresses, the buttons of the assassin's coat, the white waistcoat of Mr. Perceval, the spot of blood upon it, the countenances and attitudes of the parties present were exactly what I had dreamed.

"The singularity of the case, when mentioned among my friends and acquaintances, naturally made it the subject of conversation in London, and in consequence my friend, the late Mr. Rennie, was requested by some of the commissioners of the navy that they might be permitted to hear the circumstances from myself. Two of them accordingly met me at Mr. Rennie's house, and to them I detailed at the time the particulars, then fresh in my memory, which form the subject of the above statement.

"I forbear to make any comment on the above narrative, further than to declare solemnly that it is a faithful account of facts as they actually occurred.

(Signed) "JOHN WILLIAMS."[1]

When we come to dreams of the future, great historical examples are scarce indeed, that is, dreams respectably authenticated. We have to put up with curious trivialities. One has an odd feature.

[1] *Proceedings of the Society for Psychical Research*, vol. v., pp. 324, 325.

THE RATTLESNAKE.

Dr. Kinsolving, of the Church of the Epiphany in Philadelphia, dreamed that he "came across a rattlesnake," which "when killed had *two* black-looking rattles and a peculiar projection of bone from the tail, while the skin was unusually light in colour". Next day, while walking with his brother, Dr. Kinsolving nearly trod on a rattlesnake, "the same snake in every particular with the one I had had in my mind's eye". This would be very well, but Dr. Kinsolving's brother, who helped to kill the unlucky serpent, says "*he had a single rattle*". The letters of these gentlemen were written without communication to each other. If Mr. Kinsolving is right, the real snake with *one* rattle was *not* the dream snake with *two* rattles. The brothers were in a snaky country, West Virginia.[1]

The following is trivial, but good. It is written by Mr. Alfred Cooper, and attested by the dreamer, the Duchess of Hamilton.

THE RED LAMP.

Mr. Cooper says : "A fortnight before the death of the late Earl of L—— in 1882, I called upon the Duke of Hamilton, in Hill Street, to see him professionally. After I had finished seeing him, we went into the drawing-room, where the duchess was, and the duke said, 'Oh, Cooper, how is the earl ?'

[1] *Proceedings*, S.P.R., vol. xi., p. 495.

" The duchess said, ' What earl ? ' and on my answering ' Lord L——,' she replied : ' That is very odd. I have had a most extraordinary vision. I went to bed, but after being in bed a short time, I was not exactly asleep, but thought I saw a scene as if from a play before me. The actors in it were Lord L—— as if in a fit, with a man standing over him with a red beard. He was by the side of a bath, over which a red lamp was distinctly shown.

" I then said : ' I am attending Lord L—— at present ; there is very little the matter with him ; he is not going to die ; he will be all right very soon'.

" Well he got better for a week and was nearly well, but at the end of six or seven days after this I was called to see him suddenly. He had in-flammation of both lungs.

" I called in Sir William Jenner, but in six days he was a dead man. There were two male nurses attending on him ; one had been taken ill. But when I saw the other, the dream of the duchess was exactly represented. He was standing near a bath over the earl, and strange to say, his beard was red. There was the bath with the red lamp over it. It is rather rare to find a bath with a red lamp over it, and this brought the story to my mind. . . ."

This account, written in 1888, has been revised by the late Duke of Manchester, father of the Duchess of Hamilton, who heard the vision from his daughter on the morning after she had seen it.

The duchess only knew the earl by sight, and

had not heard that he was ill. She knew she was not asleep, for she opened her eyes to get rid of the vision, and, shutting them, saw the same thing again.[1]

In fact, the "vision" was an *illusion hypnagogique*. Probably most readers know the procession of visions which sometimes crowd on the closed eyes just before sleep.[2] They commonly represent with vivid clearness unknown faces or places, occasionally known faces. The writer has seen his own in this way and has occasionally "opened his eyes to get rid of" the appearances. In his opinion the pictures are unconsciously constructed by the half-sleeping mind out of blurs of light or dark seen with closed eyes. Mr. Cooper's story would be more complete if he had said whether or not the earl, when visited by him, was in a chair as in the vision. But beds are not commonly found in bathrooms.

THE SCAR IN THE MOUSTACHE.

This story was told to the writer by his old head-master, the Rev. Dr. Hodson, brother of Hodson, of Hodson's Horse, a person whom I never heard make any other allusion to such topics. Dr. Hodson was staying with friends in Switzerland during the holidays. One morning, as he lay awake, he seemed to see into a room as if the wall of his bedroom had been cut out. In the room were a

---

[1] Signed by Mr. Cooper and the Duchess of Hamilton.
[2] See Galton, *Inquiries into Human Faculty*, p. 91.

lady well known to him and a man whom he did
not know. The man's back was turned to the
looker-on. The scene vanished, and grew again.
Now the man faced Dr. Hodson; the face was
unfamiliar, and had a deep white scar seaming the
moustache. Dr. Hodson mentioned the circumstance
to his friends, and thought little of it. He returned
home, and, one day, in Perth station, met the lady
at the book-stall. He went up to accost her, and
was surprised by the uneasiness of her manner.
A gentleman now joined them, with a deep white
scar through his moustache. Dr. Hodson now
recalled, what had slipped his memory, that
the lady during his absence from Scotland had
eloped with an officer, the man of the vision and
the railway station. He did not say, or perhaps
know, whether the elopement was prior to the kind
of dream in Switzerland.

Here is a dream representing a future event, with
details which could not be guessed beforehand.

THE CORAL SPRIGS.

Mrs. Weiss, of St. Louis, was in New York in
January, 1881, attending a daughter, Mrs. C., who
was about to have a child. She writes:—

"On Friday night (Jan. 21) I dreamed that my
daughter's time came; that owing to some cause
not clearly defined, we failed to get word to Mr. C.,
who was to bring the doctor; that we sent for
the nurse, who came; that as the hours passed
and neither Mr. C. nor the doctor came we both

got frightened; that at last I heard Mr. C. on the stairs, and cried to him : ' Oh, Chan, for heaven's sake get a doctor! Ada may be confined at any moment'; that he rushed away, and I returned to the bedside of my daughter, who was in agony of mind and body; that suddenly I seemed to know what to do, . . . and that shortly after Mr. C. came, bringing a tall young doctor, having brown eyes, dark hair, ruddy *brun* complexion, grey trousers and grey vest, and wearing a bright blue cravat, picked out with coral sprigs; the cravat attracted my attention particularly. The young doctor pronounced Mrs. C. properly attended to, and left."

Mrs. Weiss at breakfast told the dream to Mr. C. and her daughter; none of them attached any importance to it. However, as a snowstorm broke the telegraph wires on Saturday, the day after the dream, Mrs. Weiss was uneasy. On Tuesday the state of Mrs. C. demanded a doctor. Mrs. Weiss sent a telegram for Mr. C.; he came at last, went out to bring a doctor, and was long absent. Then Mrs. Weiss suddenly felt a calm certainty that *she* (though inexperienced in such cares) could do what was needed. " I heard myself say in a peremptory fashion : ' Ada, don't be afraid, I know just what to do; all will go well'." All did go well; meanwhile Mr. C. ran to seven doctors' houses, and at last returned with a young man whom Mrs. Weiss vaguely recognised. Mrs. C. whispered, " Look at the doctor's cravat ". It was blue and coral sprigged, and then first did Mrs. Weiss remember her dream of Friday night.

Mrs. Weiss's story is corroborated by Mr. Blanchard, who heard the story "a few days after the event". Mrs. C. has read Mrs. Weiss's statement, "and in so far as I can remember it is quite correct". Mr. C. remembers nothing about it; "he declares that he has no recollection of it, *or of any matters outside his business*, and knowing him as I do," says Mrs. Weiss, "I do not doubt the assertion".

Mr. C. must be an interesting companion. The nurse remembers that after the birth of the baby Mrs. C. called Mr. C.'s attention to "the doctor's necktie," and heard her say, "Why, I know him by mamma's description as the doctor she saw in her dreams ".[1]

The only thing even more extraordinary than the dream is Mr. C.'s inability to remember anything whatever "outside of his business". Another witness appears to decline to be called, "as it would be embarrassing to him in his business". This it is to be Anglo-Saxon!

We now turn to a Celtic dream, in which knowledge supposed to be only known to a dead man was conveyed to his living daughter.

THE SATIN SLIPPERS.

On 1st February, 1891, Michael Conley, a farmer living near Ionia, in Chichasow county, Iowa, went to Dubuque, in Iowa, to be medically treated. He left at home his son Pat and his daughter Elizabeth,

[1] *Proceedings*, S.P.R., vol. xi., p. 522.

a girl of twenty-eight, a Catholic, in good health. On February 3 Michael was found dead in an out-house near his inn. In his pocket were nine dollars, seventy-five cents, but his clothes, including his shirt, were thought so dirty and worthless that they were thrown away. The body was then dressed in a white shirt, black clothes and satin slippers of a new pattern. Pat Conley was telegraphed for, and arrived at Dubuque on February 4, accompanied by Mr. George Brown, "an intelligent and reliable farmer". Pat took the corpse home in a coffin, and on his arrival Elizabeth fell into a swoon, which lasted for several hours. Her own account of what followed on her recovery may be given in her own words :—

"When they told me that father was dead I felt very sick and bad ; I did not know anything. Then father came to me. He had on a white shirt" (his own was grey), "and black clothes and slippers. When I came to, I told Pat I had seen father. I asked Pat if he had brought back father's old clothes. He said 'No,' and asked me why I wanted them. I told him father said he had sewed a roll of bills inside of his grey shirt, in a pocket made of a piece of my old red dress. I went to sleep, and father came to me again. When I awoke I told Pat he must go and get the clothes"—her father's old clothes.

Pat now telephoned to Mr. Hoffman, Coroner of Dubuque, who found the old clothes in the back yard of the local morgue. They were wrapped up in a bundle. Receiving this news, Pat went to Dubuque on February 9, where Mr. Hoffman opened the bundle in Pat's presence. Inside the old grey shirt was found a pocket of red stuff, sewn with a man's long, uneven stitches, and in the pocket notes for thirty-five dollars.

The girl did not see the body in the coffin, but asked about the *old* clothes, because the figure of her father in her dream wore clothes which she did not recognise as his. To dream in a faint is nothing unusual.[1]

THE DEAD SHOPMAN.

Swooning, or slight mental mistiness, is not very unusual in ghost seers. The brother of a friend of my own, a man of letters and wide erudition, was, as a boy, employed in a shop in a town, say Wexington. The overseer was a dark, rather hectic-looking man, who died. Some months afterwards the boy was sent on an errand. He did his business, but, like a boy, returned by a longer and more interesting route. He stopped as a bookseller's shop to stare at the books and pictures, and while doing so felt a kind of mental vagueness. It was just before his dinner hour, and he may have been hungry. On resuming his way, he looked up and found the dead overseer beside him. He had no sense of surprise,

[1] The case was reported in the *Herald* (Dubuque) for 12th February, 1891. It was confirmed by Mr. Hoffman, by Mr. George Brown and by Miss Conley, examined by the Rev. Mr. Crum, of Dubuque.— *Proceedings*, S.P.R., viii., 200-205. Pat Conley, too, corroborated, and had no theory of explanation. That the girl knew beforehand of the dollars is conceivable, but she did not know of the change of clothes.

and walked for some distance, conversing on ordinary topics with the appearance. He happened to notice such a minute detail as that the spectre's boots were laced in an unusual way. At a crossing, something in the street attracted his attention; he looked away from his companion, and, on turning to resume their talk, saw no more of him. He then walked to the shop, where he mentioned the occurrence to a friend. He has never during a number of years had any such experience again, or suffered the preceding sensation of vagueness.

This, of course, is not a ghost story, but leads up to the old tale of the wraith of Valogne. In this case, two boys had made a covenant, the first who died was to appear to the other. He *did* appear before news of his death arrived, but after a swoon of his friend's, whose health (like that of Elizabeth Conley) suffered in consequence.

NOTE.

"Perceval Murder." *Times*, 25*th May*, 1812.

"A Dumfries paper states that on the night of Sunday, the 10th instant, *twenty-four hours before the fatal deed was perpetrated*, a report was brought to Bude Kirk, two miles from Annan, that *Mr. Perceval was shot on his way to the House of Commons, at the door or in the lobby of that House.* This the whole inhabitants of the village are ready to attest, as the report quickly spread and became the topic of conversation. A clergyman investigated the rumour, with the view of tracing it to its source, but without success."

The Times of 2nd June says, "Report without foundation".

Perth Courier, 28th May, quoting from the *Dumfries and Galloway Courier*, repeats above almost verbatim. " . . . The clergyman to whom we have alluded, and who allows me to make use of his name, is Mr. Yorstoun, minister of Hoddam. This gentleman

went to the spot and carefully investigated the rumour, but has not
hitherto been successful, although he has obtained the most satisfactory proof of its having existed at the time we have mentioned.
We forbear to make any comments on this wonderful circumstance,
but should anything further transpire that may tend to throw light
upon it, we shall not fail to give the public earliest information."

The *Dumfries and Galloway Courier* I cannot find! It is not in
the British Museum.

CHAPTER III.

FROM dreams, in sleep or swoon, of a character difficult to believe in we pass by way of "hallucinations" to ghosts. Everybody is ready to admit that dreams do really occur, because almost everybody has dreamed. But everybody is not so ready to admit that sane and sensible men and women can have hallucinations, just because everybody has not been hallucinated.

On this point Mr. Francis Galton, in his *Inquiries into Human Faculty* (1833), is very instructive. Mr. Galton drew up a short catechism, asking people how clearly or how dimly they saw things " in their mind's eye ".

" Think of your breakfast-table," he said; " is your mental picture of it as clearly illuminated and as complete as your actual view of the scene ? " Mr. Galton began by questioning friends in the scientific world, F.R.S.'s and other *savants*. " The earliest results of my inquiry amazed me. . . . The great majority of the men of science to whom I first applied, protested that *mental imagery was unknown to them*, and they looked on me as fanciful and fantastic in supposing that the words ' mental imagery ' really expressed what I believed everybody supposed them to mean." One gentleman wrote : " It is only by a figure of speech that I can describe my recollection of a scene as a ' mental image ' which I can ' see ' with ' my mind's eye '. I do not see it," so he seems to have supposed that nobody else did.

When he made inquiries in general society, Mr. Galton found plenty of people who " saw " mental imagery with every degree of brilliance or dimness, from " quite comparable to the real object " to " I recollect the table, but do not see it "—my own position.

Mr. Galton was next " greatly struck by the frequency of the replies in which my correspondents " (sane and healthy) " described themselves as subject to 'visions'". These varied in degree, "some were so vivid as actually to deceive the judgment". Finally, " a notable proportion of sane persons have had not only visions, but actual hallucinations of sight at one or more periods of their life. I have a considerable packet of instances contributed by my personal friends." Thus one " distinguished authoress" saw "the principal character of one of her novels glide through the door straight up to her. It was about the size of a large doll." Another heard unreal music, and opened the door to hear it better. Another was plagued by voices, which said " Pray," and so forth.

Thus, on scientific evidence, sane and healthy people may, and " in a notable proportion *do*, experience hallucinations ". That is to say, they see persons, or hear them, or believe they are touched by them, or all their senses are equally affected at once, when no such persons are really present. This kind of thing is always going on, but " when popular opinion is of a matter-of-fact kind, the seers of visions keep quiet ; they do not like to be thought fanciful or mad, and they hide their experiences, which only come to light through inquiries such as those that I have been making ".

We may now proceed to the waking hallucinations of sane and healthy people, which Mr. Galton declares to be so far from uncommon. Into the *causes* of these hallucinations which may actually deceive the judgment, Mr. Galton does not enter.

STORY OF THE DIPLOMATIST.[1]

For example, there is a living diplomatist who knows men and cities, and has, moreover, a fine sense of humour. "My Lord," said a famous Russian statesman to him, "you have all the qualities of a diplomatist, but you cannot control your smile." This gentleman, walking alone in a certain cloister at Cambridge, met a casual acquaintance, a well-known London clergyman, and was just about shaking hands with him, when the clergyman vanished. Nothing in particular happened to either of them ; the clergyman was not in the seer's mind at the moment.

This is a good example of a solitary hallucination in the experience of a very cool-headed observer. The *causes* of such experiences are still a mystery to science. Even people who believe in "mental telegraphy," say when a distant person, at death or in any other crisis, impresses himself as present on the senses of a friend, cannot account for an experience like that of the diplomatist, an experience not very uncommon, and little noticed except when it happens to coincide with some remarkable event.[2] Nor are such hallucinations of an origin easily detected, like those of delirium, insanity, intoxication, grief, anxiety, or remorse. We can only suppose that a past impression of the aspect of a friend is recalled by some association of ideas so vividly

[1] Told by the nobleman in question to the author.
[2] The author knows some eight cases among his friends of a solitary meaningless hallucination like this.

that (though we are not *consciously* thinking of him) we conceive the friend to be actually present in the body when he is absent.

These hallucinations are casual and unsought. But between these and the dreams of sleep there is a kind of waking hallucinations which some people can purposely evoke. Such are the visions of *crystal gazing*.

Among the superstitions of almost all ages and countries is the belief that "spirits" will show themselves, usually after magical ceremonies, to certain persons, commonly children, who stare into a crystal ball, a cup, a mirror, a blob of ink (in Egypt and India), a drop of blood (among the Maoris of New Zealand), a bowl of water (Red Indian), a pond (Roman and African), water in a glass bowl (in Fez), or almost any polished surface. The magical ceremonies, which have probably nothing to do with the matter, have succeeded in making this old and nearly universal belief seem a mere fantastic superstition. But occasionally a person not superstitious has recorded this experience. Thus George Sand in her *Histoire de ma Vie* mentions that, as a little girl, she used to see wonderful moving landscapes in the polished back of a screen. These were so vivid that she thought they must be visible to others.

Recent experiments have proved that an unexpected number of people have this faculty. Gazing into a ball of crystal or glass, a crystal or other smooth ring stone, such as a sapphire or ruby, or even into a common ink-pot, they will see visions very brilliant. These are often mere reminiscences of faces or places, occasionally of faces or places sunk deep below the ordinary memory. Still more frequently they represent fantastic landscapes and romantic scenes, as in an historical novel, with people in odd costumes coming, going and acting. Thus I have been present when a lady saw in a glass ball a man in white Oriental costume kneeling beside a leaping fountain of fire. Presently a hand appeared pointing downwards through the flame. The *first* vision seen pretty often represents an invalid in bed. Printed words are occasionally read in the glass, as also happens in the visions beheld with shut eyes before sleeping.

All these kinds of things, in fact, are common in our visions between sleeping and waking (*illusions hypnagogiques*). The singularity is that they are seen by people wide awake in glass balls and so forth. Usually the seer is a person whose ordinary " mental imagery" is particularly vivid. But every " visualiser " is not a crystal seer. A novelist of my acquaintance can " visualise " so well that, having forgotten an address and lost the letter on which it was written, he called up a mental picture of the letter, and so discovered the address. But this very popular writer can see no visions in a crystal ball. Another very popular novelist can see them ; little dramas are acted out in the ball for his edification.[1]

[1] As to the fact of such visions, I have so often seen crystal gazing, and heard the pictures described by persons whose word I could not doubt, men and women of unblemished character, free from super-

These things are as unfamiliar to men of science as Mr. Galton found ordinary mental imagery, pictures in memory, to be. Psychology may or may not include them in her province; they may or may not come to be studied as ordinary dreams are studied. But, like dreams, these crystal visions enter the domain of the ghostly only when they are *veracious*, and contribute information previously unknown as to past, present or future. There are plenty of stories to this effect. To begin with an easy, or comparatively easy, exercise in belief.

UNDER THE LAMP.

I had given a glass ball to a young lady, who believed that she could play the "willing game" successfully without touching the person "willed," and when the person did not even know that "willing" was going on. This lady, Miss Baillie, had scarcely any success with the ball. She lent it to Miss Leslie, who saw a large, square, old-fashioned red sofa covered with muslin, which she found in the next country house she visited. Miss Baillie's brother, a young athlete (at short odds for the amateur golf championship), laughed at these experiments, took the ball into the study, and came back looking "gey gash". He admitted that he had seen a vision, somebody he knew "under a lamp". He would discover during the week whether

stition, that I am obliged to believe in the fact as a real though hallucinatory experience. Mr. Clodd attributes it to disorder of the liver. If no more were needed I could "scry" famously!

he saw right or not. This was at 5·30 on a Sunday afternoon. On Tuesday, Mr. Baillie was at a dance in a town some forty miles from his home, and met a Miss Preston. "On Sunday," he said, "about half-past five you were sitting under a standard lamp in a dress I never saw you wear, a blue blouse with lace over the shoulders, pouring out tea for a man in blue serge, whose back was towards me, so that I only saw the tip of his moustache."

"Why, the blinds must have been up," said Miss Preston.

"I was at Dulby," said Mr. Baillie, as he undeniably was.[1]

This is not a difficult exercise in belief. Miss Preston was not unlikely to be at tea at tea-time.

Nor is the following very hard.

THE COW WITH THE BELL.

I had given a glass ball to the wife of a friend, whose visions proved so startling and on one occasion so unholy that she ceased to make experiments. One day my friend's secretary, a young student and golfer, took up the ball.

"I see a field I know very well," he said, "but there is a cow in it that I never saw; brown, with white markings, and, this is odd in Scotland, she has a bell hanging from her neck. I'll go and look at the field."

He went and found the cow as described, bell and all.[2]

---

[1] Facts attested and signed by Mr. Baillie and Miss Preston.
[2] Story told to me by both my friends and the secretary.

In the spring of 1897 I gave a glass ball to a young lady, previously a stranger to me, who was entirely unacquainted with crystal gazing, even by report. She had, however, not infrequent experience of spontaneous visions, which were fulfilled, including a vision of the Derby (Persimmon's year), which enriched her friends. In using the ball she, time after time, succeeded in seeing and correctly describing persons and places familiar to people for whom she " scried," but totally strange to herself. In one case she added a detail quite unknown to the person who consulted her, but which was verified on inquiry. These experiments will probably be published elsewhere. Four people, out of the very small number who tried on these occasions, saw fancy pictures in the ball : two were young ladies, one a man, and one a schoolboy. I must confess that, for the first time, I was impressed by the belief that the lady's veracious visions, however they are to be explained, could not possibly be accounted for by chance coincidence. They were too many (I was aware of five in a few days), too minute, and too remote from the range of ingenious guessing. But " thought transference," tapping the mental wires of another person, would have accounted for every case, with, perhaps, the exception of that in which an unknown detail was added. This confession will, undoubtedly, seem weakly credulous, but not to make it would be unfair and unsportsmanlike. My statement, of course, especially without the details, is not evidence for other people.

The following case is a much harder exercise in

belief. It is narrated by the Duc de Saint Simon.[1] The events were described to Saint Simon on the day after their occurrence by the Duc d'Orléans, then starting for Italy, in May, 1706. Saint Simon was very intimate with the duke, and they corresponded by private cypher without secretaries. Owing to the death of the king's son and grandson (not seen in the vision), Orléans became Regent when Louis XIV. died in 1714. Saint Simon is a reluctant witness, and therefore all the better.

THE DEATHBED OF LOUIS XIV.

" Here is a strange story that the Duc d'Orléans told me one day in a *tête-à-tête* at Marly, he having just run down from Paris before he started for Italy ; and it may be observed that all the events predicted came to pass, though none of them could have been foreseen at the time. His interest in every kind of art and science was very great, and in spite of his keen intellect, he was all his life subject to a weakness which had been introduced (with other things) from Italy by Catherine de Medici, and had reigned supreme over the courts of her children. He had exercised every known method of inducing the devil to appear to him in person, though, as he has himself told me, without the smallest success. He had spent much time in investigating matters that touched on the super-natural, and dealt with the future.

" Now La Sery (his mistress) had in her house

[1] *Mémoires*, v., 120. Paris, 1829.

a little girl of eight or nine years of age, who had never resided elsewhere since her birth. She was to all appearance a very ordinary child, and from the way in which she had been brought up, was more than commonly ignorant and simple. One day, during the visit of M. d'Orléans, La Sery produced for his edification one of the charlatans with whom the duke had long been familiar, who pretended that by means of a glass of water he could see the answer to any question that might be put. For this purpose it was necessary to have as a go-between some one both young and innocent, to gaze into the water, and this little girl was at once sent for. They amused themselves by asking what was happening in certain distant places; and after the man had murmured some words over the water, the child looked in and always managed to see the vision required of her.

" M. le duc d'Orléans had so often been duped in matters of this kind that he determined to put the water-gazer to a severe test. He whispered to one of his attendants to go round to Madame de Nancre's, who lived close by, and ascertain who was there, what they were all doing, the position of the room and the way it was furnished, and then, without exchanging a word with any one, to return and let him know the result. This was done speedily and without the slightest suspicion on the part of any person, the child remaining in the room all the time. When M. le duc d'Orléans had learned all he wanted to know, he bade the child look in the water and tell him who was at Madame de

Nancre's and what they were all doing. She repeated
word for word the story that had been told by the
duke's messenger; described minutely the faces,
dresses and positions of the assembled company,
those that were playing cards at the various tables,
those that were sitting, those that were standing,
even the very furniture! But to leave nothing in
doubt, the Duke of Orleans despatched Nancre back
to the house to verify a second time the child's
account, and like the valet, he found she had been
right in every particular.

"As a rule he said very little to me about these
subjects, as he knew I did not approve of them,
and on this occasion I did not fail to scold him,
and to point out the folly of being amused by such
things, especially at a time when his attention should
be occupied with more serious matters. 'Oh, but
I have only told you half,' he replied; 'that was
just the beginning,' and then he went on to say
that, encouraged by the exactitude of the little girl's
description of Madame de Nancre's room, he resolved
to put to her a more important question, namely, as
to the scene that would occur at the death of
the king. The child had never seen any one who
was about the court, and had never even heard of
Versailles, but she described exactly and at great
length the king's bedroom at Versailles and all the
furniture which was in fact there at the date of his
death. She gave every detail as to the bed, and
cried out on recognising, in the arms of Madame
de Ventadour, a little child decorated with an order
whom she had seen at the house of Mademoiselle

la Sery; and again at the sight of M. le duc
d'Orléans. From her account, Madame de Main-
tenon, Fagon with his odd face, Madame la duchesse
d'Orléans, Madame la duchesse, Madame la prin-
cesse de Conti, besides other princes and nobles,
and even the valets and servants were all present
at the king's deathbed. Then she paused, and
M. le duc d'Orléans, surprised that she had never
mentioned Monseigneur, Monsieur le duc de Bourgogne, Madame la duchesse de Bourgogne, nor M.
le duc de Berri, inquired if she did not see such
and such people answering to their description.
She persisted that she did not, and went over the
others for the second time. This astonished M. le
duc d'Orléans deeply, as well as myself, and we
were at a loss to explain it, but the event proved
that the child was perfectly right. This *séance* took
place in 1706. These four members of the royal
family were then full of health and strength; and
they all died before the king. It was the same
thing with M. le prince, M. le duc, and M. le
prince de Conti, whom she likewise did not see,
though she beheld the children of the two last
named; M. du Maine, his own (Orléans), and M. le
comte de Toulouse. But of course this fact was
unknown till eight years after."

Science may conceivably come to study crystal
visions, but veracious crystal visions will be treated
like veracious dreams. That is to say, they will
be explained as the results of a chance coincidence
between the unknown fact and the vision, or of
imposture, conscious or unconscious, or of confusion

of memory, or the fact of the crystal vision will be simply denied. Thus a vast number of well-authenticated cases of veracious visions will be required before science could admit that it might be well to investigate hitherto unacknowledged faculties of the human mind. The evidence can never be other than the word of the seer, with whatever value may attach to the testimony of those for whom he "sees," and describes, persons and places unknown to himself. The evidence of individuals as to their own subjective experiences is accepted by psychologists in other departments of the study.[1]

[1] Readers curious in crystal-gazing will find an interesting sketch of the history of the practice, with many modern instances, in *Proceedings*, *S.P.R.*, vol. v., p. 486, by " Miss X.". There are also experiments by Lord Stanhope and Dr. Gregory in Gregory's *Letters on Animal Magnetism*, p. 370 (1851). It is said that, as sights may be seen in a glass ball, so articulate voices, by a similar illusion, can be heard in a sea shell, when

" It remembers its august abodes,
And murmurs as the ocean murmurs there ".

CHAPTER IV.

IN "crystal-gazing" anybody can make experiments for himself and among such friends as he thinks he can trust. They are hallucinations consciously sought for, and as far as possible, provoked or induced by taking certain simple measures. Unsought, spontaneous waking hallucinations, according to the result of Mr. Galton's researches, though not nearly so common as dreams, are as much facts of *sane* mental experience. Now every ghost or wraith is a hallucination. You see your wife in the dining-

room when she really is in the drawing-room;
you see your late great-great-grandfather anywhere.
Neither person is really present. The first appearance in popular language is a "wraith"; the second
is a "ghost" in ordinary speech. Both are hallucinations.

So far Mr. Galton would go, but mark what
follows! Everybody allows the existence of dreams,
but comparatively few believe in dream stories of
veracious dreams. So every scientific man believes
in hallucinations,[1] but few believe in *veracious* hallucinations. A veracious hallucination is, for our
purpose, one which communicates (as veracious
dreams do) information not otherwise known, or, at
least, not known to the knower to be known. The
communication of the knowledge may be done by
audible words, with or without an actual apparition,
or with an apparition, by words or gestures. Again, if a
hallucination of Jones's presence tallies with a great
crisis in Jones's life, or with his death, the hallucination is so far veracious in that, at least, it does not
seem meaningless. Or if Jones's appearance has
some unwonted feature not known to the seer, but
afterwards proved to be correct in fact, that is
veracious. Next, if several persons successively in
the same place, or simultaneously, have a similar
hallucination not to be accounted for physically,

---

[1] A set of scientific men, as Lélut and Lombroso, seem to think
that a hallucination stamps a man as *mad*. Napoleon, Socrates,
Pascal, Jeanne d'Arc, Luther were all lunatics. They had lucid
intervals of considerable duration, and the belief in their lunacy is
peculiar to a small school of writers.

that is, if not a veracious, a curious hallucination.
Once more, if a hallucinatory figure is afterwards
recognised in a living person previously unknown,
or a portrait previously unseen, that (if the recognition be genuine) is a veracious hallucination. The
vulgar call it a wraith of the living, or a ghost of
the dead.

Here follow two cases. The first, *The Family
Coach*,[1] gave no verified intelligence, and would be
styled a "subjective hallucination". The second
contributed knowledge of facts not previously known
to the witness, and so the vulgar would call it a
ghost. Both appearances were very rich and full
of complicated detail. Indeed, any ghost that wears
clothes is a puzzle. Nobody but savages thinks that
clothes have ghosts, but Tom Sawyer conjectures that
ghosts' clothes "are made of ghost stuff".

As a rule, not very much is seen of a ghost;
he is "something of a shadowy being". Yet we
very seldom hear of a ghost stark naked; that of
Sergeant Davies, murdered in 1749, is one of three
or four examples in civilised life.[2] Hence arises
the old question, "How are we to account for the
clothes of ghosts?" One obvious reply is that
there is no ghost at all, only a hallucination. We
do not see people naked, as a rule, in our dreams;
and hallucinations, being waking dreams, conform
to the same rule. If a ghost opens a door or lifts
a curtain in our sight, that, too, is only part of

[1] A crowd of phantom coaches will be found in Messrs. Myers
and Gurney's *Phantasms of the Living*.

[2] See *The Slaying of Sergeant Davies of Guise's*.

the illusion. The door did not open; the curtain was not lifted. Nay, if the wrist or hand of the seer is burned or withered, as in a crowd of stories, the ghost's hand did not produce the effect. It was produced in the same way as when a hypnotised patient is told that "his hand is burned," his fancy then begets real blisters, or so we are informed, truly or not. The stigmata of St. Francis and others are explained in the same way.[1] How ghosts pull bed-clothes off and make objects fly about is another question: in any case the ghosts are not *seen* in the act.

Thus the clothes of ghosts, their properties, and their actions affecting physical objects, are not more difficult to explain than a naked ghost would be, they are all the "stuff that dreams are made of". But occasionally things are carried to a great pitch, as when a ghost drives off in a ghostly dogcart, with a ghostly horse, whip and harness. Of this complicated kind we give two examples; the first reckons as a "subjective," the second as a veracious hallucination.

THE OLD FAMILY COACH.

A distinguished and accomplished country gentle-man and politician, of scientific tastes, was riding in the New Forest, some twelve miles from the place where he was residing. In a grassy glade he discovered that he did not very clearly know

---

[1] *Principles of Psychology*, by Prof. James of Harvard, vol. ii., p. 612. Charcot is one of sixteen witnesses cited for the fact.

his way to a country town which he intended to
visit. At this moment, on the other side of some
bushes a carriage drove along, and then came into
clear view where there was a gap in the bushes.
Mr. Hyndford saw it perfectly distinctly; it was
a slightly antiquated family carriage, the sides were
in that imitation of wicker work on green panel
which was once so common. The coachman was
a respectable family servant, he drove two horses:
two old ladies were in the carriage, one of them
wore a hat, the other a bonnet. They passed, and
then Mr. Hyndford, going through the gap in the
bushes, rode after them to ask his way. There
was no carriage in sight, the avenue ended in a
cul-de-sac of tangled brake, and there were no traces
of wheels on the grass. Mr. Hyndford rode back
to his original point of view, and looked for any
object which could suggest the illusion of one old-
fashioned carriage, one coachman, two horses and
two elderly ladies, one in a hat and one in a
bonnet. He looked in vain—and that is all!

Nobody in his senses would call this appearance
a ghostly one. The name, however, would be
applied to the following tale of

RIDING HOME FROM MESS.

In 1854, General Barter, C.B., was a subaltern
in the 75th Regiment, and was doing duty at the
hill station of Murree in the Punjaub. He lived
in a house built recently by a Lieutenant B., who
died, as researches at the War Office prove, a

Peshawur on 2nd January, 1854. The house was on a spur of the hill, three or four hundred yards under the only road, with which it communicated by a "bridle path," never used by horsemen. That path ended in a precipice; a footpath led into the bridle path from Mr. Barter's house.

One evening Mr. Barter had a visit from a Mr. and Mrs. Deane, who stayed till near eleven o'clock. There was a full moon, and Mr. Barter walked to the bridle path with his friends, who climbed it to join the road. He loitered with two dogs, smoking a cigar, and just as he turned to go home, he heard a horse's hoofs coming down the bridle path. At a bend of the path a tall hat came into view, then round the corner, the wearer of the hat, who rode a pony and was attended by two native grooms. "At this time the two dogs came, and crouching at my side, gave low frightened whimpers. The moon was at the full, a tropical moon, so bright that you could see to read a newspaper by its light, and I saw the party above me advance as plainly as if it were noon-day; they were above me some eight or ten feet on the bridle road. . . . On the party came, . . . and now I had better describe them. The rider was in full dinner dress, with white waistcoat and a tall chimney-pot hat, and he sat on a powerful hill pony (dark-brown, with black mane and tail) in a listless sort of way, the reins hanging loosely from both hands." Grooms led the pony and supported the rider. Mr. Barter, knowing that there was no place they could go to but his own house, cried "*Quon hai?*" (who is it?), adding in English, "Hullo, what the devil do you want here?" The group halted, the rider gathered up the reins with both hands, and turning, showed Mr. Barter the known features of the late Lieutenant B.

He was very pale, the face was a dead man's face, he was stouter than when Mr. Barter knew him and he wore *a dark Newgate fringe.*

Mr. Barter dashed up the bank, the earth thrown up in making the bridle path crumbled under him, he fell, scrambled on, reached the bridle path where the group had stopped, and found nobody. Mr. Barter ran up the path for a hundred yards, as nobody could go *down* it except over a precipice, and neither heard nor saw anything. His dogs did not accompany him.

Next day Mr. Barter gently led his friend Deane to talk of Lieutenant B., who said that the lieutenant " grew very bloated before his death, and while on the sick list he allowed the fringe to grow in spite of all we could say to him, and I believe he was buried with it ". Mr. Barter then asked where he got the pony, describing it minutely.

" He bought him at Peshawur, and killed him one day, riding in his reckless fashion down the hill to Trete."

Mr. Barter and his wife often heard the horse's hoofs later, though he doubts if any one but B. had ever ridden the bridle path. His Hindoo bearer he found one day armed with a *lattie*, being determined to waylay the sound, which " passed him

like a typhoon".[1]   Here the appearance gave correct
information unknown previously to General Barter,
namely, that Lieutenant B. grew stout and wore
a beard before his death, also that he had owned
a brown pony, with black mane and tail.   Even
granting that the ghosts of the pony and lieutenant
were present (both being dead), we are not informed
that the grooms were dead also.   The hallucination,
on the theory of " mental telegraphy," was telegraphed to General Barter's mind from some one
who had seen Lieutenant B. ride home from mess
not very sober, or from the mind of the defunct
lieutenant, or, perhaps, from that of the deceased
pony.   The message also reached and alarmed
General Barter's dogs.

Something of the same kind may or may not
explain Mr. Hyndford's view of the family coach,
which gave no traceable information.

The following story, in which an appearance of
the dead conveyed information not known to the
seer, and so deserving to be called veracious, is a
little ghastly.

THE BRIGHT SCAR.

In 1867, Miss G., aged eighteen, died suddenly of
cholera in St. Louis.   In 1876 a brother, F. G., who
was much attached to her, had done a good day's
business in St. Joseph.   He was sending in his

---

[1] Story written by General Barter, 28th April, 1888.   (S.P.R.)
Corroborated by Mrs. Barter and Mr. Stewart, to whom General
Barter told his adventure at the time.

orders to his employers (he is a commercial traveller) and was smoking a cigar, when he became conscious that some one was sitting on his left, with one arm on the table. It was his dead sister. He sprang up to embrace her (for even on meeting a stranger whom we take for a dead friend, we never realise the impossibility in the half moment of surprise) but she was gone. Mr. G. stood there, the ink wet on his pen, the cigar lighted in his hand, the name of his sister on his lips. He had noted her expression, features, dress, the kindness of her eyes, the glow of the complexion, and what he had never seen before, *a bright red scratch on the right side of her face*.

Mr. G. took the next train home to St. Louis, and told the story to his parents. His father was inclined to ridicule him, but his mother nearly fainted. When she could control herself, she said that, unknown to any one, she had accidentally scratched the face of the dead, apparently with the pin of her brooch, while arranging something about the corpse. She had obliterated the scratch with powder, and had kept the fact to herself. "She told me she *knew* at least that I had seen my sister." A few weeks later Mrs. G. died.[1]

Here the informatian existed in one living mind, the mother's, and if there is any "mental telegraphy," may thence have been conveyed to Mr. F. G.

[1] Statement by Mr. F. G., confirmed by his father and brother, who were present when he told his tale first, in St. Louis. *S.P.R. Proceedings*, vol. vi., p. 17.

Another kind of cases which may be called veracious, occurs when the ghost seer, after seeing the ghost, recognises it in a portrait not previously beheld. Of course, allowance must be made for fancy, and for conscious or unconscious hoaxing. You see a spook in Castle Dangerous. You then recognise the portrait in the hall, or elsewhere. The temptation to recognise the spook rather more clearly than you really do, is considerable, just as one is tempted to recognise the features of the Stuarts in the royal family, of the parents in a baby, or in any similar case.

Nothing is more common in literary ghost stories than for somebody to see a spectre and afterwards recognise him or her in a portrait not before seen. There is an early example in Sir Walter Scott's *Tapestried Chamber*, which was told to him by Miss Anna Seward. Another such tale is by Théophile Gautier. In an essay on Illusions by Mr. James Sully, a case is given. A lady (who corroborated the story to the present author) was vexed all night by a spectre in armour. Next morning she saw, what she had not previously observed, a portrait of the spectre in the room. Mr. Sully explains that she had seen the portrait *unconsciously*, and dreamed of it. He adds the curious circumstance that other people have had the same experience in the same room, which his explanation does not cover. The following story is published by the Society for Psychical Research, attested by the seer and her husband, whose real names are known, but not published.[1]

[1] *S.P.R.*, viii., p. 178.

THE VISION AND THE PORTRAIT.

Mrs. M. writes (December 15, 1891) that before her vision she had heard nothing about hauntings in the house occupied by herself and her husband, and nothing about the family sorrows of her predecessors there.

" One night, on retiring to my bedroom about 11 o'clock, I thought I heard a peculiar moaning sound, and some one sobbing as if in great distress of mind. I listened very attentively, and still it continued ; so I raised the gas in my bedroom, and then went to the window on the landing, drew the blind aside, and there on the grass was a very beautiful young girl in a kneeling posture, before a soldier in a general's uniform, sobbing and clasping her hands together, entreating for pardon, but alas ! he only waved her away from him. So much did I feel for the girl that I ran down the staircase to the door opening upon the lawn, and begged her to come in and tell me her sorrow. The figures then disappeared gradually, as in a dissolving view. Not in the least nervous did I feel then ; went again to my bedroom, took a sheet of writing-paper, and wrote down what I had seen." [1]

Mrs. M., whose husband was absent, began to feel nervous, and went to another lady's room.

She later heard of an old disgrace to the youngest daughter of the proud family, her predecessors in

---

[1] Mrs. M. sent the memorandum to the S.P.R. " March 13, 1886. Have just seen visions on lawn—a soldier in general's uniform, a young lady kneeling to him, 11·40 P.M."

the house.   The poor girl tried in vain to win
forgiveness, especially from a near relative, a soldier,
Sir X. Y.

"So vivid was my remembrance of the features
of the soldier, that some months after the occurrence
[of the vision] when I called with my husband at
a house where there was a portrait of him, I
stepped before it and said, 'Why, look! there is
the General!'   And sure enough it *was*."

Mrs. M. had not heard that the portrait was in
the room where she saw it.   Mr. M. writes that
he took her to the house where he knew it to be
without telling her of its existence.   Mrs. M. turned
pale when she saw it.   Mr. M. knew the sad old
story, but had kept it to himself.   The family in
which the disgrace occurred, in 1847 or 1848, were
his relations.[1]

This vision was a veracious hallucination;   it
gave intelligence not otherwise known to Mrs. M.,
and capable of confirmation, therefore the appearances would be called "ghosts".   The majority of
people do not believe in the truth of any such stories
of veracious hallucinations, just as they do not
believe in veracious dreams.   Mr. Galton, out of
all his packets of reports of hallucinations, does
not even allude to a veracious example, whether he
has records of such a thing or not.   Such reports,
however, are ghost stories, "which we now proceed,"
or continue, "to narrate".   The reader will do well
to remember that while everything ghostly, and
not to be explained by known physical facts, is in

[1] *S.P.R.*, viii., p. 178.   The real names are intentionally reserved.

the view of science a hallucination, every hallucination is not a ghost for the purposes of story-telling. The hallucination must, for story-telling purposes, be *veracious.*

Following our usual method, we naturally begin with the anecdotes least trying to the judicial faculties, and most capable of an ordinary explanation. Perhaps of all the senses, the sense of touch, though in some ways the surest, is in others the most easily deceived. Some people who cannot call up a clear mental image of things seen, say a salt-cellar, can readily call up a mental revival of the feeling of touching salt. Again, a slight accidental throb, or leap of a sinew or vein, may feel so like a touch that we turn round to see who touched us. These familiar facts go far to make the following tale more or less conceivable.

THE RESTRAINING HAND.

" About twenty years ago," writes Mrs. Elliot, " I received some letters by post, one of which contained £15 in bank notes. After reading the letters I went into the kitchen with them in my hands. I was alone at the time. . . . Having done with the letters, I made an effort to throw them into the fire, when I distinctly felt my hand arrested in the act. It was as though another hand were gently laid upon my own, pressing it back. Much surprised, I looked at my hand and then saw it contained, not the letters I had intended to destroy, but the bank notes, and that the letters were in the other hand. I was so surprised that I called out, 'Who's here?'"[1]

Nobody will call this "the touch of a vanished hand". Part of Mrs. Elliot's mind knew what she was about, and started an unreal but veracious feeling to warn her. We shall come to plenty of Hands not so readily disposed of.

Next to touch, the sense most apt to be deceived is hearing. Every one who has listened anxiously for an approaching carriage, has often heard it come before it came. In the summer of 1896 the writer, with a lady and another companion, were standing on the veranda at the back of a house in Dumfries-shire, waiting for a cab to take one of them to the station. They heard a cab arrive and draw up, went round to the front of the house, saw the servant open the door and bring out the luggage, but wheeled vehicle there was none in sound or sight. Yet all four persons had heard it, probably by dint of expectation.

To hear articulate voices where there are none is extremely common in madness,[2] but not very rare, as Mr. Galton shows, among the sane. When the voices are veracious, give unknown information, they are in the same case as truthful dreams. I offer a few from the experience, reported to me by himself, of a man of learning whom I shall call a Benedictine monk, though that is not his real position in life.

[1] Corroborated by Mr. Elliot. Mrs. Elliot nearly fainted. *S.P.R.*, viii., 344-345.

[2] Oddly enough, maniacs have many more hallucinations of hearing than of sight. In sane people the reverse is the case.

THE BENEDICTINE'S VOICES.

My friend, as a lad, was in a strait between the choice of two professions. He prayed for enlightenment, and soon afterwards heard an *internal* voice, advising a certain course. " Did you act on it ? " I asked.

" No ; I didn't. I considered that in my circumstances it did not demand attention."

Later, when a man grown, he was in his study merely idling over some books on the table, when he heard a loud voice from a corner of the room assert that a public event of great importance would occur at a given date. It did occur. About the same time, being abroad, he was in great anxiety as to a matter involving only himself. Of this he never spoke to any one. On his return to England his mother said, " You were very wretched about so and so ".

" How on earth did you know ? "

" I heard ——'s voice telling me."

Now —— had died years before, in childhood.

In these cases the Benedictine's own conjecture and his mother's affection probably divined facts, which did not present themselves as thoughts in the ordinary way, but took the form of unreal voices.

There are many examples, as of the girl in her bath who heard a voice say " Open the door " four times, did so, then fainted, and only escaped drowning by ringing the bell just before she swooned. Of course she might not have swooned if she had

not been alarmed by hearing the voices. These
tales are dull enough, and many voices, like Dr.
Johnson's mother's, when he heard her call his
name, she being hundreds of miles away, lead to
nothing and are not veracious. When they are
veracious, as in the case of dreams, it may be by
sheer accident.

In a similar class are " warnings " conveyed by
the eye, not by the ear. The Maoris of New Zealand believe that if one sees a body lying across
a path or oneself on the opposite side of a river, it
is wiser to try another path and a different ford.

THE MAN AT THE LIFT.

In the same way, in August, 1890, a lady in a
Boston hotel in the dusk rang for the lift, walked
along the corridor and looked out of a window,
started to run to the door of the lift, saw a man
in front of it, stopped, and when the lighted lift
came up, found that the door was wide open and
that, had she run on as she intended, she would
have fallen down the well. Here part of her mind
may have known that the door was open, and
started a ghost (for there was no real man there)
to stop her. Pity that these things do not occur
more frequently. They do—in New Zealand.[1]

These are a few examples of useful veracious
waking dreams. The sort of which we hear most

---

[1] Anecdote by the lady. *Boston Budget*, 31st August, 1890.
S.P.R., viii., 345.

are "wraiths". A, when awake, meets B, who is dead or dying or quite well at a distance. The number of these stories is legion. To these we advance, under their Highland title, *spirits of the living*.

CHAPTER V.

" SPIRITS of the living " is the Highland term for the appearances of people who are alive and well—but elsewhere. The common Highland belief is that they show themselves to second-sighted persons, very frequently before the arrival of a stranger or a visitor, expected or unexpected. Probably many readers have had the experience of meeting an acquaintance in the street. He passes us, and within a hundred yards we again meet and talk with our friend. When he is of very marked appearance, or has any strong peculiarity, the experience is rather perplexing. Perhaps a few bits of hallucination are sprinkled over a real object. This ordinary event leads on to what are called " Arrivals," that is when a person is seen, heard and perhaps spoken to in a place to which he is travelling, but whither he has not yet arrived. Mark Twain gives an instance in his own experience. At a large crowded reception he saw approaching him in the throng a lady whom he had known and liked many years before. When she was near him, he lost sight of her, but met her at supper, dressed as he had seen her in the " levee ". At that moment she was travelling by railway to the town in which he was.[1]

A large number of these cases have been printed.[2] In one case a gentleman and lady from their window saw his brother and sister-in-law drive past, with a horse which they knew had not been out for some weeks. The seers were presently joined by the visitors' daughter, who had met the party on the road, she having just left them at their house. Ten minutes later the real pair arrived, horse and all.[3]

This last affair is one of several tales of " Phantom Coaches," not only heard but seen, the coach being a coach of the living. In 1893 the author was staying at a Highland castle, when one of the ladies observed to her nephew, " So you and Susan *did* drive in the dogcart ; I saw you pass my window ".

---

[1] *Tom Sawyer, Detective.*

[2] *Phantasms of the Living*, by Gurney and Myers.

[3] The story is given by Mr. Mountford, one of the seers.

" No, we didn't ; but we spoke of doing it." The
lady then mentioned minute details of the dress
and attitudes of her relations as they passed her
window, where the drive turned from the hall door
through the park ; but, in fact, no such journey
had been made.   Dr. Hack Tuke published the
story of the " Arrival" of Dr. Boase at his house
a quarter of an hour before he came, the people
who saw him supposing him to be in Paris.[1]

When a person is seen in "Arrival" cases before
he arrives, the affair is not so odd if he is expected.
Undoubtedly, expectation does sometimes conjure up
phantasms, and the author once saw (as he supposed)
a serious accident occur which in fact did not take
place, though it seemed unavoidable.

Curiously enough, this creation of phantasms by
expectant attention seems to be rare where "ghosts"
are expected.   The author has slept in several
haunted houses, but has never seen what he was
led to expect.   In many instances, as in " The
Lady in Black " (*infra*), a ghost who is a frequent
visitor is never seen when people watch for her.
Among the many persons who have had delusions
as to the presence of the dead, very few have been
hoping, praying for and expecting them.

> " I look for ghosts, but none will force
>   Their way to me : 'Tis falsely said
> That there was ever intercourse
>   Between the living and the dead,
>   For surely then I should have sight
>   Of him I wait for day and night
>   With love and longings infinite."

Journal of Medical Science, April, 1880, p. 151.

The Affliction of Margaret has been the affliction of most of us. There are curious historical examples of these appearances of the living. Goethe declares that he once met himself at a certain place in a certain dress, and several years later found himself there in that costume. Shelley was seen by his friends at Lerici to pass along a balcony whence there was no exit. However, he could not be found there. The story of the wraith of Catherine the Great is variously narrated. We give it as told by an eye-witness, the Comte de Ribaupierre, about 1862 to Lady Napier and Ettrick. The Count, in 1862, was a very old man, and more than thirty years have passed since he gave the tale to Lady Napier, whose memory retains it in the following form :—

THE WRAITH OF THE CZARINA.

" In the exercise of his duties as one of the pages-in-waiting, Ribaupierre followed one day his august mistress into the throne-room of the palace. When the Empress, accompanied by the high officers of her court and the ladies of her household, came in sight of the chair of state which she was about to occupy, she suddenly stopped, and to the horror and astonished awe of her courtiers, she pointed to a visionary being seated on the imperial throne. The occupant of the chair was an exact counterpart of herself. All saw it and trembled, but none dared to move towards the mysterious presentment of their sovereign.

"After a moment of dead silence the great Catherine raised her voice and ordered her guard to advance and fire on the apparition. The order was obeyed, a mirror beside the throne was shattered, the vision had disappeared, and the Empress, with no sign of emotion, took the chair from which her semblance had passed away." It is a striking barbaric scene!

"Spirits of the living" of this kind are common enough. In the Highlands "second sight" generally means a view of an event or accident some time before its occurrence. Thus an old man was sitting with a little boy on a felled tree beside a steep track in a quarry at Ballachulish. Suddenly he jerked the boy to one side, and threw himself down on the further side of the tree. While the boy stared, the old man slowly rose, saying, "The spirits of the living are strong to-day!" He had seen a mass of rock dashing along, killing some quarrymen and tearing down the path. The accident occurred next day. It is needless to dwell on second sight, which is not peculiar to Celts, though the Highlanders talk more about it than other people.

These appearances of the living but absent, whether caused by some mental action of the person who appears or not, are, at least, *unconscious* on his part.[1] But a few cases occur in which a living person is said, by a voluntary exertion of mind, to have made himself visible to a friend at a distance. One case is vouched for by Baron von

---

[1] Catholic theology recognises, under the name of "Bilocation," the appearance of a person in one place when he is really in another.

Schrenck-Notzig, a German psychologist, who himself made the experiment with success. Others are narrated by Dr. Gibotteau. A curious tale is told by several persons as follows :—

AN "ASTRAL BODY".

Mr. Sparks and Mr. Cleave, young men of twenty and nineteen, were accustomed to "mesmerise" each other in their dormitory at Portsmouth, where they were students of naval engineering. Mr. Sparks simply stared into Mr. Cleave's eyes as he lay on his bed till he "went off". The experiments seemed so curious that witnesses were called, Mr. Darley and Mr. Thurgood. On Friday, 15th January, 1886, Mr. Cleave determined to try to see, when asleep, a young lady at Wandsworth to whom he was in the habit of writing every Sunday. He also intended, if possible, to make *her* see *him*. On awaking, he said that he had seen her in the dining-room of her house, that she had seemed to grow restless, had looked at him, and then had covered her face with her hands. On Monday he tried again, and he thought he had frightened her, as after looking at him for a few minutes she fell back in her chair in a kind of faint. Her little brother was in the room with her at the time. On Tuesday next the young lady wrote, telling Mr. Cleave that she had been startled by seeing him on Friday evening (this is an error), and again on Monday evening, ' much clearer," when she nearly fainted.

All this Mr. Sparks wrote to Mr. Gurney in

the same week. He was inviting instructions on hypnotic experiments, and "launched a letter into space," having read something vague about Mr. Gurney's studies in the newspapers. The letter, after some adventures, arrived, and on 15th March Mr. Cleave wrote his account, Mr. Darley and Mr. Thurgood corroborating as to their presence during the trance and as to Mr. Cleave's statement when he awoke. Mr. Cleave added that he made experiments "for five nights running" before seeing the lady. The young lady's letter of 19th January, 1886, is also produced (postmark, Portsmouth, 20th January). But the lady mentions her *first* vision of Mr. Cleave as on last *Tuesday* (not Friday), and her second, while she was alone with her little brother, at supper on Monday. "I was so frightened that I nearly fainted."

These are all young people. It may be said that all five were concerned in a complicated hoax on Mr. Gurney. Nor would such a hoax argue any unusual moral obliquity. Surtees of Mainsforth, in other respects an honourable man, took in Sir Walter Scott with forged ballads, and never undeceived his friend. Southey played off a hoax with his book *The Doctor*. Hogg, Lockhart, and Wilson, with Allan Cunningham and many others, were constantly engaged in such mystifications, and a "ghost-hunter" might seem a fair butt.

But the very discrepancy in Miss ———'s letter is a proof of fairness. Her first vision of Mr. Cleave was on "Tuesday last". Mr. Cleave's first impression of success was on the Friday following.

But he had been making the experiment for five nights previous, including the Tuesday of Miss ——'s letter. Had the affair been a hoax, Miss —— would either have been requested by him to re-write her letter, putting Friday for Tuesday, or what is simpler, Mr. Sparks would have adopted her version and written "Tuesday" in place of "Friday" in his first letter to Mr. Gurney. The young lady, naturally, requested Mr. Cleave not to try his experiment on her again.

A similar case is that of Mrs. Russell, who tried successfully, when awake and in Scotland, to appear to one of her family in Germany. The sister corroborates and says, "Pray don't come appearing to me again".[1]

These spirits of the living lead to the subject of spirits of the dying. No kind of tale is so common as that of dying people appearing at a distance. Hundreds have been conscientiously published.[2] The belief is prevalent among the Maoris of New Zealand, where the apparition is regarded as a proof of death.[3] Now there is nothing in savage philosophy to account for this opinion of the Maoris. A man's "spirit" leaves his body in dreams, savages think, and as dreaming is infinitely more common than death, the Maoris should argue that the appearance is that of a man's spirit wandering in his sleep. However, they, like many

---

[1] *Phantasms*, ii., pp. 671-677. [2] *Phantasms of the Living*.

[3] Mr. E. B. Tylor gives a Maori case in *Primitive Culture*. Another is in *Phantasms*, ii., 557. See also Polack's *New Zealand* for the prevalence of the belief.

Europeans, associate a man's apparition with his death. Not being derived from their philosophy, this habit may be deduced from their experience.

As there are, undeniably, many examples of hallucinatory appearances of persons in perfect health and ordinary circumstances, the question has been asked whether there are *more* cases of an apparition coinciding with death than, according to the doctrine of chances, there ought to be. Out of about 18,000 answers to questions on this subject, has been deduced the conclusion that the deaths do coincide with the apparitions to an extent beyond mere accident. Even if we had an empty hallucination for every case coinciding with death, we could not set the coincidences down to mere chance. As well might we say that if " at the end of an hour's rifle practice at long-distance range, the record shows that for every shot that has hit the bull's eye, another has missed the target, therefore the shots that hit the target did so by accident ".[1] But as empty hallucinations are more likely to be forgotten than those which coincide with a death ; as exaggeration creeps in, as the collectors of evidence are naturally inclined to select and question people whom they know to have a good story to tell, the evidence connecting apparitions, voices, and so on with deaths is not likely to be received with favour.

One thing must be remembered as affecting the theory that the coincidence between the wraith and

[1] Gurney, *Phantasms*, ii., 6.

the death is purely an accident. Everybody dreams, and out of the innumerable dreams of mankind, a few must hit the mark by a fluke. But *hallucinations* are not nearly so common as dreams. Perhaps, roughly speaking, one person in ten has had what he believes to be a waking hallucination. Therefore, so to speak, compared with dreams, but a small number of shots of this kind are fired. Therefore, bull's eyes (the coincidence between an appearance and a death) are infinitely less likely to be due to chance in the case of waking hallucinations than in the case of dreams, which all mankind are firing off every night of their lives. Stories of these coincidences between appearances and deaths are as common as they are dull. Most people come across them in the circle of their friends. They are all very much alike, and make tedious reading. We give a few which have some picturesque features.

IN TAVISTOCK PLACE.[1]

" In the latter part of the autumn of 1878, between half-past three and four in the morning, I was leisurely walking home from the house of a sick friend. A middle-aged woman, apparently a nurse, was slowly following, going in the same direction. We crossed Tavistock Square together, and emerged simultaneously into Tavistock Place. The streets and squares were deserted, the morning bright and

[1] The late Surgeon-Major Armand Leslie, who was killed at the battle of El Teb, communicated the following story to the *Daily Telegraph* in the autumn of 1881, attesting it with his signature.

calm, my health excellent, nor did I suffer from anxiety or fatigue. A man suddenly appeared, striding up Tavistock Place, coming towards me, and going in a direction opposite to mine. When first seen he was standing exactly in front of my own door (5 Tavistock Place). Young and ghastly pale, he was dressed in evening clothes, evidently made by a foreign tailor. Tall and slim, he walked with long measured strides noiselessly. A tall white hat, covered thickly with black crape, and an eye-glass, completed the costume of this strange form. The moonbeams falling on the corpse-like features revealed a face well known to me, that of a friend and relative. The sole and only person in the street beyond myself and this being was the woman already alluded to. She stopped abruptly, as if spell-bound, then rushing towards the man, she gazed intently and with horror unmistakable on his face, which was now upturned to the heavens and smiling ghastly. She indulged in her strange contemplation but during very few seconds, then with extraordinary and unexpected speed for her weight and age she ran away with a terrific shriek and yell. This woman never have I seen or heard of since, and but for her presence I could have explained the incident: called it, say, subjection of the mental powers to the domination of physical reflex action, and the man's presence could have been termed a false impression on the retina.

"A week after this event, news of this very friend's death reached me. It occurred on the morning in question. From the family I learned that according to the rites of the Greek Church and the custom of the country he resided in, he was buried in his evening clothes made abroad by a foreign tailor, and strange to say, he wore goloshes over his boots, according also to the custom of the country he died in. . . . When in England, he lived in Tavistock Place, and occupied my rooms during my absence."[1]

THE WYNYARD WRAITH.[2]

"In the month of November (1785 or 1786), Sir John Sherbrooke and Colonel Wynyard were sitting before dinner in their barrack room at Sydney Cove, in America. It was duskish, and a candle was placed on a table at a little distance. A figure dressed in plain clothes and a good round hat, passed gently between the above people and the fire. While passing, Sir J. Sherbrooke exclaimed, 'God bless my soul, who's that?'

"Almost at the same moment Colonel W. said, 'That's my brother John Wynyard, and I am sure he is dead'. Colonel W. was much agitated,

---

This is a remarkably difficult story to believe. "The morning bright and calm" is lit by the rays of the moon. The woman (a Mrs. Gamp) must have rushed *past* Dr. Leslie. A man who died in Greece or Russia "that morning" would hardly be arrayed in evening dress for burial before 4 A.M. The custom of using goloshes as "hell-shoes" (fastened on the Icelandic dead in the Sagas) needs confirmation. Men are seldom buried in eye-glasses—never in tall white hats.—*Phantasms of the Living*, ii., 252.

[2] From a memorandum, made by General Birch Reynardson, of an oral communication made to him by Sir John Sherbrooke, one of the two seers.

and cried and sobbed a great deal. Sir John said, ' The fellow has a devilish good hat; I wish I had it'. (Hats were not to be got there, and theirs were worn out.) They immediately got up (Sir John was on crutches, having broken his leg), took a candle and went into the bedroom, into which the figure had entered. They searched the bed and every corner of the room to no effect; the windows were fastened up with mortar. . . .

"They received no communication from England for about five months, when a letter from Mr. Rush, the surgeon (Coldstream Guards), announced the death of John Wynyard at the moment, as near as could be ascertained, when the figure appeared. In addition to this extraordinary circumstance, Sir John told me that two years and a half afterwards he was walking with Lilly Wynyard (a brother of Colonel W.) in London, and seeing somebody on the other side of the way, he recognised, he thought, the person who had appeared to him and Colonel Wynyard in America. Lilly Wynyard said that the person pointed out was a Mr. Eyre (Hay ?), that he and John Wynyard were frequently mistaken for each other, and that money had actually been paid to this Mr. Eyre in mistake."

A famous tale of an appearance is Lord Brougham's. His Lordship was not reckoned precisely a veracious man; on the other hand, this was not the kind of fable he was likely to tell. He was brought up under the *régime* of common-sense. "On all such subjects my father was very sceptical," he says. To disbelieve Lord Brougham we must suppose either that he wilfully made a false entry in his diary in 1799, or that in preparing his *Autobiography* in 1862, he deliberately added a falsehood—and then explained his own marvel away!

LORD BROUGHAM'S STORY.

"*December* 19, 1799.

" . . . At one in the morning, arriving at a decent inn (in Sweden), we decided to stop for the night, and found a couple of comfortable rooms. Tired with the cold of yesterday, I was glad to take advantage of a hot bath before I turned in. And here a most remarkable thing happened to me—so remarkable that I must tell the story from the beginning.

"After I left the High School, I went with G——, my most intimate friend, to attend the classes in the University. . . . We actually committed the folly of drawing up an agreement, written with our blood, to the effect that whichever of us died the first should appear to the other, and thus solve any doubts we had entertained of 'the life after death'. G—— went to India, years passed, and," says Lord Brougham, " I had nearly forgotten his existence. I had taken, as I have said, a warm bath, and while lying in it and enjoying the comfort of the heat, I turned my head round, looking towards the chair on which I had deposited my clothes, as I was about to get out of the bath. On the chair sat G——, looking calmly at me. How I got out of the bath I know not, but on recovering my senses I found myself sprawling on the floor. The apparition, or whatever it was that had taken the likeness of G——, had disappeared. . . . So strongly was I affected by it that I have here written down the whole history, with the date, 19th December, and all the particulars as they are now fresh before me. No doubt I had fallen asleep " (he has just said that he was awake and on the point of leaving the bath), " and that the appearance presented so distinctly to my eyes was a dream I cannot for a moment doubt. . . ."

On 16th October, 1862, Lord Brougham copied this extract for his *Autobiography*, and says that on his arrival in Edinburgh he received a letter from India, announcing that G—— had died on 19th December. He remarks " singular coincidence ! " and adds that, considering the vast number of dreams, the number of coincidences is perhaps fewer than a fair calculation of chances would warrant us to expect.

This is a concession to common-sense, and argues an ignorance of the fact that sane and (apparently) waking men may have hallucinations. On the theory that we *may* have inappreciable moments of sleep when we think ourselves awake, it is not an ordinary but an extraordinary coincidence that Brougham should have had that peculiar moment of the " dream " of G—— on the day or night of G——'s death, while the circumstance that he had made a compact with G—— multiplies the odds against accident in a ratio which mathematicians may calculate. Brougham was used to dreams, like other people ; he was not shocked by them. This "dream" "produced such a shock that I had no inclination to talk about it". Even on Brougham's showing, then, this dream was a thing unique in his experience, and not one of the swarm of visions of sleep. Thus his including it among these, while his whole language shows that he himself did not really reckon it among these, is an example of the fallacies of common-sense. He completes his fallacy by saying, "It is not much more wonderful than that a person whom we had no reason to expect should appear to us at the very moment we had been thinking or speaking of him". But Lord Brougham had *not* been speaking or thinking of G——; "there had been nothing to call him to my recollection," he says. To give his logic any value, he should constantly when (as far as he knew) awake, have had dreams that "shocked" him. Then *one* coincidence would have had no assignable cause save ordinary accident.

If Lord Brougham fabled in 1799 or in 1862, he did so to make a "sensation". And then he tried to undo it by arguing that his experience was a thoroughly commonplace affair.

We now give a very old story, "The Dying Mother". If the reader will compare it with Mr. Cleave's case, "An Astral Body," in this chapter, he will be struck by the resemblance. Mr. Cleave and Mrs. Goffe were both in a trance. Both wished to see persons at a distance. Both saw, and each was seen, Mrs. Goffe by her children's nurse; Mr. Cleave by the person whom he wished to see, but *not* by a small boy also present.

THE DYING MOTHER.[1]

"Mary, the wife of John Goffe of Rochester, being afflicted with a long illness, removed to her father's house at West Mulling, about nine miles from her own. There she died on 4th June, this present year, 1691.

"The day before her departure (death) she grew very impatiently desirous to see her two children, whom she had left at home to the care of a nurse. She prayed her husband to 'hire a horse, for she must go home and die with the children'. She was too ill to be moved, but 'a minister who lives in the town was with her at ten o'clock that night, to whom she expressed good hopes in the mercies of God and a willingness to die'. 'But' said she, 'it is my misery that I cannot see my children.'

"Between one and two o'clock in the morning, she fell into a trance. One, widow Turner, who watched with her that night, says that her eyes were open and fixed and her jaw fallen. Mrs. Turner put her hand upon her mouth and nostrils, but could perceive no breath. She thought her to be in a fit; and doubted whether she were dead or alive.

"The next morning the dying woman told her

---

[1] This is an old, but good story. The Rev. Thomas Tilson, minister (non-conforming) of Aylesford, in Kent, sent it on 6th July, 1691, to Baxter for his *Certainty of the World of Spirits*. The woman Mary Goffe died on 4th June, 1691. Mr. Tilson's informants were her father, speaking on the day after her burial; the nurse, with two corroborative neighbours, on 2nd July; the mother of Mary Goffe; the minister who attended her; and one woman who sat up with her—all "sober intelligent persons". Not many stories have such good evidence in their favour.

mother that she had been at home with her children.
. . . 'I was with them last night when I was
asleep.'

"The nurse at Rochester, widow Alexander by
name, affirms, and says she will take her oath
on't before a Magistrate and receive the sacrament
upon it, that a little before two o'clock that morning
she saw the likeness of the said Mary Goffe come
out of the next chamber (where the elder child lay
in a bed by itself) the door being left open, and stood
by her bedside for about a quarter of an hour; the
younger child was there lying by her. Her eyes
moved and her mouth went, but she said nothing.
The nurse, moreover, says that she was perfectly
awake; it was then daylight, being one of the
longest days in the year. She sat up in bed and
looked steadfastly on the apparition. In that time
she heard the bridge clock strike two, and a while
after said, 'In the name of the Father, Son and
Holy Ghost, what art thou?' Thereupon the apparition removed and went away; she slipped on her
clothes and followed, but what became on't she
cannot tell.

"Mrs. Alexander then walked out of doors till six,
when she persuaded some neighbours to let her in.
She told her adventure; they failed to persuade
her that she had dreamed it. On the same day
the neighbour's wife, Mrs. Sweet, went to West
Mulling, saw Mrs. Goffe before her death, and heard
from Mrs. Goffe's mother the story of the daughter's
dream of her children, Mrs. Sweet not having mentioned the nurse's story of the apparition." That

poor Mrs. Goffe walked to Rochester and returned undetected, a distance of eighteen miles is difficult to believe.

Goethe has an *obiter dictum* on the possibility of intercommunion without the aid of the ordinary senses, between the souls of lovers. Something of the kind is indicated in anecdotes of dreams dreamed in common by husband and wife, but, in such cases, it may be urged that the same circumstance, or the same noise or other disturbing cause, may beget the same dream in both. A better instance is

THE VISION OF THE BRIDE.

Colonel Meadows Taylor writes, in *The Story of my Life* (vol. ii., p. 32): " The determination (to live unmarried) was the result of a very curious and strange incident that befel me during one of my marches to Hyderabad. I have never forgotten it, and it returns to this day to my memory with a strangely vivid effect that I can neither repel nor explain. I purposely withhold the date of the year. In my very early life I had been deeply and devotedly attached to one in England, and only relinquished the hope of one day winning her when the terrible order came out that no furlough to Europe would be granted.

" One evening I was at the village of Dewas Kudea, after a very long afternoon and evening march from Muktul, and I lay down very weary; but the barking of village dogs, the baying of jackals and over-fatigue and heat prevented sleep, and I was wide awake and restless. Suddenly, for my tent door was wide open, I saw the face and figure so familiar to me, but looking older, and with a sad and troubled expression ; the dress was white and seemed covered with a profusion of lace and glistened in the bright moonlight. The arms were stretched out, and a low plaintive cry of ' Do not let me go! Do not let me go!' reached me. I sprang forward, but the figure receded, growing fainter and fainter till I could see it no more, but the low plaintive tones still sounded. I had run barefooted across the open space where my tents were pitched, very much to the astonishment of the sentry on guard, but I returned to my tent without speaking to him. I wrote to my father. I wished to know whether there were any hope for me. He wrote back to me these words : ' Too late, my dear son—on the very day of the vision you describe to me, A. was married '."

The colonel did not keep his determination not to marry, for his *Life* is edited by his daughter, who often heard her father mention the incident, " precisely in the same manner, and exactly as it is in the book ".[1]

If thinking of friends and lovers, lost or dead, could bring their forms and voices before the eye and ear of flesh, there would be a world of hallucinations around us. " But it wants heaven-sent moments for this skill," and few bridal nights send a vision and a voice to the bed of a wakeful lover far away.

Stories of this kind, appearances of the living or

[1] *Phantasms*, ii., 528.

dying really at a distance, might be multiplied to any extent. They are all capable of explanation, if we admit the theory of telepathy, of a message sent by an unknown process from one living man's mind to another. Where more than one person shares the vision, we may suppose that the influence comes directly from A to B, C and D, or comes from A to B, and is by him unconsciously "wired" on to B and C, or is "suggested" to them by B's conduct or words.

In that case animals may be equally affected, thus, if B seems alarmed, that may frighten his dog, or the alarm of a dog, caused by some noise or smell, heard or smelt by him, may frighten B, C and D, and make one or all of them see a ghost.

Popular opinion is strongly in favour of beasts seeing ghosts. The people of St. Kilda, according to Martin, held that cows shared the visions of second-sighted milk-maids. Horses are said to shy on the scene of murders. Scott's horse ran away (home) when Sir Walter saw the bogle near Ashiestiel. In a case given later the dog shut up in a room full of unexplained noises, yelled and whined. The same dog (an intimate friend of my own) bristled up his hair and growled before his master saw the Grey Lady. The Rev. J. G. Wood gives a case of a cat which nearly went mad when his mistress saw an apparition. Jeremy Taylor tells of a dog which got quite used to a ghost that often appeared to his master, and used to follow it. In "The Lady in Black," a dog would jump up and fawn on the ghost and then run away in a fright. Mr. Wesley's mastiff was much alarmed by the family ghost. Not to multiply cases, dogs and other animals are easily affected by whatever it is that makes people think a ghost is present, or by the conduct of the human beings on these occasions.

Absurd as the subject appears, there are stories of the ghosts of animals. These may be discussed later; meanwhile we pass from appearances of the living or dying to stories of appearances of the dead.

CHAPTER VI.

APPEARANCES OF THE DEAD.

WE now pass beyond the utmost limits to which a "scientific" theory of things ghostly can be pushed. Science admits, if asked, that it does not know everything. It is not *inconceivable* that living minds may communicate by some other channel than that of the recognised senses. Science now admits the fact of hypnotic influence, though, sixty years ago, Braid was not allowed to read a paper on it before the British Association. Even now the topic is not welcome. But perhaps only one eminent man of science declares that hypnotism is *all* imposture and malobservation. Thus it is not wholly beyond the scope of fancy to imagine that some day official science may glance at the evidence for "telepathy".

But the stories we have been telling deal with living men supposed to be influencing living men. When the dead are alleged to exercise a similar power, we have to suppose that some consciousness survives the grave, and manifests itself by causing hallucinations among the living. Instances of this have already been given in "The Ghost and the Portrait," "The Bright Scar" and "Riding Home after Mess". These were adduced as examples of *veracity* in hallucinations. Each appearance gave information to the seer which he did not previously possess. In the first case, the lady who saw the soldier and the suppliant did not know of their previous existence and melancholy adventure. In the second, the brother did not know that his dead sister's face had been scratched. In the third, the observer did not know that Lieutenant B. had grown a beard and acquired a bay pony with black mane and tail. But though the appearances were *veracious*, they were *purposeless*, and again, as in each case the information existed in living minds, it *may* have been wired on from them.

Thus the doctrine of telepathy puts a ghost of the dead in a great quandary, If he communicates no verifiable information, he may be explained as a mere empty illusion. If he does yield fresh information, and if that is known to any living mind, he and his intelligence may have been wired on from that mind. His only chance is to communicate facts which are proved to be true, facts which nobody living knew before. Now it is next to impossible to demonstrate that the facts communicated were absolutely unknown to everybody.

Far, however, from conveying unknown intelligence, most ghosts convey none at all, and appear to have no purpose whatever.

It will be observed that there was no traceable reason why the girl with a scar should appear to Mr. G., or the soldier and suppliant to Mrs. M., or Lieutenant B. to General Barker. The appearances came in a vague, casual, aimless way, just as the living and healthy clergyman appeared to the diplomatist. On St. Augustine's theory the dead persons who appeared may have known no more about the matter than did the living clergyman. It is not even necessary to suppose that the dead man was dreaming about the living person to whom, or about the place in which, he appeared. But on the analogy of the tales in which a dream or thought of the living seems to produce a hallucination of their presence in the minds of other and distant living people, so a dream of the dead may (it is urged) have a similar effect if "in that sleep of death such dreams may come". The idea occurred to Shakespeare! In any case the ghosts of our stories hitherto have been so aimless and purposeless as to resemble what we might imagine a dead man's dream to be.

This view of the case (that a " ghost " may be a reflection of a dead man's dream) will become less difficult to understand if we ask ourselves what natural thing most resembles the common idea of a ghost. You are reading alone at night, let us say, the door opens and a human figure glides into the room. To you it pays no manner of attention ; it does not answer if you speak; it may trifle with some object in the chamber and then steal quietly out again.

It is the House-maid walking in her Sleep.

This perfectly accountable appearance, in its aimlessness, its unconsciousness, its irresponsiveness, is undeniably just like the common notion of a ghost. Now, if ordinary ghosts are not of flesh and blood, like the sleep-walking house-maid, yet are as irresponsive, as unconscious, and as vaguely wandering as she, then (if the dead are somewhat) a ghost *may* be a hallucination produced in the living by the *unconscious* action of the mind of the dreaming dead. The conception is at least conceivable. If adopted, merely for argument's sake, it would first explain the purposeless behaviour of ghosts, and secondly, relieve people who see ghosts of the impression that they see "spirits". In the Scotch phrase the ghost obviously "is not all there," any more than the sleep walker is intellectually "all there". This incomplete, incoherent presence is just what might be expected if a dreaming disembodied mind could affect an embodied mind with a hallucination.

But the good old-fashioned ghost stories are usually of another type. The robust and earnest ghosts of our ancestors " had their own purpose sun-clear before them," as Mr. Carlyle would have said. They knew what they wanted, asked for it, and saw that they got it.

As a rule their bodies were unburied, and so they demanded sepulture; or they had committed a wrong, and wished to make restitution; or they had left debts which they were anxious to pay; or they had advice, or warnings, or threats to com-municate; or they had been murdered, and were determined to bring their assassins to the gibbet.

Why, we may ask, were the old ghost stories so different from the new? Well, first they were not all different. Again, probably only the more dramatic tales were as a rule recorded. Thirdly, many of the stories may have been either embellished—a fancied purpose being attributed to a purposeless ghost—or they may even have been invented to protect witnesses who gave information against mur-derers. Who could disobey a ghost?

In any case the old ghost stories are much more dramatic than the new. To them we turn, beginning with the appearances of Mr. and Mrs. Furze at Spraiton, in Devonshire, in 1682. Our author is Mr. Richard Bovet, in his *Pandæmonium, or the Devil's Cloister opened* (1683). The motive of the late Mr. Furze was to have some small debts paid; his wife's spectre was influenced by a jealousy of Mr. Furze's spectre's relations with another lady.

THE DAEMON OF SPRAITON IN DEVON.[1]

ANNO 1682.

" About the month of November in the year 1682, in the parish of Spraiton, in the county of Devon, one Francis Fey (servant to Mr. Philip Furze) being in a field near the dwelling-house of his said master, there appeared unto him the *resemblance* of an *aged gentleman* like his master's father, with a pole or staff in his hand, resembling that he was wont to carry when living to kill the moles withal. The *spectrum* approached near the young man, whom you may imagin not a little surprized at the *appearance* of one that he knew to be dead, but the *spectrum bid him not be afraid of him, but tell his master* (who was his son) that several *legacies which by his testament he had bequeathed were unpaid, naming ten shillings to one and ten shillings to another, both which persons he named* to the young man, who replyed that the party he last named was dead, and so it could not be paid to him. The ghost answered *he knew that, but it must be paid to the next relation*, whom he also named. The spectrum likewise ordered him to carry

[1] " That which was published in May, 1683, concerning the Daemon, or Daemons of *Spraiton* was the extract of a letter from T. C., Esquire, a near neighbour to the place ; and though it needed little confirmation further than the credit that the learning and quality of that gentleman had stampt upon it, yet was much of it likewise known to and related by the Reverend Minister of Barnstaple, of the vicinity to Spraiton. Having likewise since had fresh testimonials of the veracity of that relation, and it being at first designed to fill this place, I have thought it not amiss (for the strangeness of it) to print it here a second time, exactly as I had transcribed it then."—BOVET.

twenty shillings to a gentlewoman, sister to the
deceased, living near Totness in the said county,
and promised, if these things were performed, to
trouble him no further ; but at the same time the
spectrum, speaking of his *second wife* (who was also
dead) *called her wicked woman*, though the gentleman
who writ the letter knew her and esteemed her a
very good woman. And (having thus related him
his mind) the spectrum left the young man, who
according to the *direction* of the *spirit* took care to
see the small legacies satisfied, and carried the
twenty shillings that was appointed to be paid the
gentlewoman near Totness, but she utterly refused to
receive it, being sent her (as she said) from the devil.
The same night the young man lodging at her
house, the aforesaid spectrum appeared to him
again ; whereupon the young man challenged his
promise not to trouble him any more, saying he had
performed all according to his appointment, but
that the gentlewoman, his sister, would not receive
the money.

" *To which the spectrum replied that was true indeed ;*
but withal *directed* the young man to ride to *Totness*
and buy for her *a ring of that value, which the spirit
said she would accept of*, which being provided accordingly, she received. Since the performance of
which the ghost or apparition of the old gentleman
hath seemed to be at rest, having never given the
young man any further trouble.

" But the next day after having delivered the ring,
the young man was riding home to his master's
house, accompanyed by a servant of the gentle-

woman's near *Totness*, and near about the time of their entrance (or a little before they came) into the parish of *Spraiton* aforesaid, there appeared to be upon the horse behind the young man, the resemblance of the *second wife* of the old gentleman spoken of before.

"This daemon often threw the young man off his horse, and cast him with such violence to the ground as was great astonishment, not only to the gentlewoman's servant (with him), but to divers others who were spectators of the frightful action, the ground resounding with great noise by reason of the incredible force with which he was cast upon it. At his coming into his master's yard, the horse which he rid, though very poor and out of case, leaped at one spring twenty-five foot, to the amazement of all that saw it. Soon after the she-spectre shewed herself to divers in the house, *viz.*, the aforesaid young man, *Mistress Thomasin Gidly*, *Ann Langdon*, born in that parish, and a little child, which, by reason of the troublesomeness of the spirit, they were fain to remove from that house. She appeared sometimes in her own shape, sometimes in forms very horrid; now and then like a monstrous dog belching out fire; at another time it flew out at the window, in the shape of a horse, carrying with it only one pane of glass and a small piece of iron.

"One time the young man's head was thrust into a very strait place betwixt a bed's head and a wall, and forced by the strength of divers men to be removed thence, and that not without being much

hurt and bruised, so that much blood appeared about
it : upon this it was advised he should be bleeded,
to prevent any ill accident that might come of the
bruise; after bleeding, the ligature or binder of his
arm was removed from thence and conveyed about
his middle, where it was strained with such violence
that the girding had almost stopp'd his breath and
kill'd him, and being cut asunder it made *a strange
and dismal noise*, so that the standers by were
affrighted at it. At divers other times he hath been
in danger to be strangled with cravats and hand-
kerchiefs that he hath worn about his neck, which
have been drawn so close that with the sudden
violence he hath near been choaked, and hardly
escaped death.

"The spectre hath shewed great offence at the
perriwigs which the young man used to wear, for
they are often torn from his head after a very
strange manner; one that he esteemed above the
rest he put in a small box, and that box he placed
in another, which he set against the wall of his
chamber, placing a joint-stool with other weight
a top of it, but in short time the boxes were broken
in sunder and the perriwig rended into many small
parts and tatters. Another time, lying in his
master's chamber with his perriwig on his head, to
secure it from danger, within a little time it was
torn from him and reduced into very small fragments. At another time one of his shoe-strings
was observed (without the assistance of any hand)
to come of its own accord out of its shoe and fling
itself to the other side of the room ; the other was

crawling after it, but a maid espying that, with her hand drew it out, and it strangely *clasp'd* and *curl'd* about her hand like a living *eel* or *serpent;* this is testified by a lady of considerable quality, too great for exception, who was an eye-witness. The same lady shewed Mr. *C.* one of the young man's gloves, which was torn in his pocket while she was by, which is so dexterously tatter'd and so artificially torn that it is conceived a cutler could not have contrived an instrument to have laid it abroad so accurately, and all this was done in the pocket in the compass of one minute. It is further observable that if the aforesaid young man, or another person who is a servant maid in the house, do wear their own clothes, they are certainly torn in pieces on their backs, but if the clothes belong to any other, they are not injured after that manner.

" Many other strange and fantastical freaks have been done by the said daemon or spirit in the view of divers persons ; a barrel of salt of considerable quantity hath been observed to march from room to room without any human assistance.

"An hand-iron hath seemed to lay itself cross overthwart a pan of milk that hath been scalding over the fire, and two flitches of bacon have of their own accord descended from the chimney where they were hung, and placed themselves upon the handiron.

" When the spectre appears in resemblance of her own person, she seems to be habited in the same cloaths and dress which the gentlewoman of the house (her daughter-in-law) hath on at the same time. Divers times the feet and legs of the young man aforesaid have been so entangled about his neck that he hath been loosed with great difficulty, sometimes they have been so twisted about the frames of chairs and stools that they have hardly been set at liberty. But one of the most considerable instances of the malice of the spirit against the young man happened on Easter Eve, when Mrs. *C.* the relator, was passing by the door of the house, and it was thus :—

" When the young man was returning from his labour, he was taken up by the *skirt* of his *doublet* by this *female daemon*, and carried a height into the air. He was soon missed by his Master and some other servants that had been at labour with him, and after diligent enquiry no news could be heard of him, until at length (near half an hour after) he was heard singing and whistling in a bog or quagmire, where they found him in a kind of trance or *extatick fit*, to which he hath sometimes been accustomed (but whether before the affliction he met with from this spirit I am not certain). He was affected much after such sort, as at the time of those *fits*, so that the people did not give that *attention* and *regard* to what he said as at other times ; but when he returned again to himself (which was about an hour after) he solemnly protested to them that the daemon had carried him so high that his master's house seemed to him to be but *as a hay-cock*, and *that during all that time he was in perfect sense, and prayed to Almighty God not to suffer the devil to destroy him ;* and that he was suddenly set down in that quagmire.

The workmen found one shoe on one side of his master's house, and the other on the other side, and in the morning espied his perriwig hanging on the top of a tree; by which it appears he had been carried a considerable height, and that what he told them was not a fiction.

"After this it was observed that that part of the young man's body which had been on the mud in the quagmire was somewhat benummbed and seemingly deader than the other, whereupon the following *Saturday*, which was the day before *Low Sunday*, he was carried to *Crediton, alias Kirton,* to be bleeded, which being done accordingly, and the company having left him for some little space, at their return they found him in one of his fits, with his *forehead* much *bruised,* and *swoln* to a *great bigness,* none being able to guess how it happened, until his recovery from that *fit,* when upon enquiry he gave them this account of it: *that a bird had with great swiftness and force flown in at the window with a stone in its beak, which it had dashed against his forehead, which had occasioned the swelling which they saw.*

"The people much wondering at the strangeness of the accident, diligently sought the stone, and under the place where he sat they found not such a stone as they expected but a weight of brass or copper, which it seems the daemon had made use of on that occasion to give the poor young man that hurt in his forehead.

"The persons present were at the trouble to break it to pieces, every one taking a part and preserving it in memory of so strange an accident. After this

the spirit continued to molest the young man in a
very severe and rugged manner, often handling him
with great extremity, and whether it hath yet left
its violences to him, or whether the young man be
yet alive, I can have no certain account."

I leave the reader to consider of the extraordinary
strangeness of the relation.

The reader, considering the exceeding strangeness
of the relation, will observe that we have now reached
" great swingeing falsehoods," even if that opinion
had not hitherto occurred to his mind. But if he
thinks that such stories are no longer told, and even
sworn to on Bible oath, he greatly deceives himself.
In the chapter on " Haunted Houses " he will find
statements just as hard narrated of the years 1870
and 1882. In these, however, the ghosts had no
purpose but mischief.[1]

We take another " ghost with a purpose ".

SIR GEORGE VILLIERS' GHOST.

The variations in the narratives of Sir George
Villiers' appearance to an old servant of his, or old
protégé, and the warning communicated by this man
to Villiers' son, the famous Duke of Buckingham,
are curious and instructive. The tale is first told
in print by William Lilly, the astrologer, in the
second part of a large tract called *Monarchy or No
Monarchy in England* (London, 1651), twenty-three
years after Buckingham's murder. But while prior

---

[1] Shchapoff case of " The Dancing Devil " and " The Great
Amherst Mystery ".

in publication, Lilly's story was probably written after, though independent of Lord Clarendon's, in the first book of his *History of the Rebellion*, begun on 18th March, 1646, that is within eighteen years of the events. Clarendon, of course, was in a position to know what was talked of at the time. Next, we have a letter of Mr. Douch to Glanvil, undated, but written after the Restoration, and, finally, an original manuscript of 1652.

Douch makes the warning arrive "some few days" before the murder of Buckingham, and says that the ghost of Sir George, " in his morning gown," bade one Parker tell Buckingham to abandon the expedition to La Rochelle or expect to be murdered. On the third time of appearing the vision pulled a long knife from under his gown, as a sign of the death awaiting Buckingham. He also communicated a " private token " to Parker, the " percipient," Sir George's old servant. On each occasion of the appearance, Parker was reading at midnight. Parker, *after* the murder, told one Ceeley, who told it to a clergyman, who told Douch, who told Glanvil.

In Lilly's version the ghost had a habit of walking in Parker's room, and finally bade him tell Buckingham to abstain from certain company, "or else he will come to destruction, and that suddenly ". Parker, thinking he had dreamed, did nothing ; the ghost reappeared, and communicated a secret "which he (Buckingham) knows that none in the world ever knew but myself and he ". The duke, on hearing the story from Parker, backed by the secret, was amazed, but did not alter his conduct. On the third time the spectre produced the knife, but at *this* information the duke only laughed. Six weeks later he was stabbed. Douch makes the whole affair pass immediately before the assassination. "And Mr. Parker died soon after," as the ghost had foretold to him.

Finally, Clarendon makes the appearances set in six months before Felton slew the duke. The percipient, unnamed, was in bed. The narrative now develops new features; the token given on the ghost's third coming obviously concerns Buckingham's mother, the Countess, the "one person more" who knew the secret communicated. The ghost produces no knife from under his gown; no warning of Buckingham's death by violence is mentioned. A note in the MS. avers that Clarendon himself had papers bearing on the subject, and that he got his information from Sir Ralph Freeman (who introduced the unnamed percipient to the duke), and from some of Buckingham's servants, "who were informed of much of it before the murder of the duke". Clarendon adds that, in general, "no man looked on relations of that sort with less reverence and consideration" than he did. This anecdote he selects out of "many stories scattered abroad at the time" as "upon a better foundation of credit". The percipient was an officer in the king's wardrobe at Windsor, "of a good reputation for honesty and discretion," and aged about fifty. He was bred at a school in Sir George's parish, and as a boy was kindly treated by Sir George, "whom afterwards he never saw". On first beholding the spectre in his room, the seer recognised Sir George's costume, then antiquated. At last the seer went to Sir Ralph Freeman, who introduced him to the duke on a hunting morning at Lambeth Bridge. They talked earnestly apart, observed by Sir Ralph, Clarendon's informant. The duke seemed abstracted all day; left the field early, sought his mother, and after a heated conference of which the sounds reached the ante-room, went forth in visible trouble and anger, a thing never before seen in him after talk with his mother. She was found "overwhelmed with tears and in the highest agony imaginable". "It is a notorious truth" that, when told of his murder, "she seemed not in the least degree surprised."

The following curious manuscript account of the affair is, after the prefatory matter, the copy of a letter dated 1652. There is nothing said of a ghostly knife, the name of the seer is not Parker, and in its whole effect the story tallies with Clarendon's version, though the narrator knows nothing of the scene with the Countess of Buckingham.

CAVALIER VERSION.[1]

"1627. Since William Lilly the Rebells Jugler and Mountebank in his malicious and blaspheamous discourse concerning our late Martyred Soveraigne of ever blessed memory (amongst other lyes and falsehoods) imprinted a relation concerning an Aparition which foretold several Events which should

[1] Additional MSS., British Museum, 27,402, *f.* 132.

happen to the Duke of Buckingham, wherein he
falsifies boeth the person to whom it appeared and
ye circumstances; I thought it not amis to enter
here (that it may be preserved) the true account of
that Aparition as I have receaved it from the hande
and under the hande of Mr. Edmund Wyndham, of
Kellefford in the County of Somersett. I shall sett
it downe (*ipsissimis verbis*) as he delivered it to me
at my request written with his own hande.

WYNDHAM'S LETTER.

" Sr. According to your desire and my promise I
have written down what I remember (divers things
being slipt out of my memory) of the relation made
me by Mr. Nicholas Towse concerning the Aparition
wch visited him. About ye yeare 1627,[1] I and my
wife upon an occasion being in London lay att my
Brother Pyne's house without Bishopsgate, wch.
was ye next house unto Mr. Nicholas Towse's, who
was my Kinsman and familiar acquaintance, in
consideration of whose Society and friendship he
tooke a house in that place, ye said Towse being
a very fine Musician and very good company, and
for ought I ever saw or heard, a Vurtuous, religious
and wel disposed Gentleman. About that time ye
said Mr. Towse tould me that one night, being in
Bed and perfectly waking, and a Candle burning by
him (as he usually had) there came into his Chamber
and stood by his bed side an Olde Gentleman in such

---

[1] Really 1628, unless, indeed, the long-continued appearances
began in the year before Buckingham's death; old style.

an habitt as was in fashion in Q: Elizebeth's tyme, at whose first appearance Mr. Towse was very much troubled, but after a little tyme, recollecting him-selfe, he demanded of him in ye Name of God what he was, whether he were a Man. And ye Aparition replyed No. Then he asked him if he were a Divell. And ye answer was No. Then Mr. Towse said 'in ye Name of God, what art thou then?' And as I remember Mr. Towse told me that ye Apparition answered him that he was ye Ghost of Sir George Villiers, Father to ye then Duke of Buckingham, whom he might very well remember, synce he went to schoole at such a place in Leicester-shire (naming ye place which I have forgotten). And Mr. Towse tould me that ye Apparition had perfectly ye resemblance of ye said Sr George Vil-liers in all respects and in ye same habitt that he had often seene him weare in his lifetime.

" The said Apparition then tould Mr. Towse that he could not but remember ye much kindness that he, ye said Sr George Villiers, had expressed to him whilst he was a Schollar in Leicestershire, as aforesaid, and that as out of that consideration he believed that he loved him and that therefore he made choyce of him, ye sayde Mr. Towse, to deliver a message to his sonne, ye Duke of Buckingham; thereby to prevent such mischiefe as would otherwise befall ye said Duke whereby he would be inevitably ruined. And then (as I remember) Mr. Towse tould me that ye Apparition instructed him what message he should deliver unto ye Duke. Vnto wch. Mr. Towse replyed that he should be very unwilling to

goe to ye Duke of Buckingham upon such an errand,
whereby he should gaine nothing but reproach and
contempt, and to be esteemed a Madman, and therefore desired to be exscused from ye employment,
but ye Apparition pressd him wth. much earnestness
to undertake it, telling him that ye Circumstances
and secret Discoveries which he should be able to
make to ye Duke of such passages in ye course of
his life which were known to none but himselfe,
would make it appeare that ye message was not ye
fancy of a Distempered Brayne, but a reality, and
so ye Apparition tooke his leave of him for that
night and telling him that he would give him leave
to consider till the next night, and then he would
come to receave his answer wheather he would
undertake to deliver his message or no.

" Mr. Towse past that day wth. much trouble
and perplexity, debating and reasoning wth. him-
selfe wether he should deliver his message or not
to ye Duke but, in ye conclusion, he resolved to doe
it, and ye next night when ye Apparition came he
gave his answer accordingly, and then receaved his
full instruction. After which Mr. Towse went and
founde out Sr. Thomas Bludder and Sr. Ralph Freeman, by whom he was brought to ye Duke of
Buckingham, and had sevarall private and lone
audiences of him, I my selfe, by ye favoure of a
freinde (Sr. Edward Savage) was once admitted to
see him in private conference with ye Duke, where
(although I heard not there discourses) I observed
much earnestnessse in their actions and gestures.
After wch. conference Mr. Towse tould me that

ye Duke would not follow ye advice that was given him, which was (as I remember) that he intimated ye casting of, and ye rejecting of some Men who had great interest in him, which was, and as I take it he named, Bp. Laud and that ye Duke was to doe some popular Acts in ye ensuing Parliament, of which Parliament ye Duke would have had Mr. Towse to have been a Burgesse, but he refused it, alleadging that unless ye Duke followed his directions, he must doe him hurt if he were of ye Parliament. Mr. Towse then toalde that ye Duke of Buckingham confessed that he had toalde him those things wch. no Creature knew but himself, and that none but God or ye Divell could reveale to him. Ye Duke offered Mr. Towse to have ye King knight him, and to have given him preferment (as he tould me), but that he refused it, saying that vnless he would follow his advice he would receave nothing from him.

" Mr. Towse, when he made me this relation, he tolde me that ye Duke would inevitably be destroyed before such a time (wch. he then named) and accordingly ye Duke's death happened before that time. He likewise tolde that he had written downe all ye severall discourses that he had had wth. ye Apparition, and that at last his coming was so familiar that he was as litle troubled with it as if it had beene a friende or acquayntance that had come to visitt him. Mr. Towse told me further that ye Archbishop of Canterbury, then Bishop of London, Dr. Laud, should by his Councells be ye authoure of very great troubles to ye Kingdome, by which it should be reduced to ye extremity of disorder and confusion, and that it should seeme to be past all hope of recovery without a miracle, but when all people were in dispayre of seeing happy days agayne, ye Kingdome should suddenly be reduced and resettled agayne in a most happy condition.

"At this tyme my father Pyne was in trouble and comitted to ye Gatehouse by ye Lords of ye Councell about a Quarrel betweene him and ye Lord Powlett, upon which one night I saide to my Cosin Towse, by way of jest, 'I pray aske your Appairition what shall become of my father Pyne's business,' which he promised to doe, and ye next day he tolde me that my father Pyne's enemyes were ashamed of their malicious prosecution, and that he would be at liberty within a week or some few days, which happened according.

"Mr. Towse, his wife, since his death tolde me that her husband and she living at Windsor Castle, where he had an office that Sumer that ye Duke of Buckingham was killed, tolde her that very day that the Duke was sett upon by ye mutinous Mariners att Portesmouth, saying then that ye next attempt agaynst him would be his Death, which accordingly happened. And att ye instant ye Duke was killed (as she vnderstood by ye relation afterwards) Mr. Towse was sitting in his chayre, out of which he suddenly started vp and sayd, 'Wyfe, ye Duke of Buckingham is slayne!'

"Mr. Towse lived not long after that himselfe, but tolde his wife ye tyme of his Death before itt

happened. I never saw him after I had seen some
effects of his discourse, which before I valued not,
and therefore was not curious to enquire after more
than he voluntaryly tolde me, which I then enter-
tayned not wth. these serious thoughts which I
have synce reflected on in his discourse. This is
as much as I can remember on this business which,
according to youre desire, is written by

> " Sr. Yor., &c.,
>
> > " EDMUND WINDHAM.

" BOULOGNE, 5th August, 1652."

This version has, over all others, the merit of being
written by an acquaintance of the seer, who was
with him while the appearances were going on.
The narrator was also present at an interview between the seer and Buckingham. His mention of
Sir Ralph Freeman tallies with Clarendon's, who
had the story from Freeman. The ghost predicts
the Restoration, and this is recorded before that
happy event. Of course Mr. Towse may have been
interested in Buckingham's career and may have
invented the ghost (after discovering the secret
token)[1] as an excuse for warning him.

The reader can now take his choice among versions of Sir George Villiers' ghost. He must
remember that, in 1642, Sir Henry Wotton " spent
some inquiry whether the duke had any ominous

---

[1] It may fairly be argued, granting the ghost, his advice and his
knowledge of a secret known to the countess, that he was a hallucination unconsciously wired on to old Towse by the mind of the
anxious countess herself!

presagement before his end," but found no evidence. Sir Henry told Izaak Walton a story of a dream of an ancestor of his own, whereby some robbers of the University chest at Oxford were brought to justice. Anthony Wood consulted the records of the year mentioned, and found no trace of any such robbery.

We now approach a yet more famous ghost than Sir George's. This is Lord Lyttelton's. The ghost had a purpose, to warn that bad man of his death, but nobody knows whose ghost she was!

LORD LYTTELTON'S GHOST.

"Sir," said Dr. Johnson, "it is the most extraordinary thing that has happened in my day." The doctor's day included the rising of 1745 and of the Wesleyans, the seizure of Canada, the Seven Years' War, the American Rebellion, the Cock Lane ghost, and other singular occurrences, but "the most extraordinary thing" was—Lord Lyttelton's ghost! Famous as is that spectre, nobody knows what it was, nor even whether there was any spectre at all.

Thomas, Lord Lyttelton, was born in 1744. In 1768 he entered the House of Commons. In 1769 he was unseated for bribery. He then vanishes from public view, probably he was playing the prodigal at home and abroad, till February, 1772, when he returned to his father's house, and married. He then went abroad (with a barmaid) till 1773, when his father died. In January, 1774, he took his seat in the House of Lords. In November, 1779,

Lyttelton went into Opposition. On Thursday, 25th November, he denounced Government in a magnificent speech. As to a sinecure which he held, he said, " Perhaps I shall not keep it long!"

Something had Happened !

On the night before his speech, that of Wednesday, 24th November, Lyttelton had seen the ghost, and had been told that he would die in three days. He mentioned this to Rowan Hamilton on the Friday.[1] On the same day, or on Friday, he mentioned it to Captain Ascough, who told a lady, who told Mrs. Thrale.[2] On the Friday he went to Epsom with friends, and mentioned the ghost to them, among others to Mr. Fortescue.[3] About midnight on 28th November, Lord Lyttelton died suddenly in bed, his valet having left him for a moment to fetch a spoon for stirring his medicine. The cause of death was not stated; there was no inquest.

This, literally, is all that is *known* about Lord Lyttelton's ghost. It is variously described as : (1) " a young woman and a robin " (Horace Walpole) ; (2) " a spirit " (Captain Ascough) ; (3) a bird in a dream, " which changed into a woman in white " (Lord Westcote's narrative of 13th February, 1780, collected from Lord Lyttelton's guests and servants); (4) " a bird turning into a woman " (Mrs. Delany,

---

[1] Hamilton's *Memoirs*.
[2] Mrs. Thrale's *Diary*, 28th November, 1779.
[3] *Diary* of Lady Mary Coke, 30th November, 1779.

9th December, 1779); (5) a dream of a bird, followed by a woman, Mrs. Amphlett, in white (Pitt Place archives after 1789); (6) "a fluttering noise, as of a bird, followed by the apparition of a woman who had committed suicide after being seduced by Lyttelton" (Lady Lyttelton, 1828); (7) a bird "which vanished when a female spirit in white raiment presented herself" (*Scots Magazine*, November-December, 1779).

Out of seven versions, a bird, or a fluttering noise as of a bird (a common feature in ghost stories),[1] with a woman following or accompanying, occurs in six. The phenomena are almost equally ascribed to dreaming and to waking hallucination, but the common-sense of the eighteenth century called all ghosts "dreams". In the Westcote narrative (1780) Lyttelton explains the dream by his having lately been in a room with a lady, Mrs. Dawson, when a robin flew in. Yet, in the same narrative, Lyttelton says on Saturday morning "that he was very well, and believed he should bilk the *ghost*". He was certainly in bed at the time of the experience, and probably could not be sure whether he was awake or asleep.[2]

---

[1] See *Phantasms*, ii., 586.

[2] The difficulty of knowing whether one is awake or asleep, just about the moment of entering or leaving sleep is notorious. The author, on awaking in a perfectly dark room, has occasionally seen it in a dim light, and has even been aware, or seemed to be aware, of the pattern of the wall paper. In a few moments this effect of light disappears, and all is darkness. This is the confused mental state technically styled " Borderland," a haunt of ghosts, who are really flitting dreams.

Considering the remoteness of time, the story is very well recorded. It is chronicled by Mrs. Thrale before the news of Lyttelton's death reached her, and by Lady Mary Coke two days later, by Walpole on the day after the peer's decease, of which he had heard. Lord Lyttelton's health had for some time been bad; he had made his will a few weeks before, and his nights were horror-haunted. A little boy, his nephew, to whom he was kind, used to find the wicked lord sitting by his bed at night, because he dared not be alone. So Lockhart writes to his daughter, Mrs. Hope Scott.[1] He had strange dreams of being in hell with the cruel murderess, Mrs. Brownrigg, who "whipped three female 'prentices to death and hid them in the coal-hole". Such a man might have strange fancies, and a belief in approaching death might bring its own fulfilment. The hypothesis of a premeditated suicide, with the story of the ghost as a last practical joke, has no corroboration. It occurred to Horace Walpole at once, but he laid no stress on it.

Such is a plain, dry, statistical account of the most extraordinary event that happened in Dr. Johnson's day.

However, the story does not end here. On the fatal night, 27th November, 1779, Mr. Andrews, M.P., a friend of Lyttelton's was awakened by finding Lord Lyttelton drawing his curtains. Suspecting a practical joke, he hunted for his lordship both in his house and in the garden. Of course

[1] *Life of Lockhart.*

he never found him.   The event was promptly
recorded in the next number of the *Scots Magazine*,
December, 1779.[1]

[1] The author has given authorities in *Blackwood's Magazine*,
March, 1895.   A Mr. Coulton (not Croker as erroneously stated)
published in the *Quarterly Review*, No. 179, an article to prove that
Lyttelton committed suicide, and was Junius.   See also the author's
Life of Lockhart.

CHAPTER VII.

MORE GHOSTS WITH A PURPOSE.

The Slaying of Sergeant Davies in 1749. The Trial. Scott's Theory. Curious recent Corroboration of Sir Walter's Hypothesis. Other Trials involving Ghostly Evidence. Their Want of Authenticity. "Fisher's Ghost" criticised. The Aylesbury Murder. The Dog o' Mause. The Ghosts of Dogs. Peter's Ghost.

MUCH later in time than the ghost of Sir George Villiers is the ghost of Sergeant Davies, of Guise's regiment. His purpose was, first, to get his body buried ; next, to bring his murderers to justice. In this latter desire he totally failed.

THE SLAYING OF SERGEANT DAVIES.

We now examine a ghost with a purpose ; he wanted to have his bones buried. The Highlands, in spite of Culloden, were not entirely pacified in the year 1749. Broken men, robbers, fellows with wrongs unspeakable to revenge, were out in the heather. The hills that seemed so lonely were not bare of human life. A man was seldom so solitary but that eyes might be on him from cave, corry, wood, or den. The Disarming Act had been obeyed in the usual style : old useless weapons were given up to the military. But the spirit of the clans was not wholly broken. Even the old wife of Donald Ban, when he was " sair hadden down by a Bodach " (ghost) asked the spirit to answer one question, "Will the Prince come again?" The song expressed the feelings of the people :—

> The wind has left me bare indeed,
> And blawn my bonnet off my heid,
> But something's hid in Hieland brae,
> The wind's no blawn my sword away!

Traffickers came and went from Prince Charles to Cluny, from Charles in the Convent of St. Joseph to Cluny lurking on Ben Alder. Kilt and tartan were worn at the risk of life or liberty, in short, the embers of the rising were not yet extinct.

At this time, in the summer of 1749, Sergeant Arthur Davies, of Guise's regiment, marched with eight privates from Aberdeen to Dubrach in Braemar, while a corporal's guard occupied the Spital of Glenshee, some eight miles away. "A more waste tract of mountain and bog, rocks and ravines, without habitations of any kind till you reach Glenclunie, is scarce to be met with in Scotland," says Sir Walter.

The sergeant's business was the general surveillance of the country side. He was a kindly prosperous man, liked in the country, fond of children, newly married, and his wife bore witness "that he and she lived together in as great amity and love as any couple could do, and that he never was in use to stay away a night from her".

The sergeant had saved fifteen guineas and a half;
he carried the gold in a green silk purse, and was
not averse to displaying it. He wore a silver watch,
and two gold rings, one with a peculiar knob on the
bezel. He had silver buckles to his brogues, silver
knee-buckles, two dozen silver buttons on a striped
lute-string waistcoat, and he carried a gun, a present
from an officer in his regiment. His dress, on the
fatal 28th of September, was "a blue surtout coat,
with a striped silk vest, and *teiken* breeches and
brown stockings". His hair, of "a dark mouse
colour," was worn in a silk ribbon, his hat was
silver laced, and bore his initials cut in the felt.
Thus attired, "a pretty man," Sergeant Davies
said good-bye to his wife, who never saw him again,
and left his lodgings at Michael Farquharson's early
on 28th September. He took four men with him,
and went to meet the patrol from Glenshee. On
the way he met John Growar in Glenclunie, who
spoke with him "about a tartan coat, which the
sergeant had observed him to drop, and after strictly
enjoining him not to use it again, dismissed him,
instead of making him prisoner".

This encounter was after Davies left his men,
before meeting the patrol, it being his intention to
cross the hill and try for a shot at a stag.

The sergeant never rejoined his men or met the
patrol! He vanished as if the fairies had taken
him. His captain searched the hill with a band
of men four days after the disappearance, but to no
avail. Various rumours ran about the country,
among others a clatter that Davies had been killed

by Duncan Clerk and Alexander Bain Macdonald.
But the body was undiscovered.

In June, one Alexander Macpherson came to
Donald Farquharson, son of the man with whom
Davies had been used to lodge. Macpherson (who
was living in a sheiling or summer hut of shepherds
on the hills) said that he "was greatly troubled by
the ghost of Sergeant Davies, who insisted that he
should bury his bones, and that, he having declined
to bury them, the ghost insisted that he should apply
to Donald Farquharson". Farquharson " could not
believe this," till Macpherson invited him to come
and see the bones. Then Farquharson went with
the other, "as he thought it might possibly be true,
and if it was, he did not know but the apparition
might trouble himself".

The bones were found in a peat moss, about half
a mile from the road taken by the patrols. There,
too, lay the poor sergeant's mouse-coloured hair,
with rags of his blue cloth and his brogues, without
the silver buckles, and there did Farquharson and
Macpherson bury them all.

Alexander Macpherson, in his evidence at the
trial, declared that, late in May, 1750, "when he
was in bed, a vision appeared to him as of a man
clothed in blue, who said, '*I am Sergeant Davies!*'".
At first Macpherson thought the figure was "a real
living man," a brother of Donald Farquharson's. He
therefore rose and followed his visitor to the door,
where the ghost indicated the position of his bones,
and said that Donald Farquharson would help to
inter them. Macpherson next day found the bones,

and spoke to Growar, the man of the tartan coat
(as Growar admitted at the trial). Growar said if
Macpherson did not hold his tongue, he himself
would inform Shaw of Daldownie. Macpherson
therefore went straight to Daldownie, who advised
him to bury the bones privily, not to give the country
a bad name for a rebel district. While Macpherson
was in doubt, and had not yet spoken to Farquharson, the ghost revisited him at night and repeated
his command. He also denounced his murderers,
Clerk and Macdonald, which he had declined to do
on his first appearance. He spoke in Gaelic, which,
it seems, was a language not known by the sergeant.

Isobel MacHardie, in whose service Macpherson
was, deponed that one night in summer, June, 1750,
while she lay at one end of the sheiling (a hill hut
for shepherds or neatherds) and Macpherson lay at
the other, "she saw something naked come in at
the door, which frighted her so much that she drew
the clothes over her head. That when it appeared
it came in in a bowing posture, and that next
morning she asked Macpherson what it was that
had troubled them in the night before. To which
he answered that she might be easy, for it would not
trouble them any more."

All this was in 1750, but Clerk and Macdonald
were not arrested till September, 1753. They were
then detained in the Tolbooth of Edinburgh on
various charges, as of wearing the kilt, till June,
1754, when they were tried, Grant of Prestongrange
prosecuting, aided by Haldane, Home and Dundas,
while Lockhart and Mackintosh defended. It was

proved that Clerk's wife wore Davies's ring, that
Clerk, after the murder, had suddenly become rela-
tively rich and taken a farm, and that the two men,
armed, were on the hill near the scene of the murder
on 28th September, 1749. Moreover, Angus Cameron
swore that he saw the murder committed. His
account of his position was curious. He and another
Cameron, since dead, were skulking near sunset in
a little hollow on the hill of Galcharn. There he had
skulked all day, "waiting for Donald Cameron, *who
was afterwards hanged*, together with some of the
said Donald's companions from Lochaber". No
doubt they were all honest men who had been
"out," and they may well have been on Cluny's
business of conveying gold from the Loch Arkaig
hoard to Major Kennedy for the prince.

On seeing Clerk and Macdonald strike and shoot
the man in the silver-laced hat, Cameron and his
companion ran away, nor did Cameron mention
the matter till nine months later, and then only to
Donald (not he who was hanged). Donald advised
him to hold his tongue. This Donald corroborated
at the trial. The case against Clerk and Macdonald
looked very black, especially as some witnesses fled
and declined to appear. Scott, who knew Macintosh, the counsel for the prisoners, says that their
advocates and agent "were convinced of their guilt".
Yet a jury of Edinburgh tradesmen, moved by
Macintosh's banter of the apparition, acquitted the
accused solely, as Scott believes, because of the
ghost and its newly-learned Gaelic. It is indeed extraordinary that Prestongrange, the patron of David

Balfour, allowed his witnesses to say what the ghost said, which certainly "is not evidence". Sir Walter supposes that Macpherson and Mrs. Mac-Hardie invented the apparition as an excuse for giving evidence. "The ghost's commands, according to Highland belief, were not to be disobeyed." Macpherson must have known the facts "by ordinary means". We have seen that Clerk and Macdonald were at once suspected; there was "a clatter" against them. But Angus Cameron had not yet told his tale of what he saw. Then who *did* tell?

Here comes in a curious piece of evidence of the year 1896. A friend writes (29th December, 1896) :—

"DEAR LANG,

"I enclose a tradition connected with the murder of Sergeant Davies, which my brother picked up lately before he had read the story in your *Cock Lane*. He had heard of the event before, both in Athole and Braemar, and it was this that made him ask the old lady (see next letter) about it.

"He thinks that Glenconie of your version (p. 256) must be Glenclunie, into which Allt Chriostaidh falls. He also suggests that the person who was chased by the murderers may have got up the ghost, in order to shift the odium of tale-bearing to other shoulders. The fact of being mixed up in the affair lends some support to the story here related."

Here follows my friend's brother's narrative, the name of the witness being suppressed.

CONCERNING THE MURDER OF SERGEANT DAVIES.

There is at present living in the neighbourhood of —— an old lady, about seventy years of age. Her maiden name is ——,[1] and she is a native of Braemar, but left that district when about twenty years old, and has never been back to it even for a visit. On being asked whether she had ever heard the story of Sergeant Davies, she at first persisted in denying all knowledge of it. The ordinary version was then related to her, and she listened quietly until it was finished, when she broke out with :—

"That isn't the way of it at all, for the men *were* seen, and it was a forbear of my own that saw them. He had gone out to try to get a stag, and had his gun and a deer-hound with him. He saw the men on the hill doing something, and thinking they had got a deer, he went towards them. When he got near them, the hound began to run on in front of him, and at that minute *he saw what it was they had*. He called to the dog, and turned to run away, but saw at once that he had made a mistake, for he had called their attention to himself, and a shot was fired after him, which wounded the dog. He then ran home as fast as he could, never looking behind him, and did not know how far the men followed him. Some time afterwards the dog came home, and he went to see whether it was much hurt, whereupon it flew at him, and had to be killed.

---

[1] A prominent name among the witnesses at the trial.

They thought that it was trying to revenge itself on him for having left it behind."

At this point the old lady became conscious that she was telling the story, and no more could be got out of her. The name of the lady who keeps a secret of 145 years' standing, is the name of a witness in the trial. The whole affair is thoroughly characteristic of the Highlanders and of Scottish jurisprudence after Culloden, while the verdict of "Not Guilty" (when "Not Proven" would have been stretching a point) is evidence to the "common-sense" of the eighteenth century.[1]

There are other cases, in Webster, Aubrey and Glanvil of ghosts who tried more successfully to bring their murderers to justice. But the reports of the trials do not exist, or cannot be found, and Webster lost a letter which he once possessed, which would have been proof that ghostly evidence was given and was received at a trial in Durham (1631 or 1632). Reports of old men present were collected for Glanvil, but are entirely too vague.

The case of *Fisher's Ghost*, which led to evidence being given as to a murder in New South Wales, cannot be wholly omitted. Fisher was a convict settler, a man of some wealth. He disappeared from his station, and his manager (also a convict) declared that he had returned to England. Later,

---

[1] The report of the trial in the *Scots Magazine* of June, 1754 (magazines appeared at the end of the month), adds nothing of interest. The trial lasted from 7 A.M. of June 11 till 6 A.M. of June 14. The jury deliberated for two hours before arriving at a verdict.

a man returning from market saw Fisher sitting on
a rail; at his approach Fisher vanished. Black
trackers were laid on, found human blood on the
rail, and finally discovered Fisher's body. The
manager was tried, was condemned, acknowledged
his guilt and was hanged.

The story is told in *Household Words*, where Sir
Frederick Forbes is said to have acted as judge.
No date is given. In *Botany Bay*,[1] the legend is
narrated by Mr. John Lang, who was in Sydney
in 1842. He gives no date of the occurrence, and
clearly embellishes the tale. In 1835, however, the
story is told by Mr. Montgomery Martin in volume
iv. of his *History of the British Colonies*. He gives
the story as a proof of the acuteness of black
trackers. Beyond saying that he himself was in
the colony when the events and the trial occurred,
he gives no date. I have conscientiously investigated the facts, by aid of the Sydney newspapers,
and the notes of the judge, Sir Frederick Forbes.
Fisher disappeared at the end of June, 1826, from
Campbeltown. Suspicion fell on his manager,
Worral. A reward was offered late in September.
Late in October the constable's attention was drawn
to blood-stains on a rail. Starting thence, the
black trackers found Fisher's body. Worral was
condemned and hanged, after confession, in February, 1827. Not a word is said about *why* the
constable went to, and examined, the rail. But
Mr. Rusden, author of a *History of Australia*, knew

---

[1] Sydney, no date.

the medical attendant Farley (who saw Fisher's ghost, and pointed out the bloody rail), and often discussed it with Farley. Mr. Souttar, in a work on Colonial traditions, proves the point that Farley told his ghost story *before* the body of Fisher was found. But, for fear of prejudicing the jury, the ghost was kept out of the trial, exactly as in the following case.

THE GARDENER'S GHOST.

Perhaps the latest ghost in a court of justice (except in cases about the letting of haunted houses) "appeared" at the Aylesbury Petty Session on 22nd August, 1829. On 25th October, 1828, William Edden, a market gardener, was found dead, with his ribs broken, in the road between Aylesbury and Thame. One Sewell, in August, 1829, accused a man named Tyler, and both were examined at the Aylesbury Petty Sessions. Mrs. Edden gave evidence that she sent five or six times for Tyler " to come and see the corpse. . . . I had some particular reasons for sending for him which I never did divulge. . . . I will tell you my reasons, gentlemen, if you ask me, in the face of Tyler, even if my life should be in danger for it." The reasons were that on the night of her husband's murder, " something rushed over me, and I thought my husband came by me. I looked up, and I thought I heard the voice of my husband come from near my mahogany table. . . . I thought I saw my husband's apparition, and the man that had done it, and that

man was Tyler. . . . I ran out and said, 'O dear
God! my husband is murdered, and his ribs are
broken'."

Lord Nugent—"What made you think your husband's ribs were broken?"

"He held up his hands like this, and I saw a
hammer, or something like a hammer, and it came
into my mind that his ribs were broken." Sewell
stated that the murder was accomplished by means
of a hammer.

The prisoners were discharged on 13th September.
On 5th March, 1830, they were tried at the Buckingham Lent Assizes, were found guilty and were
hanged, protesting their innocence, on 8th March,
1830.

"In the report of Mrs. Edden's evidence (at the
Assizes) no mention is made of the vision."[1]

Here end our ghosts in courts of justice; the
following ghost gave evidence of a murder, or rather,
confessed to one, but was beyond the reach of human
laws.

This tale of 1730 is still current in Highland
tradition. It has, however, been improved and made
infinitely more picturesque by several generations of
narrators. As we try to be faithful to the best
sources, the contemporary manuscript version is
here reprinted from *The Scottish Standard-Bearer*, an
organ of the Scotch Episcopalians (October and
November, 1894).

---

[1] *Phantasms*, ii., 586, quoting (apparently) the *Buckingham Gazette*
of the period.

THE DOG O' MAUSE.

Account of an apparition that appeared to William Soutar,[1] in the Mause, 1730.

[This is a copy from that in the handwriting of Bishop Rattray, preserved at Craighall, and which was found at Meikleour a few years ago, to the proprietor of which, Mr. Mercer, it was probably sent by the Bishop.—W. W. H., 3rd August, 1846.]

"I have sent you an account of an apparition as remarkable, perhaps, as anything you ever heard of, and which, considered in all its circumstances, leaves, I think, no ground of doubt to any man of common-sense. The person to whom it appeared is one William Soutar, a tenant of Balgowan's, who lives in Middle Mause, within about half a mile from this place on the other side of the river, and in view from our windows of Craighall House. He is about thirty-seven years of age, as he says, and has a wife and bairns.

"The following is an account from his own mouth; and because there are some circumstances fit to be taken in as you go along, I have given them with reference at the end,[2] that I may not interrupt the sense of the account, or add anything to it. Therefore, it begins :—

"'In the month of December in the year 1728, about sky-setting, I and my servant, with several others living in the town (farm-steading) heard a

[1] Oddly enough a Mr. William Soutar, of Blairgowrie, tells a ghost story of his own to the S.P.R. !

[2] I put them for convenience at the foot.—W. L. L.

scraiching (screeching, crying), and I followed the
noise, with my servant, a little way from the town
(farm-steading throughout). We both thought we
saw what had the appearance to be a fox, and
hounded the dogs at it, but they would not pursue
it.[1]

"'About a month after, as I was coming from Blair[2]
alone, about the same time of the night, a big dog
appeared to me, of a dark greyish colour, between
the Hilltown and Knockhead[3] of Mause, on a lea
rig a little below the road, and in passing by it
touched me sonsily (firmly) on the thigh at my
haunch-bane (hip-bone), upon which I pulled my staff
from under my arm and let a stroke at it ; and I
had a notion at the time that I hit it, and my
haunch was painful all that night. However, I
had no great thought of its being anything particular
or extraordinary, but that it might be a mad dog
wandering. About a year after that, to the best
of my memory, in December month, about the
same time of the night and in the same place,
when I was alone, it appeared to me again as before,
and passed by me at some distance ; and then I
began to think it might be something more than
ordinary.

[1] The dogs in all these towns (farms) of Mause are very well
accustomed with hunting the fox.

[2] Blair (Blairgowrie) is the kirk-town of that parish, where there
is also a weekly market : it lies about a mile below Middle Mause
on the same side of the river.

[3] Knockhead is within less than half a mile of Middle Mause,
and the Hilltown lies betwixt the two. We see both of them from
our window of Craighall House.

"'In the month of December, 1730, as I was coming from Perth, from the Claith (cloth) Market a little before sky-setting, it appeared to me again, being alone, at the same place, and passed by me just as before. I had some suspicion of it then likewise, but I began to think that a neighbour of mine in the Hilltown having an ox lately dead, it might be a dog that had been at the carrion, by which I endeavoured to put the suspicion out of my head.

"'On the second Monday of December, 1730, as I was coming from Woodhead, a town (farm) in the ground of Drumlochy, it appeared to me again in the same place just about sky-setting; and after it had passed me as it was going out of my sight, it spoke with a low voice so that I distinctly heard it, these words, "Within eight or ten days do or die," and it thereupon disappeared. No more passed at that time. On the morrow I went to my brother, who dwells in the Nether Aird of Drumlochy, and told him of the last and of all the former appearances, which was the first time I ever spoke of it to anybody. He and I went to see a sister of ours at Glenballow, who was dying, but she was dead before we came. As we were returning home, I desired my brother, whose name is James Soutar, to go forward with me till we should be passed the place where it used to appear to me; and just as we had come to it, about ten o'clock at night, it appeared to me again just as formerly; and as it was passing over some ice I pointed to it with my finger and asked my brother if he saw it, but he said he did not, nor did his servant, who was with us. It spoke nothing at that time, but just disappeared as it passed the ice.

"'On the Saturday after, as I was at my own sheep-cots putting in my sheep, it appeared to me again just after daylight, betwixt day and skylight, and upon saying these words, "Come to the spot of ground within half an hour," it just disappeared; whereupon I came home to my own house, and took up a staff and also a sword off the head of the bed, and went straight to the place where it used formerly to appear to me; and after I had been there some minutes and had drawn a circle about me with my staff, it appeared to me. And I spoke to it saying, "In the name of God and Jesus Christ, what are you that troubles me?" and it answered me, "I am David Soutar, George Soutar's brother.[1] I killed a man more than five-and-thirty years ago, when you was new born, at a bush be-east the road, as you go into the Isle."[2] And as I was going away, I stood again and said, "David Soutar was a man, and you appear like a dog," whereupon it spoke to me again, saying, "I killed him with a dog, and therefore I am made to speak out of the mouth of a dog, and tell you you must go and bury these bones". Upon this I went straight to my brother to his house, and told him what had happened to me. My brother having told the minister of Blair, he and I came to the minister on Monday

[1] This George Soutar died about two or three years ago, and was very well known to William.

[2] The Isle is a spot of ground in the wood of Rychalzie, about a mile above Middle Mause, on the same side of the river.

thereafter, as he was examining in a neighbour's house in the same town where I live. And the minister, with my brother and me and two or three more, went to the place where the apparition said the bones were buried, when Rychalzie met us accidentally; and the minister told Rychalzie the story in the presence of all that were there assembled, and desired the liberty from him to break up the ground to search for the bones. Rychalzie made some scruples to allow us to break up the ground, but said he would go along with us to Glasclune[1]; and if he advised, he would allow search to be made. Accordingly he went straight along with my brother and me and James Chalmers, a neighbour who lives in the Hilltown of Mause, to Glasclune, and told Glasclune the story as above narrated; and he advised Rychalzie to allow the search to be made, whereupon he gave his consent to it.

"'The day after, being Friday, we convened about thirty or forty men and went to the Isle, and broke up the ground in many places, searching for the bones, but we found nothing.

"'On Wednesday the 23rd December, about twelve o'clock, when I was in my bed, I heard a voice but saw nothing; the voice said, "Come away".[2] Upon this I rose out of my bed, cast on my coat and went to the door, but did not see it. And I said, "In the name of God, what do you demand

[1] Glasclune is a gentleman of the name of Blair, whose house lies about three-quarters of a mile south-west from Middle Mause.

[2] He said the voice answered him as if it had been some distance without the door.

of me now?" It answered, "Go, take up these
bones". I said, "How shall I get these bones?"
It answered again, "At the side of a withered
bush,[1] and there are but seven or eight of them
remaining". I asked, "Was there any more guilty
of that action but you?" It answered, "No". I
asked again, "What is the reason you trouble me?"
It answered, "Because you are the youngest".
Then said I to it, "Depart from me, and give me
a sign that I may know the particular spot, and
give me time". [Here there is written on the margin
in a different hand, "You will find the bones at
the side of a withered bush. There are but eight
of them, and for a sign you will find the print of a
cross impressed on the ground."] On the morrow,
being Thursday, I went alone to the Isle to see if
I could find any sign, and immediately I saw both
the bush, which was a small bush, the greatest
stick in it being about the thickness of a staff, and
it was withered about half-way down; and also the
sign, which was about a foot from the bush. The
sign was an exact cross, thus X; each of the two
lines was about a foot and a half in length and

[1] Besides the length of time since the murder was committed,
there is another reason why all the bones were not found, *viz.*, that
there is a little burn or brook which had run for the space of twenty
years, at least, across upon the place when the bones were found, and
would have carried them all away had it not been that the bush, at
the side of which they were buried, had turned the force of the
stream a little from off that place where they lay, for they were not
more than a foot, or at most a foot and a half, under ground, and
it is only within these three years that a water-spate has altered
the course of the burn.

near three inches broad, and more than an inch deeper than the rest of the ground, as if it had been pressed down, for the ground was not cut. On the morrow, being Friday, I went and told my brother of the voice that had spoken to me, and that I had gone and seen the bush which it directed me to and the above-mentioned sign at it. The next day, being Saturday, my brother and I went, together with seven or eight men with us, to the Isle. About sun-rising we all saw the bush and the sign at it; and upon breaking up the ground just at the bush, we found the bones, *viz.*, the chaft-teeth (jaw-teeth-molars) in it, one of the thigh bones, one of the shoulder blades, and a small bone which we supposed to be a collar bone, which was more consumed than any of the rest, and two other small bones, which we thought to be bones of the sword-arm. By the time we had digged up those bones, there convened about forty men who also saw them. The minister and Rychalzie came to the place and saw them.

"'We immediately sent to the other side of the water, to Claywhat,[1] to a wright that was cutting timber there, whom Claywhat brought over with him, who immediately made a coffin for the bones, and my wife brought linen to wrap them in, and I wrapped the bones in the linen myself and put them in the coffin before all these people, and sent for the mort-cloth and buried them in the churchyard of Blair that evening. There were near an hundred

[1] The course of the river (the Ericht) is from north to south. Middle Mause lies on the west side of it, and Craighall on the east.

persons at the burial, and it was a little after sunset when they were buried.'"

"This above account I have written down as dictated to me by William Soutar in the presence of Robert Graham, brother to the Laird of Balgowan, and of my two sons, James and John Rattray, at Craighall, 30th December, 1730.

"We at Craighall heard nothing of this history till after the search was over, but it was told us on the morrow by some of the servants who had been with the rest at the search; and on Saturday Glasclune's son came over to Craighall and told us that William Soutar had given a very distinct account of it to his father.

"On St. Andrew's Day, the 1st of December, this David Soutar (the ghost) listed himself a soldier, being very soon after the time the apparition said the murder was committed, and William Soutar declares he had no remembrance of him till that apparition named him as brother to George Soutar; then, he said, he began to recollect that when he was about ten years of age he had seen him once at his father's in a soldier's habit, after which he went abroad and was never more heard of; neither did William ever before hear of his having listed as a soldier, neither did William ever before hear of his having killed a man, nor, indeed, was there ever anything heard of it in the country, and it is not yet known who the person was that was killed, and whose bones are now found.

"My son John and I went within a few days after to visit Glasclune, and had the account from him

as William had told him over. From thence we
went to Middle Mause to hear it from himself; but
he being from home, his father, who also lives in
that town, gave us the same account of it which
Glasclune had done, and the poor man could not
refrain from shedding tears as he told it, as Glasclune told us his son was under very great concern
when he spoke of it to him. We all thought this
a very odd story, and were under suspense about
it because the bones had not been found upon the
search.

"(Another account that also seems to have been
written by the bishop mentions that the murderer
on committing the deed went home, and on looking
in at the window he saw William Soutar lying in
a cradle—hence it was the ghaist always came to
him, and not to any of the other relations.)"

Mr. Hay Newton, of Newton Hall, a man of
great antiquarian tastes in the last generation, wrote
the following notes on the matter:—

"Widow M'Laren, aged seventy-nine, a native of
Braemar, but who has resided on the Craighall estate
for sixty years, says that the tradition is that the man
was murdered for his money; that he was a Highland drover on his return journey from the south;
that he arrived late at night at the Mains of Mause
and wished to get to Rychalzie; that he stayed
at the Mains of Mause all night, but left it early
next morning, when David Soutar with his dog
accompanied him to show him the road; but that
with the assistance of the dog he murdered the
drover and took his money at the place mentioned;

that there was a tailor at work in his father's house
that morning when he returned after committing
the murder (according to the custom at that date
by which tailors went out to make up customers'
own cloth at their own houses), and that his mother
being surprised at his strange appearance, asked
him what he had been about, to which inquiry he
made no reply; that he did not remain long in the
country afterwards, but went to England and never
returned. The last time he was seen he went down
by the Brae of Cockridge. A man of the name of
Irons, a fisherman in Blairgowrie, says that his
father, who died a very old man some years ago,
was present at the getting of the bones. Mr. Small,
Finzyhan, when bringing his daughter home from
school in Edinburgh, saw a coffin at the door of a
public house near Rychalzie where he generally
stopped, but he did not go in as usual, thinking
that there was a death in the family. The inn-
keeper came out and asked him why he was passing
the door, and told him the coffin contained the bones
of the murdered man which had been collected, upon
which he went into the house.

"The Soutars disliked much to be questioned on
the subject of the Dog of Mause. Thomas Soutar,
who was tenant in Easter Mause, formerly named
Knowhead of Mause, and died last year upwards of
eighty years of age, said that the Soutars came
originally from Annandale, and that their name was
Johnston; that there were three brothers who fled
from that part of the country on account of their
having killed a man; that they came by Soutar's

Hill, and having asked the name of the hill, were told 'Soutar,' upon which they said, 'Soutar be it then,' and took that name. One of the brothers went south and the others came north."[1]

The appearance of human ghosts in the form of beasts is common enough; in Shropshire they usually "come" as bulls. (See Miss Burne's *Shropshire Folklore*.) They do not usually speak, like the Dog o' Mause. M. d'Assier, a French Darwinian, explains that ghosts revert "atavistically" to lower forms of animal life![2]

We now, in accordance with a promise already made, give an example of the ghosts of beasts! Here an explanation by the theory that the consciousness of the beast survives death and affects with a hallucination the minds of living men and animals, will hardly pass current. But if such cases were as common and told on evidence as respectable as that which vouches for appearances of the dead, believers in these would either have to shift their ground, or to grant that

> Admitted to that equal sky,
> Our faithful dog may bear us company.

We omit such things as the dripping death wraith of a drowned cat who appeared to a lady, or the illused monkey who died in a Chinese house, after which he haunted it by rapping, secreting objects, and, in short, in the usual way.[3] We adduce

---

[1] With reference to the last statement in Mr. Newton's notes see the *Journal* of Sir Walter Scott (edit., 1891, p. 210) under date 13th June, 1826.

[2] *L'Homme Posthume.*   [3] Denny's *Folklore of China*

PETER'S GHOST.

A naval officer visited a friend in the country. Several men were sitting round the smoking-room fire when he arrived, and a fox-terrier was with them. Presently the heavy, shambling footsteps of an old dog, and the metallic shaking sound of his collar, were heard coming up stairs.

"Here's old Peter!" said his visitor.

"*Peter's dead!*" whispered his owner.

The sounds passed through the closed door, heard by all; they pattered into the room; the fox-terrier bristled up, growled, and pursued a viewless object across the carpet; from the hearth-rug sounded a shake, a jingle of a collar and the settling weight of a body collapsing into repose.[1]

This pleasing anecdote rests on what is called *nautical evidence*, which, for reasons inexplicable to me, was (in these matters) distrusted by Sir Walter Scott.

[1] Story received in a letter from Lieutenant —— of H.M.S gunboat ——.

CHAPTER VIII.

More Ghosts with a Purpose. Ticonderoga. The Beres-
ford Ghost. Sources of Evidence. The Family
Version. A New Old-Fashioned Ghost. Half-
past One o'clock. Put out the Light!

THE ghost in the following famous tale had a
purpose. He was a Highland ghost, a Campbell,
and desired vengeance on a Macniven, who murdered
him. The ghost, practically, " cried *Cruachan*," and
tried to rouse the clan. Failing in this, owing to
Inverawe's loyalty to his oath, the ghost uttered a
prophecy.

The tale is given in the words of Miss Elspeth
Campbell, who collected it at Inverawe from a Highland narrator. She adds a curious supplementary
tradition in the Argyle family.

TICONDEROGA.

It was one evening in the summer of the year
1755 that Campbell of Inverawe [1] was on Cruachan
hill side. He was startled by seeing a man coming
towards him at full speed ; a man ragged, bleeding,
and evidently suffering agonies of terror. " The

[1] He fought at Culloden, of course for King George, and was
appealed to for protection by old Glengarry.

avengers of blood are on my track, Oh, save me!" the poor wretch managed to gasp out. Inverawe, filled with pity for the miserable man, swore " By the word of an Inverawe which never failed friend or foe yet " to save him.

Inverawe then led the stranger to the secret cave on Cruachan hill side.

None knew of this cave but the laird of Inverawe himself, as the secret was most carefully kept and had been handed down from father to son for many generations. The entrance was small, and no one passing would for an instant suspect it to be other than a tod's hole,[1] but within were fair-sized rooms, one containing a well of the purest spring water. It is said that Wallace and Bruce had made use of this cave in earlier days.

Here Inverawe left his guest. The man was so overcome by terror that he clung on to Inverawe's plaid,[2] imploring him not to leave him alone. Inverawe was filled with disgust at this cowardly conduct, and already almost repented having plighted his word to save such a worthless creature.

On Inverawe's return home he found a man in a state of great excitement waiting to see him. This man informed him of the murder of his (Inverawe's) foster-brother by one Macniven. "We have," said he, "tracked the murderer to within a short distance of this place, and I am here to warn you in case he should seek your protection." Inverawe turned pale and remained silent, not knowing what

[1] Fox's hole.
[2] How did Inverawe get leave to wear the Highland dress?

answer to give. The man, knowing the love that subsisted between the foster-brothers, thought this silence arose from grief alone, and left the house to pursue the search for Macniven further.

The compassion Inverawe felt for the trembling man he had left in the cave turned to hate when he thought of his beloved foster-brother murdered; but as he had plighted his word to save him, save him he must and would. As soon, therefore, as night fell he went to the cave with food, and promised to return with more the next day.

Thoroughly worn out, as soon as he reached home he retired to rest, but sleep he could not. So taking up a book he began to read. A shadow fell across the page. He looked up and saw his foster-brother standing by the bedside. But, oh, how changed! His fair hair clotted with blood; his face pale and drawn, and his garments all gory. He uttered the following words: "Inverawe, shield not the murderer; blood must flow for blood," and then faded away out of sight.

In spite of the spirit's commands, Inverawe remained true to his promise, and returned next day to Macniven with fresh provisions. That night his foster-brother again appeared to him uttering the same warning: "Inverawe, Inverawe, shield not the murderer; blood must flow for blood". At daybreak Inverawe hurried off to the cave, and said to Macniven: "I can shield you no longer; you must escape as best you can". Inverawe now hoped to receive no further visit from the vengeful spirit. In this he was disappointed, for at the usual hour the ghost appeared, and in anger said, "I have warned you once, I have warned you twice; it is too late now. We shall meet again at TICONDEROGA."

Inverawe rose before dawn and went straight to the cave. Macniven was gone!

Inverawe saw no more of the ghost, but the adventure left him a gloomy, melancholy man. Many a time he would wander on Cruachan hill side, brooding over his vision, and people passing him would see the far-away look in his eyes, and would say one to the other: "The puir laird, he is aye thinking on him that is gone". Only his dearest friends knew the cause of his melancholy.

In 1756 the war between the English and French in America broke out. The 42nd regiment embarked, and landed at New York in June of that year. Campbell of Inverawe was a major in the regiment. The lieut.-colonel was Francis Grant. From New York the 42nd proceeded to Albany, where the regiment remained inactive till the spring of 1757. One evening when the 42nd were still quartered at this place, Inverawe asked the colonel "if he had ever heard of a place called Ticonderoga".[1] Colonel Grant replied he had never heard

[1] In every version of the story that I have heard or read Ticonderoga is called St. Louis, and Inverawe was ignorant of its other name. Yet in all the histories of the war that I have seen, the only name given to the place is Ticonderoga. There is no mention of its having a French name. Even if Inverawe knew the fort they were to storm was called Ticonderoga, he cannot have known it when the ghost appeared to him in Scotland. At that time there was not even a fort at Ticonderoga, as the French only erected it

the name before. Inverawe then told his story. Most of the officers were present at the time; some were impressed, others were inclined to look upon the whole thing as a joke, but seeing how very much disturbed Inverawe was about it all, even the most unbelieving refrained from bantering him.

In 1758 an expedition was to be directed against Ticonderoga, on Lake George, a fort erected by the French. The Highlanders were to form part of this expedition. The force was under Major-General Abercromby.

Ticonderoga was called by the French St. Louis [really "Fort Carillon"], and Inverawe knew it by no other name. One of the officers told Colonel Grant that the Indian name of the place was Ticonderoga. Grant, remembering Campbell's story, said: "For God's sake don't let Campbell know this, or harm will come of it".

The troops embarked on Lake George and landed without opposition near the extremity of the lake early in July. They marched from there, through woods, upon Ticonderoga, having had one successful skirmish with the enemy, driving them back with considerable loss. Lord Howe was killed in this engagement.

On the 10th of July the assault was directed to

in 1756. Inverawe had told his story to friends in Scotland before the war broke out in America, so even if in 1758 he did know the real name of the fort that the expedition was directed against, I don't see that it lessens the interest of the story.—E. A. C.

The French really called the place Fort Carillon, which disguised the native name Ticonderoga. See *Memoirs of the Chevalier Johnstone.*—A. L.

be commenced by the picquets.[1] The Grenadiers
were to follow, supported by the battalions and re-
serves. The Highlanders and 55th regiment formed
the reserve.

In vain the troops attempted to force their way
through the abbatis, they themselves being exposed
to a heavy artillery and musket fire from an enemy
well under cover. The Highlanders could no longer
be restrained, and rushed forward from the reserve,
cutting and carving their way through trees and
other obstacles with their claymores. The deadly
fire still continued from the fort. As no ladders
had been provided for scaling the breastwork, the
soldiers climbed on to one another's shoulders, and
made holes for their feet in the face of the work
with their swords and bayonets, but as soon as a
man reached the top he was thrown down. Captain
John Campbell and a few men succeeded at last in
forcing their way over the breastworks, but were
immediately cut down.

After a long and desperate struggle, lasting in
fact nearly four hours, General Abercromby gave
orders for a retreat. The troops could hardly be
prevailed upon to retire, and it was not till the
order had been given for the third time that the
Highlanders withdrew from the hopeless encounter.

---

[1] Abercromby's force consisted of the 27th, 42nd, 44th, 46th,
55th, and battalions of the 60th Royal Americans, with about 9000
Provincials and a train of artillery. The assault, however, took
place before the guns could come up, matters having been hastened
by the information that M. de Lévy was approaching with 3000
French troops to relieve Ticonderoga garrison.

The loss sustained by the regiment was as follows: eight officers, nine sergeants and 297 men killed ; seventeen officers, ten sergeants and 306 men wounded.

Inverawe, after having fought with the greatest courage, received at length his death wound. Colonel Grant hastened to the dying man's side, who looked reproachfully at him, and said : " You deceived me ; this is Ticonderoga, for I have seen him ". Inverawe never spoke again. Inverawe's son, an officer in the same regiment, also lost his life at Ticonderoga.

On the very day that these events were happening in far-away America, two ladies, Miss Campbell of Ederein and her sister, were walking from Kilmalieu to Inveraray, and had reached the then new bridge over the Aray. One of them happened to look up at the sky. She gave a call to her sister to look also. They both of them saw in the sky what looked like a siege going on. They saw the different regiments with their colours, and recognised many of their friends among the Highlanders. They saw Inverawe and his son fall, and other men whom they knew. When they reached Inveraray they told all their friends of the vision they had just seen. They also took down the names of those they had seen fall, and the time and date of the occurrence.

The well-known Danish physician, Sir William Hart, was, together with an Englishman and a servant, walking round the Castle of Inveraray. These men saw the same phenomena, and confirmed the statements made by the two ladies. Weeks after the gazette corroborated their statements in its

account of the attempt made on Ticonderoga. Every
detail was correct in the vision, down to the actual
number of the killed and wounded.

But there was sorrow throughout Argyll long
before the gazette appeared.

.   .   .   .

We now give the best attainable version of a yet
more famous legend, " The Tyrone Ghost ".

The literary history of " The Tyrone Ghost " is
curious. In 1802 Scott used the tale as the foundation of his ballad, *The Eve of St. John*, and
referred to the tradition of a noble Irish family in
a note. In 1858 the subject was discussed in *Notes
and Queries*. A reference was given to Lyon's
privately printed *Grand Juries of Westmeath from*
1751. The version from that rare work, a version
dated " Dublin, August, 1802," was published in
Notes and Queries of 24th July, 1858. In December,
1896, a member of the Beresford family published
in *The Nines* (a journal of the Wiltshire regiment),
the account which follows, derived from a MS. at
Curraghmore, written by Lady Betty Cobbe, grand-
daughter of the ghost-seer, Lady Beresford. The
writer in *The Nines* remembers Lady Betty. The
account of 1802 is clearly derived from the Curraghmore MS., but omits dates; calls Sir Tristram Beresford " Sir Marcus "; leaves out the visit to Gill Hall,
where the ghost appeared, and substitutes blanks
for the names of persons concerned. Otherwise
the differences in the two versions are mainly
verbal.

THE BERESFORD GHOST.

" There is at Curraghmore, the seat of Lord Waterford, in Ireland, a manuscript account of the tale,
such as it was originally received and implicitly
believed in by the children and grandchildren of the
lady to whom Lord Tyrone is supposed to have
made the supernatural appearance after death. The
account was written by Lady Betty Cobbe, the
youngest daughter of Marcus, Earl of Tyrone, and
granddaughter of Nicola S., Lady Beresford. She
lived to a good old age, in full use of all her faculties,
both of body and mind. I can myself remember
her, for when a boy I passed through Bath on a
journey with my mother, and we went to her house
there, and had luncheon. She appeared to my
juvenile imagination a very appropriate person to
revise and transmit such a tale, and fully adapted
to do ample justice to her subject-matter. It never
has been doubted in the family that she received
the full particulars in early life, and that she heard
the circumstances, such as they were believed
to have occurred, from the nearest relatives of the
two persons, the supposed actors in this mysterious
interview, *viz.*, from her own father, Lord Tyrone,
who died in 1763, and from her aunt, Lady Riverston,
who died in 1763 also.

" These two were both with their mother, Lady
Beresford, on the day of her decease, and they, without assistance or witness, took off from their parent's
wrist the black bandage which she had always worn on
all occasions and times, even at Court, as some very

old persons who lived well into the eighteenth century testified, having received their information from eye-witnesses of the fact. There was an oil painting of this lady in Tyrone House, Dublin, representing her with a black ribbon bound round her wrist. This portrait disappeared in an unaccountable manner. It used to hang in one of the drawing-rooms in that mansion, with other family pictures. When Henry, Marquis of Waterford, sold the old town residence of the family and its grounds to the Government as the site of the Education Board, he directed Mr. Watkins, a dealer in pictures, and a man of considerable knowledge in works of art and vertu, to collect the pictures, etc., etc., which were best adapted for removal to Curraghmore. Mr. Watkins especially picked out this portrait, not only as a good work of art, but as one which, from its associations, deserved particular care and notice. When, however, the lot arrived at Curraghmore and was unpacked, no such picture was found ; and though Mr. Watkins took great pains and exerted himself to the utmost to trace what had become of it, to this day (nearly forty years), not a hint of its existence has been received or heard of.

"John le Poer, Lord Decies, was the eldest son of Richard, Earl of Tyrone, and of Lady Dorothy Annesley, daughter of Arthur, Earl of Anglesey. He was born 1665, succeeded his father 1690, and died 14th October, 1693. He became Lord Tyrone at his father's death, and is the 'ghost' of the story.

"Nicola Sophie Hamilton was the second and

youngest daughter and co-heiress of Hugh, Lord Glenawley, who was also Baron Lunge in Sweden. Being a zealous Royalist, he had, together with his father, migrated to that country in 1643, and returned from it at the Restoration. He was of a good old family, and held considerable landed property in the county Tyrone, near Ballygawley. He died there in 1679. His eldest daughter and co-heiress, Arabella Susanna, married, in 1683, Sir John Macgill, of Gill Hall, in the county Down.

"Nicola S. (the second daughter) was born in 1666, and married Sir Tristram Beresford in 1687. Between that and 1693 two daughters were born, but no son to inherit the ample landed estates of his father, who most anxiously wished and hoped for an heir. It was under these circumstances, and at this period, that the manuscripts state that Lord Tyrone made his appearance after death; and all the versions of the story, without variation, attribute the same cause and reason, *viz.*, a solemn promise mutually interchanged in early life between John le Poer, then Lord Decies, afterwards Lord Tyrone, and Nicola S. Hamilton, that whichever of the two died the first, should, if permitted, appear to the survivor for the object of declaring the approval or rejection by the Deity of the revealed religion as generally acknowledged : of which the departed one must be fully cognisant, but of which they both had in their youth entertained unfortunate doubts.

"In the month of October, 1693, Sir Tristram and Lady Beresford went on a visit to her sister, Lady Macgill, at Gill Hall, now the seat of Lord Clan-william, whose grandmother was eventually the heiress of Sir J. Macgill's property. One morning Sir Tristram rose early, leaving Lady Beresford asleep, and went out for a walk before breakfast. When his wife joined the table very late, her appearance and the embarrassment of her manner attracted general attention, especially that of her husband. He made anxious inquiries as to her health, and asked her apart what had occurred to her wrist, which was tied up with black ribbon tightly bound round it. She earnestly entreated him not to inquire more then, or thereafter, as to the cause of her wearing or continuing afterwards to wear that ribbon; 'for,' she added, 'you will never see me without it'. He replied, 'Since you urge it so vehemently, I promise you not to inquire more about it'.

"After completing her hurried breakfast she made anxious inquiries as to whether the post had yet arrived. It had not yet come in; and Sir Tristram asked: 'Why are you so particularly eager about letters to-day?' 'Because I expect to hear of Lord Tyrone's death, which took place on Tuesday.' 'Well,' remarked Sir Tristram, 'I never should have put you down for a superstitious person; but I suppose that some idle dream has disturbed you.' Shortly after, the servant brought in the letters; one was sealed with black wax. 'It is as I expected,' she cries; 'he is dead.' The letter was from Lord Tyrone's steward to inform them that his master had died in Dublin, on Tuesday, 14th October, at 4 P.M. Sir Tristram endeavoured to console her, and begged her to restrain her grief, when she assured him that she felt relieved and easier now that she knew the actual fact. She added, ' I can now give you a most satisfactory piece of intelligence, *viz.*, that I am with child, and that it will be a boy '. A son was born in the following July. Sir Tristram survived its birth little more than six years. After his death Lady Beresford continued to reside with her young family at his place in the county of Derry, and seldom went from home. She hardly mingled with any neighbours or friends, excepting with Mr. and Mrs. Jackson, of Coleraine. He was the principal personage in that town, and was, by his mother, a near relative of Sir Tristram. His wife was the daughter of Robert Gorges, LL.D. (a gentleman of good old English family, and possessed of a considerable estate in the county Meath), by Jane Loftus, daughter of Sir Adam Loftus, of Rathfarnham, and sister of Lord Lisburn. They had an only son, Richard Gorges, who was in the army, and became a general officer very early in life. With the Jacksons Lady Beresford maintained a constant communication and lived on the most intimate terms, while she seemed determined to eschew all other society and to remain in her chosen retirement.

" At the conclusion of three years thus passed, one luckless day " Young Gorges " most vehemently professed his passion for her, and solicited her hand, urging his suit in a most passionate appeal, which was evidently not displeasing to the fair widow, and which, unfortunately for her, was successful. They were married in 1704. One son and two daughters were born to them, when his abandoned and dissolute conduct forced her to seek and to obtain a separation. After this had continued for four years, General Gorges pretended extreme penitence for his past misdeeds, and with the most solemn promises of amendment induced his wife to live with him again, and she became the mother of a second son. The day month after her confinement happened to be her birthday, and having recovered and feeling herself equal to some exertion, she sent for her son, Sir Marcus Beresford, then twenty years old, and her married daughter, Lady Riverston. She also invited Dr. King, the Archbishop of Dublin (who was an intimate friend), and an old clergyman who had christened her, and who had always kept up a most kindly intercourse with her during her whole life, to make up a small party to celebrate the day.

" In the early part of it Lady Beresford was engaged in a kindly conversation with her old friend the clergyman, and in the course of it said : ' You know that I am forty-eight this day '. ' No, indeed,' he replied ; ' you are only forty-seven, for your mother had a dispute with me once on the very subject of your age, and I in consequence sent and consulted the registry, and can most confidently assert that you are only forty-seven this day.' ' You have signed my death-warrant, then,' she cried ; ' leave me, I pray, for I have not much longer to live, but have many things of grave importance to settle before I die. Send my son and my daughter to me immediately.' The clergyman did as he was bidden. He directed Sir Marcus and his sister to go instantly to their mother ; and he sent to the archbishop and a few other friends to put them off from joining the birthday party.

"When her two children repaired to Lady Beresford, she thus addressed them : ' I have something of deep importance to communicate to you, my dear children, before I die. You are no strangers to the intimacy and the affection which subsisted in early life between Lord Tyrone and myself. We were educated together when young, under the same roof, in the pernicious principles of Deism. Our real friends afterwards took every opportunity to convince us of our error, but their arguments were insufficient to overpower and uproot our infidelity, though they had the effect of shaking our confidence in it, and thus leaving us wavering between the two opinions. In this perplexing state of doubt we made a solemn promise one to the other, that whichever died first should, if permitted, appear to the other for the purpose of declaring what religion was the one acceptable to the Almighty. One night, years after this interchange of promises, I was sleeping with your father at Gill Hall, when I suddenly awoke and discovered Lord Tyrone sitting visibly by the side of the bed. I screamed out, and vainly endeavoured to rouse Sir Tristram. "Tell me," I said, "Lord Tyrone, why and wherefore are you here at this time of the night?" "Have you then forgotten our promise to each other, pledged in early life? I died on Tuesday, at four o'clock. I have been permitted thus to appear in order to assure you that the revealed religion is the true and only one by which we can be saved. I am also suffered to in-

form you that you are with child, and will produce a
son, who will marry my heiress; that Sir Tristram
will not live long, when you will marry again, and
you will die from the effects of childbirth in your
forty-seventh year." I begged from him some convincing sign or proof so that when the morning came
I might rely upon it, and feel satisfied that his appearance had been real, and that it was not the phantom
of my imagination. He caused the hangings of the
bed to be drawn in an unusual way and impossible
manner through an iron hook. I still was not
satisfied, when he wrote his signature in my pocket-
book. I wanted, however, more substantial proof of
his visit, when he laid his hand, which was cold
as marble, on my wrist; the sinews shrunk up, the
nerves withered at the touch. "Now," he said,
"let no mortal eye, while you live, ever see that
wrist," and vanished. While I was conversing
with him my thoughts were calm, but as soon as he
disappeared I felt chilled with horror and dismay, a
cold sweat came over me, and I again endeavoured
but vainly to awaken Sir Tristram; a flood of tears
came to my relief, and I fell asleep.

"'In the morning your father got up without
disturbing me; he had not noticed anything extraordinary about me or the bed-hangings. When I
did arise I found a long broom in the gallery outside
the bedroom door, and with great difficulty I un-
hooded the curtain, fearing that the position of it
might excite surprise and cause inquiry. I bound
up my wrist with black ribbon before I went down
to breakfast, where the agitation of my mind was too

visible not to attract attention. Sir Tristram made many anxious inquiries as to my health, especially as to my sprained wrist, as he conceived mine to be. I begged him to drop all questions as to the bandage, even if I continued to adopt it for any length of time. He kindly promised me not to speak of it any more, and he kept his promise faithfully. You, my son, came into the world as predicted, and your father died six years after. I then determined to abandon society and its pleasures and not mingle again with the world, hoping to avoid the dreadful predictions as to my second marriage; but, alas! in the one family with which I held constant and friendly intercourse I met the man, whom I did not regard with perfect indifference. Though I struggled to conquer by every means the passion, I at length yielded to his solicitations, and in a fatal moment for my own peace I became his wife. In a few years his conduct fully justified my demand for a separation, and I fondly hoped to escape the fatal prophecy. Under the delusion that I had passed my forty-seventh birthday, I was prevailed upon to believe in his amendment, and to pardon him. I have, however, heard from undoubted authority that I am only forty-seven this day, and I know that I am about to die. I die, however, without the dread of death, fortified as I am by the sacred precepts of Christianity and upheld by its promises. When I am gone, I wish that you, my children, should unbind this black ribbon and alone behold my wrist before I am consigned to the grave.'

" She then requested to be left that she might lie down and compose herself, and her children quitted the apartment, having desired her attendant to watch her, and if any change came on to summon them to her bedside. In an hour the bell rang, and they hastened to the call, but all was over. The two children having ordered every one to retire, knelt down by the side of the bed, when Lady Riverston unbound the black ribbon and found the wrist exactly as Lady Beresford had described it—every nerve withered, every sinew shrunk.

" Her friend, the Archbishop, had had her buried in the Cathedral of St. Patrick, in Dublin, in the Earl of Cork's tomb, where she now lies."

.   .   .   .

The writer now professes his disbelief in any spiritual presence, and explains his theory that Lady Beresford's anxiety about Lord Tyrone deluded her by a vivid dream, during which she hurt her wrist.

Of all ghost stories the Tyrone, or Beresford Ghost, has most variants. Following Monsieur Hauréau, in the *Journal des Savants*, I have tracked the tale, the death compact, and the wound inflicted by the ghost on the hand, or wrist, or brow, of the seer, through Henry More, and Melanchthon, and a mediæval sermon by Eudes de Shirton, to William of Malmesbury, a range of 700 years. Mrs. Grant of Laggan has a rather recent case, and I have heard of another in the last ten years! Calmet has a case in 1625, the spectre leaves

The sable score of fingers four

on a board of wood.

Now for a modern instance of a gang of ghosts with a purpose!

When I narrated the story which follows to an eminent moral philosopher, he remarked, at a given point, "Oh, the ghost *spoke*, did she?" and displayed scepticism. The evidence, however, left him, as it leaves me, at a standstill, not convinced, but agreeably perplexed. The ghosts here are truly old-fashioned.

My story is, and must probably remain, entirely devoid of proof, as far as any kind of ghostly influence is concerned. We find ghosts appearing, and imposing a certain course of action on a living witness, for definite purposes of their own. The course of action prescribed was undeniably pursued, and apparently the purpose of the ghosts was fulfilled, but what that purpose was their agent declines to state, and conjecture is hopelessly baffled.

The documents in the affair have been published by the Society for Psychical Research (*Proceedings*, vol. xi., p. 547), and are here used for reference. But I think the matter will be more intelligible if I narrate it exactly as it came under my own observation. The names of persons and places are all fictitious, and are the same as those used in the documents published by the S.P.R.

HALF-PAST ONE O'CLOCK.

In October, 1893, I was staying at a town which we shall call Rapingham. One night I and some kinsfolk dined with another old friend of all of us, a

Dr. Ferrier. In the course of dinner he asked *à propos de bottes :*—

"Have you heard of the ghost in Blake Street?" a sunny, pleasant street of respectable but uninteresting antiquity in Rapingham.

We had none of us heard of the ghost, and begged the doctor to enlighten our ignorance. His story ran thus—I have it in his own writing as far as its essence goes :—

"The house," he said, "belongs to my friends, the Applebys, who let it, as they live elsewhere. A quiet couple took it and lived in it for five years, when the husband died, and the widow went away. They made no complaint while tenants. The house stood empty for some time, and all I know personally about the matter is that I, my wife, and the children were in the dining-room one Sunday when we heard unusual noises in the drawing-room overhead. We went through the rooms but could find no cause or explanation of the disturbance, and thought no more about it.

"About six or seven years ago I let the house to a Mr. Buckley, who is still the tenant. He was unmarried, and his family consisted of his mother and sisters. They preceded him to put the place in order, and before his arrival came to me in some irritation complaining that I had let them *a haunted house!* They insisted that there were strange noises, as if heavy weights were being dragged about, or heavy footsteps pacing in the rooms and on the stairs. I said that I knew nothing about the matter. The stairs are of stone, water is only carried up to the first floor, there is an unused system of hot air pipes.[1]   Something went wrong with the water-main in the area once, but the noises lasted after it was mended.

"I think Mr. Buckley when he arrived never heard anything unusual. But one evening as he walked upstairs carrying an ink-bottle, he found his hand full of some liquid. Thinking that he had spilt the ink, he went to a window where he found his hand full of water, to account for which there was no stain on the ceiling, or anything else that he could discover. On another occasion one of the young ladies was kneeling by a trunk in an attic, alone, when water was switched over her face, as if from a wet brush.[2] There was a small pool of water on the floor, and the wall beyond her was sprinkled.

"Time went on, and the disturbances were very rare: in fact ceased for two years till the present week, when Mrs. Claughton, a widow accompanied by two of her children, came to stay with the Buckleys.[3] She had heard of the disturbances and the theory of hauntings—I don't know if these things interested her or not.

"Early on Monday, 9th October, Mrs. Claughton came to consult me. Her story was this: About a quarter past one on Sunday night, or Monday morning, she was in bed with one of her children, the

---

[1] I know one inveterate ghost produced in an ancient Scottish house by these appliances.—A. L.

[2] Such events are common enough in old tales of haunted houses.

[3] This lady was well known to my friends and to Dr. Ferrier. I also have had the honour to make her acquaintance.

other sleeping in the room. She was awakened by footsteps on the stair, and supposed that a servant was coming to call her to Miss Buckley, who was ill. The steps stopped at the door, then the noise was repeated. Mrs. Claughton lit her bedroom candle, opened the door and listened. There was no one there. The clock on the landing pointed to twenty minutes past one. Mrs. Claughton went back to bed, read a book, fell asleep, and woke to find the candle still lit, but low in the socket. She heard a sigh, and saw a lady, unknown to her, her head swathed in a soft white shawl, her expression gentle and refined, her features much emaciated.

"The Appearance said, 'Follow me,' and Mrs. Claughton, taking the bedroom candle, rose and followed out on to the landing, and so into the adjacent drawing-room. She cannot remember opening the door, which the housemaid had locked outside, and she owns that this passage is dreamlike in her memory. Seeing that her candle was flickering out, she substituted for it a pink one taken from a chiffonier. The figure walked nearly to the window, turned three-quarters round, said 'To-morrow!' and was no more seen. Mrs. Claughton went back to her room, where her eldest child asked :—

" 'Who is the lady in white?'

" 'Only me, mother, go to sleep,' she thinks she answered. After lying awake for two hours, with gas burning, she fell asleep. The pink candle from the drawing-room chiffonier was in her candlestick in the morning.

" After hearing the lady's narrative I told her to try

change of air, which she declined as cowardly. So, as she would stay on at Mr. Buckley's, I suggested that an electric alarm communicating with Miss Buckley's room should be rigged up, and this was done."

Here the doctor paused, and as the events had happened within the week, we felt that we were at last on the track of a recent ghost.

"Next morning, about one, the Buckleys were aroused by a tremendous peal of the alarm; Mrs. Claughton they found in a faint. Next morning[1] she consulted me as to the whereabouts of a certain place, let me call it 'Meresby'. I suggested the use of a postal directory; we found Meresby, a place extremely unknown to fame, in an agricultural district about five hours from London in the opposite direction from Rapingham. To this place Mrs. Claughton said she must go, in the interest and by the order of certain ghosts, whom she saw on Monday night, and whose injunctions she had taken down in a note-book. She has left Rapingham for London, and there," said the doctor, "my story ends for the present."

We expected it to end for good and all, but in the course of the week came a communication to the doctor in writing from Mrs. Claughton's governess. This lady, on Mrs. Claughton's arrival at her London house (Friday, 13th October), passed a night perturbed by sounds of weeping, "loud moans," and "a very odd noise over-head, like

---

[1] Apparently on Thursday morning really.

some electric battery gone wrong," in fact, much like the " warning" of a jack running down, which Old Jeffrey used to give at the Wesley's house in Epworth. There were also heavy footsteps and thuds, as of moving weighty bodies. So far the governess.

This curious communication I read at Rapingham on Saturday, 14th October, or Sunday, 15th October. On Monday I went to town. In the course of the week I received a letter from my kinsman in Rapingham, saying that Mrs. Claughton had written to Dr. Ferrier, telling him that she had gone to Meresby on Saturday; had accomplished the bidding of the ghosts, and had lodged with one Joseph Wright, the parish clerk. Her duty had been to examine the Meresby parish registers, and to compare certain entries with information given by the ghosts and written by her in her note-book. If the entries in the parish register tallied with her notes, she was to pass the time between one o'clock and half-past one, alone, in Meresby Church, and receive a communication from the spectres. All this she said that she had done, and in evidence of her journey enclosed her half ticket to Meresby, which a dream had warned her would not be taken on her arrival. She also sent a white rose from a grave to Dr. Ferrier, a gentleman in no sympathy with the Jacobite cause, which, indeed, has no connection whatever with the matter in hand.

On hearing of this letter from Mrs. Claughton, I confess that, not knowing the lady, I remained purely sceptical. The railway company, however, vouched for the ticket. The rector of Meresby, being appealed to, knew nothing of the matter. He therefore sent for his curate and parish clerk.

" Did a lady pass part of Sunday night in the church ? "

The clerk and the curate admitted that this unusual event *had* occurred. A lady had arrived from London on Saturday evening; had lodged with Wright, the parish clerk; had asked for the parish registers; had compared them with her note-book after morning service on Sunday, and had begged leave to pass part of the night in the church. The curate in vain tried to dissuade her, and finally, washing his hands of it, had left her to Wright the clerk. To him she described a Mr. George Howard, deceased (one of the ghosts). He recognised the description, and he accompanied her to the church on a dark night, starting at one o'clock. She stayed alone, without a light, in the locked-up church from 1·20 to 1·45, when he let her out.

There now remained no doubt that Mrs. Claughton had really gone to Meresby, a long and disagreeable journey, and had been locked up in the church alone at a witching hour.

Beyond this point we have only the statements of Mrs. Claughton, made to Lord Bute, Mr. Myers and others, and published by the Society for Psychical Research. She says that after arranging the alarm bell on Monday night (October 9-10) she fell asleep reading in her dressing-gown, lying outside her bed. She wakened, and found the lady of the white shawl bending over her. Mrs. Claughton

said: "Am I dreaming, or is it true?" The figure
gave, as testimony to character, a piece of information.
Next Mrs. Claughton saw a male ghost, "tall, dark,
healthy, sixty years old," who named himself as George
Howard, buried in Meresby churchyard, Meresby
being a place of which Mrs. Claughton, like most
people, now heard for the first time. He gave the
dates of his marriage and death, which are correct,
and have been seen by Mr. Myers in Mrs. Claughton's
note-book. He bade her verify these dates at Meresby, and wait at 1·15 in the morning at the grave of
Richard Harte (a person, like all of them, unknown
to Mrs. Claughton) at the south-west corner of the
south aisle in Meresby Church. This Mr. Harte died
on 15th May, 1745, and missed many events of interest
by doing so. Mr. Howard also named and described
Joseph Wright, of Meresby, as a man who would
help her, and he gave minute local information.
Next came a phantom of a man whose name Mrs.
Claughton is not free to give;[1] he seemed to be
in great trouble, at first covering his face with his
hands, but later removing them. These three
spectres were to meet Mrs. Claughton in Meresby
Church and give her information of importance on
a matter concerning, apparently, the third and only
unhappy appearance. After these promises and injunctions the phantoms left, and Mrs. Claughton
went to the door to look at the clock. Feeling
faint, she rang the alarum, when her friends came

---

[1] She gave, not for publication, the other real names, here altered
to pseudonyms.

and found her in a swoon on the floor. The hour was 1˙20.

What Mrs. Claughton's children were doing all this time, and whether they were in the room or not, does not appear.

On Thursday Mrs. Claughton went to town, and her governess was perturbed, as we have seen.

On Friday night Mrs. Claughton *dreamed* a number of things connected with her journey; a page of the notes made from this dream was shown to Mr. Myers. Thus her half ticket was not to be taken, she was to find a Mr. Francis, concerned in the private affairs of the ghosts, which needed rectifying, and so forth. These premonitions, with others, were all fulfilled. Mrs. Claughton, in the church at night, continued her conversation with the ghosts whose acquaintance she had made at Rapingham. She obtained, it seems, all the information needful to settling the mysterious matters which disturbed the male ghost who hid his face, and on Monday morning she visited the daughter of Mr. Howard in her country house in a park, "recognised the strong likeness to her father, and carried out all things desired by the dead to the full, as had been requested. . . . The wishes expressed to her were perfectly rational, reasonable and of natural importance."

The clerk, Wright, attests the accuracy of Mrs. Claughton's description of Mr. Howard, whom he knew, and the correspondence of her dates with those in the parish register and on the graves, which he found for her at her request. Mr. Myers, "from a very partial knowledge" of what the Meresby ghosts' business was, thinks the reasons for not revealing this matter "entirely sufficient". The ghosts' messages to survivors " effected the intended results," says Mrs. Claughton.

.   .   .   .

Of this story the only conceivable natural explanation is that Mrs. Claughton, to serve her private ends, paid secret preliminary visits to Meresby, "got up" there a number of minute facts, chose a haunted house at the other end of England as a first scene in her little drama, and made the rest of the troublesome journeys, not to mention the uncomfortable visit to a dark church at midnight, and did all this from a hysterical love of notoriety. This desirable boon she would probably never have obtained, even as far as it is consistent with a pseudonym, if I had not chanced to dine with Dr. Ferrier while the adventure was only beginning. As there seemed to be a chance of taking a ghost " on the half volley," I at once communicated the first part of the tale to the Psychical Society (using pseudonyms, as here, throughout), and two years later Mrs. Claughton consented to tell the Society as much as she thinks it fair to reveal.

This, it will be confessed, is a round-about way of obtaining fame, and an ordinary person in Mrs. Claughton's position would have gone to the Psychical Society at once, as Mark Twain meant to do when he saw the ghost which turned out to be a very ordinary person.

There I leave these ghosts, my mind being in a just balance of agnosticism. If ghosts at all, they were ghosts with a purpose. The species is now very rare.

The purpose of the ghost in the following instance was trivial, but was successfully accomplished. In place of asking people to do what it wanted, the ghost did the thing itself. Now the modern theory of ghosts, namely, that they are delusions of the senses of the seers, caused somehow by the mental action of dead or distant people, does not seem to apply in this case. The ghost produced an effect on a material object.

"PUT OUT THE LIGHT!"

The Rev. D. W. G. Gwynne, M.D., was a physician in holy orders. In 1853 he lived at P—— House, near Taunton, where both he and his wife "were made uncomfortable by auditory experiences to which they could find no clue," or, in common English, they heard mysterious noises. "During the night," writes Dr. Gwynne, "I became aware of a draped figure passing across the foot of the bed towards the fireplace. I had the impression that the arm was raised, pointing with the hand towards the mantel-piece on which a night-light was burning. Mrs. Gwynne at the same moment seized my arm, *and the light was extinguished!* Notwithstanding, I distinctly saw the figure returning towards the door, and being under the impression that one of the servants had found her way into our room, I leaped out of bed to intercept the intruder, but found and saw nothing. I rushed to the door and endeavoured to follow the supposed intruder, and it was not until I found the door locked, as usual, that I was painfully impressed. I need hardly say that Mrs. Gwynne was in a very nervous state. She asked me what I had seen, and I told her. She had seen the same figure," " but," writes Mrs. Gwynne, " I distinctly *saw the hand of the figure placed over the night-light, which was at once extinguished*". " Mrs. Gwynne also heard the rustle of the 'tall man-like figure's' garments. In addition to the night-light there was moonlight in the room."

Other people had suffered many things in the same house, unknown to Dr. and Mrs. Gwynne, who gave up the place soon afterwards."

In plenty of stories we hear of ghosts who draw curtains or open doors, and these apparent material effects are usually called part of the seer's delusion. But the night-light certainly went out under the figure's hand, and was relit by Dr. Gwynne. Either the ghost was an actual entity, not a mere hallucination of two people, or the extinction of the light was a curious coincidence.[1]

---

[1] *Phantasms*, ii., 202.

CHAPTER IX.

*Haunted Houses. Antiquity of Haunted Houses. Savage
Cases. Ancient Egyptian Cases. Persistence in
Modern Times. Impostures. Imaginary Noises.
Nature of Noises. The Creaking Stair. Ghostly
Effects produced by the Living but Absent. The
Grocer's Cough. Difficulty of Belief. My Gillie's
Father's Story. "Silverton Abbey." The Dream
that Opened the Door. Abbotsford Noises. Legiti-
mate Haunting by the Dead. The Girl in Pink.
The Dog in the Haunted Room. The Lady in
Black. Dogs Alarmed. The Dead Seldom Re-
cognised. Glamis. A Border Castle. Another
Class of Hauntings. A Russian Case. The
Dancing Devil. The Little Hands.*

HAUNTED houses have been familiar to man ever
since he has owned a roof to cover his head. The
Australian blacks possessed only shelters or "leans-
to," so in Australia the spirits do their rapping on
the tree trunks ; a native illustrated this by whacking
a table with a book. The perched-up houses of
the Dyaks are haunted by noisy routing agencies.
We find them in monasteries, palaces, and crofters'
cottages all through the Middle Ages. On an ancient
Egyptian papyrus we find the husband of the Lady
Onkhari protesting against her habit of haunting

his house, and exclaiming: "What wrong have I done," exactly in the spirit of the "Hymn of Donald Ban," who was "sair hadden down by a bodach" (noisy bogle) after Culloden.[1]

The husband of Onkhari does not say *how* she disturbed him, but the manners of Egyptian haunters, just what they remain at present, may be gathered from a magical papyrus, written in Greek. Spirits "wail and groan, or laugh dreadfully"; they cause bad dreams, terror and madness; finally, they "practice stealthy theft," and rap and knock. The "theft" (by making objects disappear mysteriously) is often illustrated in the following tales, as are the groaning and knocking.[2] St. Augustine speaks of hauntings as familiar occurrences, and we have a chain of similar cases from ancient Egypt to 1896. Several houses in that year were so disturbed that the inhabitants were obliged to leave them. The newspapers were full of correspondence on the subject.

The usual annoyances are apparitions (rare), flying about of objects (not very common), noises of every kind (extremely frequent), groans, screams, footsteps and fire-raising. Imposture has either been proved or made very probable in ten out of eleven cases of volatile objects between 1883 and 1895.[3] Moreover, it is certain that the noises of haunted houses are not equally audible by all persons present, even when the sounds are at their loudest. Thus Lord St. Vincent, the great admiral, heard nothing during

[1] Maspero, *Etudes Egyptiennes*, i., fascic. 2.
[2] Examples cited in *Classical Review*, December, 1896, pp. 411, 413.
[3] *Proceedings*, S.P.R., vol. xii., p. 45-116.

his stay at the house of his sister, Mrs. Ricketts, while that lady endured terrible things. After his departure she was obliged to recall him. He arrived, and slept peacefully. Next day his sister told him about the disturbances, after which he heard them as much as his neighbours, and was as unsuccessful in discovering their cause.[1]

Of course this looks as if these noises were unreal, children of the imagination. Noises being the staple of haunted houses, a few words may be devoted to them. They are usually the *frou-frou* or rustling sweep of a gown, footsteps, raps, thumps, groans, a sound as if all the heavy furniture was being knocked about, crashing of crockery and jingling of money. Of course, as to footsteps, people *may* be walking about, and most of the other noises are either easily imitated, or easily produced by rats, water pipes, cracks in furniture (which the Aztecs thought ominous of death), and other natural causes. The explanation is rather more difficult when the steps pace a gallery, passing and repassing among curious inquirers, or in this instance.

THE CREAKING STAIR.

A lady very well known to myself, and in literary society, lived as a girl with an antiquarian father in an old house dear to an antiquary. It was haunted, among other things, by footsteps. The old oak staircase had two creaking steps, numbers seventeen and eighteen from the top. The girl

---

[1] See " Lord St. Vincent's Story ".

would sit on the stair, stretching out her arms, and count the steps as they passed her, one, two, three, and so on to seventeen and eighteen, *which always creaked*.[1] In this case rats and similar causes were excluded, though we may allow for "expectant attention". But this does not generally work. When people sit up on purpose to look out for the ghost, he rarely comes; in the case of the "Lady in Black," which we give later, when purposely waited for, she was never seen at all.

Discounting imposture, which is sometimes found, and sometimes merely fabled (as in the Tedworth story), there remains one curious circumstance. Specially ghostly noises are attributed to the living but absent.

THE GROCER'S COUGH.

A man of letters was born in a small Scotch town, where his father was the intimate friend of a tradesman whom we shall call the grocer. Almost every day the grocer would come to have a chat with Mr. Mackay, and the visitor, alone of the natives, had the habit of knocking at the door before entering. One day Mr. Mackay said to his daughter, "There's Mr. Macwilliam's knock. Open the door." But there was no Mr. Macwilliam! He was just leaving his house at the other end of the street. From that day Mr. Mackay always heard the grocer's knock "a little previous," accompanied by the grocer's cough, which was peculiar. Then all the family

---

[1] Anecdote received from the lady.

heard it, including the son who later became learned. He, when he had left his village for Glasgow, reasoned himself out of the opinion that the grocer's knock did herald and precede the grocer. But when he went home for a visit he found that he heard it just as of old. Possibly some local Sentimental Tommy watched for the grocer, played the trick and ran away. This explanation presents no difficulty, but the boy was never detected.[1]

Such anecdotes somehow do not commend themselves to the belief even of people who can believe a good deal.

But "the spirits of the living," as the Highlanders say, have surely as good a chance to knock, or appear at a distance, as the spirits of the dead. To be sure, the living do not know (unless they are making a scientific experiment) what trouble they are giving on these occasions, but one can only infer, like St. Augustine, that probably the dead don't know it either.

Thus,

MY GILLIE'S FATHER'S STORY.

Fishing in Sutherland, I had a charming companion in the gillie. He was well educated, a great reader, the best of salmon fishers, and I never heard a man curse William, Duke of Cumberland, with more enthusiasm. His father, still alive, was second-sighted, and so, to a moderate extent and without theory, was my friend. Among other anec-

[1] Story at second-hand.

dotes (confirmed in writing by the old gentleman) was this:—

The father had a friend who died in the house which they both occupied. The clothes of the deceased hung on pegs in the bedroom. One night the father awoke, and saw a stranger examining and handling the clothes of the defunct. Then came a letter from the dead man's brother, inquiring about the effects. He followed later, and was the stranger seen by my gillie's father.

Thus the living but absent may haunt a house both noisily and by actual appearance. The learned even think, for very exquisite reasons, that "Silverton Abbey"[1] is haunted noisily by a "spirit of the living". Here is a case:—

THE DREAM THAT KNOCKED AT THE DOOR.

The following is an old but good story. The Rev. Joseph Wilkins died, an aged man, in 1800. He left this narrative, often printed; the date of the adventure is 1754, when Mr. Wilkins, aged twenty-three, was a schoolmaster in Devonshire. The dream was an ordinary dream, and did not announce death, or anything but a journey. Mr. Wilkins dreamed, in Devonshire, that he was going to London. He thought he would go by Gloucestershire and see his people. So he started, arrived at his father's house, found the front door locked, went in by the back door, went to his parents' room, saw his father asleep in bed and his mother

[1] See *The Standard* for summer, 1896.

awake. He said: "Mother, I am going a long journey, and have come to bid you good-bye". She answered in a fright, "Oh dear son, thou art dead!" Mr. Wilkins wakened, and thought nothing of it. As early as a letter could come, one arrived from his father, addressing him as if he were dead, and desiring him, if by accident alive, or any one into whose hands the letter might fall, to write at once. The father then gave his reasons for alarm. Mrs. Wilkins, being awake one night, heard some one try the front door, enter by the back, then saw her son come into her room and say he was going on a long journey, with the rest of the dialogue. She then woke her husband, who said she had been dreaming, but who was alarmed enough to write the letter. No harm came of it to anybody.

The story would be better if Mr. Wilkins, junior, like Laud, had kept a nocturnal of his dreams, and published his father's letter, with post-marks.

The story of the lady who often dreamed of a house, and when by chance she found and rented it was recognised as the ghost who had recently haunted it, is good, but is an invention!

A somewhat similar instance is that of the uproar of moving heavy objects, heard by Scott in Abbotsford on the night preceding and the night of the death of his furnisher, Mr. Bullock, in London. The story is given in Lockhart's *Life of Scott*, and is too familiar for repetition.

On the whole, accepting one kind of story on the same level as the other kind, the living and absent may unconsciously produce the phenomena of haunted houses just as well as the dead, to whose alleged performances we now advance. Actual appearances, as we have said, are not common, and just as all persons do not hear the sounds, so many do not see the appearance, even when it is visible to others in the same room. As an example, take a very mild and lady-like case of haunting.

THE GIRL IN PINK.

The following anecdote was told to myself, a few months after the curious event, by the three witnesses in the case. They were connections of my own, the father was a clergyman of the Anglican Church; he, his wife and their daughter, a girl of twenty, were the "percipients". All are cheerful, sagacious people, and all, though they absolutely agreed as to the facts in their experience, professed an utter disbelief in "ghosts," which the occurrence has not affected in any way. They usually reside in a foreign city, where there is a good deal of English society. One day they left the town to lunch with a young fellow-countryman who lived in a villa in the neighbourhood. There he was attempting to farm a small estate, with what measure of success the story does not say. His house was kept by his sister, who was present, of course, at the little luncheon party. During the meal some question was asked, or some remark was made, to which the clerical guest replied in English by a reference to "the maid-servant in pink".

"There is no maid in pink," said the host, and he asked both his other guests to corroborate him.

Both ladies, mother and daughter, were obliged to say that unless their eyes deceived them, they certainly *had* seen a girl in pink attending on them, or, at least, moving about in the room. To this their entertainers earnestly replied that no such person was in their establishment, that they had no woman servant but the elderly cook and house-keeper, then present, who was neither a girl nor in pink. After luncheon the guests were taken all over the house, to convince them of the absence of the young woman whom they had seen, and assuredly there was no trace of her.

On returning to the town where they reside, they casually mentioned the circumstance as a curious illusion. The person to whom they spoke said, with some interest, "Don't you know that a girl is said to have been murdered in that house before your friends took it, and that she is reported to be occasionally seen, dressed in pink?"

They had heard of no such matter, but the story seemed to be pretty generally known, though naturally disliked by the occupant of the house. As for the percipients, they each and all remain firm in the belief that, till convinced of the impossibility of her presence, they were certain they had seen a girl in pink, and rather a pretty girl, whose appearance suggested nothing out of the common. An obvious hypothesis is discounted, of course, by the presence of the sister of the young gentleman who farmed the estate and occupied the house.

Here is another case, mild but pertinacious.

THE DOG IN THE HAUNTED ROOM.

The author's friend, Mr. Rokeby, lives, and has lived for some twenty years, in an old house at Hammersmith. It is surrounded by a large garden, the drawing-room and dining-room are on the right and left of the entrance from the garden, on the ground floor. My friends had never been troubled by any phenomena before, and never expected to be. However, they found the house "noisy," the windows were apt to be violently shaken at night and steps used to be heard where no steps should be. Deep long sighs were audible at all times of day. As Mrs. Rokeby approached a door, the handle would turn and the door fly open.[1] Sounds of stitching a hard material, and of dragging a heavy weight occurred in Mrs. Rokeby's room, and her hair used to be pulled in a manner for which she could not account. "These sorts of things went on for about five years, when in October, 1875, about three o'clock in the afternoon, I was sitting" (says Mrs. Rokeby) "with three of my children in the dining-room, reading to them. I rang the bell for the parlour-maid, when the door opened, and on looking up I saw the figure of a woman come in and walk up to the side of the table, stand there a

[1] I have once seen this happen, and it is a curious thing to see, when on the other side of the door there is nobody.

second or two, and then turn to go out again, but before reaching the door she seemed to dissolve away. She was a grey, short-looking woman, apparently dressed in grey muslin. I hardly saw the face, which seemed scarcely to be defined at all. None of the children saw her," and Mrs. Rokeby only mentioned the affair at the time to her husband.

Two servants, in the next two months, saw the same figure, alike in dress at least, in other rooms both by daylight and candle light. They had not heard of Mrs. Rokeby's experience, were accustomed to the noises, and were in good health. One of them was frightened, and left her place.

A brilliant light in a dark room, an icy wind and a feeling of being "watched" were other discomforts in Mrs. Rokeby's lot. After 1876, only occasional rappings were heard, till Mr. Rokeby being absent one night in 1883, the noises broke out, " banging, thumping, the whole place shaking". The library was the centre of these exercises, and the dog, a fine collie, was shut up in the library. Mrs. Rokeby left her room for her daughter's, while the dog whined in terror, and the noises increased in violence. Next day the dog, when let out, rushed forth with enthusiasm, but crouched with his tail between his legs when invited to re-enter.

This was in 1883. Several years after, Mr. Rokeby was smoking, alone, in the dining-room early in the evening, when the dog began to bristle up his hair, and bark. Mr. Rokeby looked up and saw the woman in grey, with about half her figure passed through the slightly open door. He ran to the door, but she was gone, and the servants were engaged in their usual business.[1]

Our next ghost offered many opportunities to observers.

THE LADY IN BLACK.

A ghost in a haunted house is seldom observed with anything like scientific precision. The spectre in the following narrative could not be photographed, attempts being usually made in a light which required prolonged exposure. Efforts to touch it were failures, nor did it speak. On the other hand, it did lend itself, perhaps unconsciously, to one scientific experiment. The story is unromantic; the names are fictitious.[2]

Bognor House, an eligible family residence near a large town, was built in 1860, and occupied, till his death in 1876, by Mr. S. He was twice married, and was not of temperate ways. His second wife adopted his habits, left him shortly before his death, and died at Clifton in 1878. The pair used to quarrel about some jewels which Mr. S. concealed in the flooring of a room where the ghost was never seen.

A Mr. L. now took the house, but died six months later. Bognor House stood empty for four years, during which there was vague talk of hauntings. In April, 1882, the house was taken by Captain Morton. This was in April; in June Miss Rose Morton, a lady

---

[1] *S.P.R.*, iii., 115, and from oral narrative of Mr. and Mrs. Rokeby. In 1885, when the account was published, Mr. Rokeby had not yet seen the lady in grey. Nothing of interest is known about the previous tenants of the house.

[2] *Proceedings*, *S.P.R.*, vol. viii., p. 311.

of nineteen studying medicine (and wearing spectacles), saw the first appearance. Miss Morton did not mention her experiences to her family, her mother being an invalid, and her brothers and sisters very young, but she transmitted accounts to a friend, a lady, in a kind of diary letters. These are extant, and are quoted.

Phenomena of this kind usually begin with noises, and go on to apparitions. Miss Morton one night, while preparing to go to bed, heard a noise outside, thought it was her mother, opened the door, saw a tall lady in black holding a handkerchief to her face, and followed the figure till her candle burned out. A widow's white cuff was visible on each wrist, the whole of the face was never seen. In 1882-84, Miss Morton saw the figure about six times; it was thrice seen, once through the window from outside, by other persons, who took it for a living being. Two boys playing in the garden ran in to ask who was the weeping lady in black.

On 29th January, 1884, Miss Morton spoke to her inmate, as the lady in black stood beside a sofa. "She only gave a slight gasp and moved towards the door. Just by the door I spoke to her again, but she seemed as if she were quite unable to speak."[1] In May and June Miss Morton fastened strings at different heights from the stair railings to the wall, where she attached them with glue, but she twice saw the lady pass through the cords, leaving them untouched. When Miss Morton cornered the figure and tried to touch her, or pounce on her, she dodged, or disappeared. But by a curious contradiction her steps were often

[1] Letter of 31st January, 1884.

heard by several of the family, and when she heard the steps, Miss Morton used to go out and follow the figure.

There is really no more to tell. Miss Morton's father never saw the lady, even when she sat on a sofa for half an hour, Miss Morton watching her. Other people saw her in the garden crying, and sent messages to ask what was the matter, and who was the lady in distress. Many members of the family, boys, girls, married ladies, servants and others often saw the lady in black. In 1885 loud noises, bumps and turning of door handles were common, and though the servants were told that the lady was quite harmless, they did not always stay. The whole establishment of servants was gradually changed, but the lady still walked. She appeared more seldom in 1887-1889, and by 1892 even the light footsteps ceased. Two dogs, a retriever and a Skye terrier, showed much alarm. "Twice," says Miss Morton, "I saw the terrier suddenly run up to the mat at the foot of the stairs in the hall, wagging its tail, and moving its back in the way dogs do when they expect to be caressed. It jumped up, fawning as it would do if a person had been standing there, but suddenly slunk away with its tail between its legs, and retreated, trembling, under a sofa." Miss Morton's own emotion, at first, was "a feeling of awe at something unknown, mixed with a strong desire to know more about it".[1]

---

[1] Six separate signed accounts by other witnesses are given. They add nothing more remarkable than what Miss Morton relates. No account was published till the haunting ceased, for fear of lowering the letting value of Bognor House.

This is a pretty tame case of haunting, as was conjectured, by an unhappy *revenant*, the returned spirit of the second Mrs. S. Here it may be remarked that apparitions in haunted houses are very seldom recognised as those of dead persons, and, when recognised, the recognition is usually dubious. Thus, in February, 1897, Lieutenant Carr Glyn, of the Grenadiers, while reading in the outer room of the Queen's Library in Windsor, saw a lady in black in a kind of mantilla of black lace pass from the inner room into a corner where she was lost to view. He supposed that she had gone out by a door there, and asked an attendant later who she was. There was no door round the corner, and, in the opinion of some, the lady was Queen Elizabeth! She has a traditional habit, it seems, of haunting the Library. But surely, of all people, in dress and aspect Queen Elizabeth is most easily recognised. The seer did not recognise her, and she was probably a mere casual hallucination. In old houses such traditions are common, but vague. In this connection Glamis is usually mentioned. Every one has heard of the Secret Chamber, with its mystery, and the story was known to Scott, who introduces it in *The Betrothed*. But we know when the Secret Chamber was built (under the Restoration), who built it, what he paid the masons, and where it is: under the Charter Room.[1] These cold facts rather take the "weird" effect off the Glamis legend.

The usual process is, given an old house, first a noise, then a hallucination, actual or pretended, then

[1] Mr. A. H. Millar's *Book of Glamis*, Scottish History Society.

a myth to account for the hallucination. There is a castle on the border which has at least seven or eight distinct ghosts. One is the famous Radiant Boy. He has been evicted by turning his tapestried chamber into the smoking-room. For many years not one ghost has been seen except the lady with the candle, viewed by myself, but, being ignorant of the story, I thought she was one of the maids. Perhaps she was, but she went into an empty set of rooms, and did not come out again. Footsteps are apt to approach the doors of these rooms in mirk midnight, the door handle turns, and that is all.

So much for supposed hauntings by spirits of the dead.

At the opposite pole are hauntings by agencies whom nobody supposes to be ghosts of inmates of the house. The following is an extreme example, as the haunter proceeded to arson. This is not so very unusual, and, if managed by an impostor, shows insane malevolence.[1]

---

[1] This account is abridged from Mr. Walter Leaf's translation of Aksakoff's *Predvestniki Spiritizma*, St. Petersburg, 1895. Mr. Aksakoff publishes contemporary letters, certificates from witnesses, and Mr. Akutin's hostile report. It is based on the possibility of imitating the raps, the difficulty of locating them, and the fact that the flying objects were never seen to start. If Mrs. Shchapoff threw them, they might, perhaps, have occasionally been seen to start. *S.P.R.*, vol. xii., p. 298. Precisely similar events occurred in Russian military quarters in 1853. As a quantity of Government property was burned, official inquiries were held. The reports are published by Mr. Aksakoff. The repeated verdict was that no suspicion attached to any subject of the Czar.

THE DANCING DEVIL.

On 16th November, 1870, Mr. Shchapoff, a Russian squire, the narrator, came home from a visit to a country town, Iletski, and found his family in some disarray. There lived with him his mother and his wife's mother, ladies of about sixty-nine, his wife, aged twenty, and his baby daughter. The ladies had been a good deal disturbed. On the night of the 14th, the baby was fractious, and the cook, Maria, danced and played the harmonica to divert her. The baby fell asleep, the wife and Mr. Shchapoff's miller's lady were engaged in conversation, when a shadow crossed the blind on the outside. They were about to go out and see who was passing, when they heard a double shuffle being executed with energy in the loft overhead. They thought Maria, the cook, was making a night of it, but found her asleep in the kitchen. The dancing went on but nobody could be found in the loft. Then raps began on the window panes, and so the miller and gardener patrolled outside. Nobody!

Raps and dancing lasted through most of the night and began again at ten in the morning. The ladies were incommoded and complained of broken sleep. Mr. Shchapoff, hearing all this, examined the miller, who admitted the facts, but attributed them to a pigeon's nest, which he had found under the cornice. Satisfied with this rather elementary hypothesis, Mr. Shchapoff sat down to read Livingstone's *African Travels*. Presently the double shuffle sounded in the loft. Mrs. Shchapoff was asleep in her bedroom, but was awakened by loud raps. The window was tapped at, deafening thumps were dealt at the outer wall, and the whole house thrilled. Mr. Shchapoff rushed out with dogs and a gun, there were no footsteps in the snow, the air was still, the full moon rode in a serene sky. Mr. Shchapoff came back, and the double shuffle was sounding merrily in the empty loft. Next day was no better, but the noises abated and ceased gradually.

Alas, Mr. Shchapoff could not leave well alone. On 20th December, to amuse a friend, he asked Maria to dance and play. Raps, in tune, began on the window panes. Next night they returned, while boots, slippers, and other objects, flew about with a hissing noise. A piece of stuff would fly up and fall with a heavy hard thud, while hard bodies fell soundless as a feather. The performances slowly died away.

On Old Year's Night Maria danced to please them; raps began, people watching on either side of a wall heard the raps on the other side. On 8th January, Mrs. Shchapoff fainted when a large, luminous ball floated, increasing in size, from under her bed. The raps now followed her about by day, as in the case of John Wesley's sisters. On these occasions she felt weak and somnolent. Finally Mr. Shchapoff carried his family to his town house for much-needed change of air.

Science, in the form of Dr. Shustoff, now hinted that electricity or magnetic force was at the bottom of the annoyances, a great comfort to the household, who conceived that the devil was concerned. The doctor accompanied his friends to their country house for a night, Maria was invited to oblige with a dance, and only a few taps on windows followed. The family returned to town till 21st January. No sooner was Mrs. Shchapoff in bed than knives and forks came out of a closed cupboard and flew about, occasionally sticking in the walls.

On 24th January the doctor abandoned the hypothesis of electricity, because the noises kept time to profane but not to sacred music. A Tartar hymn by a Tartar servant, an Islamite, had no accompaniment, but the *Freischütz* was warmly encored.

This went beyond the most intelligent spontaneous exercises of electricity. Questions were asked of the agencies, and to the interrogation, "Are you a devil?" a most deafening knock replied. "We all jumped backwards."

Now comes a curious point. In the Wesley and Tedworth cases, the masters of the houses, like the curé of Cideville (1851), were at odds with local "cunning men".

Mr. Shchapoff's fiend now averred that he was "set on" by the servant of a neighbouring miller, with whom Mr. Shchapoff had a dispute about a mill pond. This man had previously said, "It will be worse; they will drag you by the hair". And, indeed, Mrs. Shchapoff was found in tears, because her hair had been pulled.[1]

[1] The same freedom was taken, as has been said, with a lady of the most irreproachable character, a friend of the author, in a haunted house, of the usual sort, in Hammersmith, about 1876.

Science again intervened. A section of the Imperial Geographical Society sent Dr. Shustoff, Mr. Akutin (a Government civil engineer), and a literary gentleman, as a committee of inquiry appointed by the governor of the province. They made a number of experiments with Leyden jars, magnets, and so forth, with only negative results. Things flew about, both *from*, and *towards* Mrs. Shchapoff. Nothing volatile was ever seen to *begin* its motion, though, in March, 1883, objects were seen, by a policeman and six other witnesses, to fly up from a bin and out of a closed cupboard, in a house at Worksop.[1] Mr. Akutin, in Mrs. Shchapoff's bedroom, found the noises answer questions in French and German, on contemporary politics, of which the lady of the house knew nothing. Lassalle was said to be alive, Mr. Shchapoff remarked, "What nonsense!" but Mr. Akutin corrected him. The bogey was better informed. The success of the French in the great war was predicted.

The family now moved to their town house, and the inquest continued, though the raps were only heard near the lady. A Dr. Dubinsky vowed that she made them herself, with her tongue; then, with her pulse. The doctor assailed, and finally shook the faith of Mr. Akutin, who was to furnish a report. "He bribed a servant boy to say that his mistress made the sounds herself, and then pretended that he had caught her trying to deceive us by throwing things." Finally Mr. Akutin reported that the whole affair was a hysterical imposition by Mrs. Shchapoff.

[1] *Proceedings*, S.P.R., vol. xii., p. 49.

Dr. Dubinsky attended her, her health and spirits improved, and the disturbances ceased. But poor Mr. Shchapoff received an official warning not to do it again, from the governor of his province. That way lies Siberia.

"Imagine, then," exclaims Mr. Shchapoff, "our horror, when, on our return to the country in March, the unknown force at once set to work again. And now even my wife's presence was not essential. Thus, one day, I saw with my own eyes a heavy sofa jump off all four legs (three or four times in fact), and this when my aged mother was lying on it." The same thing occurred to Nancy Wesley's bed, on which she was sitting while playing cards in 1717. The picture of a lady of seventy, sitting tight to a bucking sofa, appeals to the brave.

Then the fire-raising began. A blue spark flew out of a wash-stand, into Mrs. Shchapoff's bedroom. Luckily she was absent, and her mother, rushing forward with a water-jug, extinguished a flaming cotton dress. Bright red globular meteors now danced in the veranda. Mr. Portnoff next takes up the tale as follows, Mr. Shchapoff having been absent from home on the occasion described.

"I was sitting playing the guitar. The miller got up to leave, and was followed by Mrs. Shchapoff. Hardly had she shut the door, when I heard, as though from far off, a deep drawn wail. The voice seemed familiar to me. Overcome with an unaccountable horror I rushed to the door, and there in the passage I saw a literal pillar of fire, in the middle of which, draped in flame, stood Mrs. Shchapoff. . . .

I rushed to put it out with my hands, but I found it burned them badly, as if they were sticking to burning pitch. A sort of cracking noise came from beneath the floor, which also shook and vibrated violently." Mr. Portnoff and the miller " carried off the unconscious victim ".

Mr. Shchapoff also saw a small pink hand, like a child's, spring from the floor, and play with Mrs. Shchapoff's coverlet, in bed. These things were too much; the Shchapoffs fled to a cottage, and took a new country house. They had no more disturbances. Mrs. Shchapoff died in child-bed, in 1878, " a healthy, religious, quiet, affectionate woman ".

CHAPTER X.

MODERN HAUNTINGS.

The Shchapoff Story of a Peculiar Type. "Demoniacal Possession." Story of Willington Mill briefly analysed. Authorities for the Story. Letters. A Journal. The Wesley Ghost. Given Critically and Why. Note on similar Stories, such as the Drummer of Tedworth. Sir Walter Scott's Scepticism about Nautical Evidence. Lord St. Vincent. Scott asks Where are his Letters on a Ghostly Disturbance. The Letters are now Published. Lord St. Vincent's Ghost Story. Reflections.

CASES like that of Mrs. Shchapoff really belong to a peculiar species of haunted houses. Our ancestors, like the modern Chinese, attributed them to diabolical possession, not to an ordinary ghost of a dead person. Examples are very numerous, and have all the same "symptoms," as Coleridge would have said, he attributing them to a contagious nervous malady of observation in the spectators. Among the most notorious is the story of Willington Mill, told by Howitt, and borrowed by Mrs. Crowe, in *The Night Side of Nature.* Mr. Procter, the occupant, a Quaker, vouched to Mrs. Crowe for the authenticity of Howitt's version. (22nd July, 1847.)

Other letters from seers are published, and the Society of Psychical Research lately printed Mr. Procter's contemporary journal. A man, a woman, and a monkey were the chief apparitions. There were noises, lights, beds were heaved about : nothing was omitted. A *clairvoyante* was turned on, but could only say that the spectral figures, which she described, "had no brains". After the Quakers left the house there seems to have been no more trouble. The affair lasted for fifteen years.

Familiar as it is, we now offer the old story of the hauntings at Epworth, mainly because a full view of the inhabitants, the extraordinary family of Wesley, seems necessary to an understanding of the affair. The famous and excessively superstitious John Wesley was not present on the occasion.

THE WESLEY GHOST.

No ghost story is more celebrated than that of *Old Jeffrey*, the spirit so named by Emily Wesley, which disturbed the Rectory at Epworth, chiefly in the December of 1716 and the spring of 1717. Yet the vagueness of the human mind has led many people, especially journalists, to suppose that the haunted house was that, not of Samuel Wesley, but of his son John Wesley, the founder of the Wesleyan Methodists. For the better intelligence of the tale, we must know who the inmates of the Epworth Rectory were, and the nature of their characters and pursuits. The rector was the Rev. Samuel Wesley, born in 1662, the son of a clergyman banished from

his living on "Black Bartholomew Day," 1666.
Though educated among Dissenters, Samuel Wesley converted himself to the truth as it is in the
Church of England, became a "poor scholar" of
Exeter College in Oxford, supported himself mainly
by hack-work in literature (he was one of the editors
of a penny paper called *The Athenian Mercury*, a sort
of *Answers*), married Miss Susanna Annesley, a lady
of good family, in 1690-91, and in 1693 was presented
to the Rectory of Epworth in Lincolnshire by Mary,
wife of William of Orange, to whom he had dedicated
a poem on the life of Christ. The living was poor,
Mr. Wesley's family multiplied with amazing velocity, he was in debt, and unpopular. His cattle
were maimed in 1705, and in 1703 his house was
burned down. The Rectory House, of which a
picture is given in Clarke's *Memoirs of the Wesleys*,
1825, was built anew at his own expense. Mr.
Wesley was in politics a strong Royalist, but having
seen James II. shake "his lean arm" at the Fellows
of Magdalen College, and threaten them "with the
weight of a king's right hand," he conceived a prejudice against that monarch, and took the side of
the Prince of Orange. His wife, a very pious woman
and a strict disciplinarian, was a Jacobite, would not
say "amen" to the prayers for "the king," and was
therefore deserted by her husband for a year or more
in 1701-1702. They came together again, however,
on the accession of Queen Anne.

Unpopular for his politics, hated by the Dissenters,
and at odds with the "cunning men," or local wizards
against whom he had frequently preached, Mr. Wesley

was certainly apt to have tricks played on him by his neighbours. His house, though surrounded by a wall, a hedge, and its own grounds, was within a few yards of the nearest dwelling in the village street.

In 1716, when the disturbances began, Mr. Wesley's family consisted of his wife ; his eldest son, Sam, aged about twenty-three, and then absent at his duties as an usher at Westminster ; John, aged twelve, a boy at Westminster School ; Charles, a boy of eight, away from home, and the girls, who were all at the parsonage. They were Emily, about twenty-two, Mary, Nancy and Sukey, probably about twenty-one, twenty and nineteen, and Hetty, who may have been anything between nineteen and twelve, but who comes after John in Dr. Clarke's list, and is apparently reckoned among " the children ".[1] Then there was Patty, who may have been only nine, and little Keziah.

All except Patty were very lively young people, and Hetty, afterwards a copious poet, " was gay and sprightly, full of mirth, good-humour, and keen wit. She indulged this disposition so much that it was said to have given great uneasiness to her parents." The servants, Robin Brown, Betty Massy and Nancy Marshall, were recent comers, but were acquitted by Mrs. Wesley of any share in the mischief. The

---

[1] John Wesley, however, places Hetty as next in seniority to Mary or Molly. We do not certainly know whether Hetty was a child, or a grown-up girl, but, as she always sat up till her father went to bed, the latter is the more probable opinion. As Hetty has been accused of causing the disturbances, her age is a matter of interest. Girls of twelve or thirteen are usually implicated in these affairs. Hetty was probably several years older.

family, though, like other people of their date, they were inclined to believe in witches and "warnings," were not especially superstitious, and regarded the disturbances, first with some apprehension, then as a joke, and finally as a bore.

The authorities for what occurred are, first, a statement and journal by Mr. Wesley, then a series of letters of 1717 to Sam at Westminster by his mother, Emily and Sukey, next a set of written statements made by these and other witnesses to John Wesley in 1726, and last and worst, a narrative composed many years after by John Wesley for *The Arminian Magazine*.

The earliest document, by a few days, is the statement of Mr. Wesley, written, with a brief journal, between 21st December, 1716, and 1st January, 1717. Comparing this with Mrs. Wesley's letter to Sam of 12th January, 1716 and Sukey's letter of 24th January, we learn that the family for some weeks after 1st December had been " in the greatest panic imaginable," supposing that Sam, Jack, or Charlie (who must also have been absent from home) was dead, " or by some misfortune killed ". The reason for these apprehensions was that on the night of 1st December the maid " heard at the dining-room door several dreadful groans, like a person in extremes ". They laughed at her, but for the whole of December "the groans, squeaks, tinglings and knockings were frightful enough ". The rest of the family (Mr. Wesley always excepted) " heard a strange knocking in divers places," chiefly in the green room, or nursery, where (apparently)

Hetty, Patty and Keziah lay. Emily heard the noises later than some of her sisters, perhaps a week after the original groans. She was locking up the house about ten o'clock when a sound came like the smashing and splintering of a huge piece of coal on the kitchen floor. She and Sukey went through the rooms on the ground floor, but found the dog asleep, the cat at the other end of the house, and everything in order. From her bedroom Emily heard a noise of breaking the empty bottles under the stairs, but was going to bed, when Hetty, who had been sitting on the lowest step of the garret stairs beside the nursery door, waiting for her father, was chased into the nursery by a sound as of a man passing her in a loose trailing gown. Sukey and Nancy were alarmed by loud knocks on the outside of the dining-room door and overhead. All this time Mr. Wesley heard nothing, and was not even told that anything unusual was heard. Mrs. Wesley at first held her peace lest he should think it " according to the vulgar opinion, a warning against his own death, which, indeed, we all apprehended". Mr. Wesley only smiled when he was informed ; but, by taking care to see all the girls safe in bed, sufficiently showed his opinion that the young ladies and their lovers were the ghost. Mrs. Wesley then fell back on the theory of rats, and employed a man to blow a horn as a remedy against these vermin. But this measure only aroused the emulation of the sprite, whom Emily began to call " Jeffrey ".

Not till 21st December did Mr. Wesley hear anything, then came thumpings on his bedroom wall. Unable to discover the cause, he procured a stout mastiff, which soon became demoralised by his experiences. On the morning of the 24th, about seven o'clock, Emily led Mrs. Wesley into the nursery, where she heard knocks on and under the bedstead ; these sounds replied when she knocked. Something "like a badger, with no head," says Emily ; Mrs. Wesley only says, "like a badger," ran from under the bed. On the night of the 25th there was an appalling *vacarme*. Mr. and Mrs. Wesley went on a tour of inspection, but only found the mastiff whining in terror. "We still heard it rattle and thunder in every room above or behind us, locked as well as open, except my study, where as yet it never came." On the night of the 26th Mr. Wesley seems to have heard of a phenomenon already familiar to Emily— "something like the quick winding up of a jack, at the corner of the room by my bed head". This was always followed by knocks, "hollow and loud, such as none of us could ever imitate". Mr. Wesley went into the nursery, Hetty, Kezzy and Patty were asleep. The knocks were loud, beneath and in the room, so Mr. Wesley went below to the kitchen, struck with his stick against the rafters, and was answered "as often and as loud as I knocked". The peculiar knock which was his own, 1—23456—7, was not successfully echoed at that time. Mr. Wesley then returned to the nursery, which was as *tapageuse* as ever. The children, three, were trembling in their sleep. Mr. Wesley invited the agency to an interview in his study, was answered by one knock outside, "all the rest were within," and then came silence. Investigations outside produced no result, but the latch of the door would rise and fall, and the door itself was pushed violently back against investigators.

"I have been with Hetty," says Emily, "when it has knocked under her, and when she has removed has followed her," and it knocked under little Kezzy, when "she stamped with her foot, pretending to scare Patty."

Mr. Wesley had requested an interview in his study, especially as the Jacobite goblin routed loudly "over our heads constantly, when we came to the prayers for King George and the prince". In his study the agency pushed Mr. Wesley about, bumping him against the corner of his desk, and against his door. He would ask for a conversation, but heard only "two or three feeble squeaks, a little louder than the chirping of a bird, but not like the noise of rats, which I have often heard".

Mr. Wesley had meant to leave home for a visit on Friday, 28th December, but the noises of the 27th were so loud that he stayed at home, inviting the Rev. Mr. Hoole, of Haxey, to view the performances. "The noises were very boisterous and disturbing this night." Mr. Hoole says (in 1726, confirmed by Mrs. Wesley, 12th January, 1717) that there were sounds of feet, trailing gowns, raps, and a noise as of planing boards : the disturbance finally went outside the house and died away. Mr. Wesley seems to have paid his visit on the 30th, and notes, "1st January, 1717. My family have had no disturbance since I went away."

To judge by Mr. Wesley's letter to Sam, of 12th January, there was no trouble between the 29th of December and that date. On the 19th of January, and the 30th of the same month, Sam wrote, full of curiosity, to his father and mother. Mrs. Wesley replied (25th or 27th January), saying that no explanation could be discovered, but "it commonly was nearer Hetty than the rest". On 24th January, Sukey said "it is now pretty quiet, but still knocks at prayers for the king." On 11th February, Mr. Wesley, much bored by Sam's inquiries, says, "we are all now quiet. . . . It would make a glorious penny book for Jack Dunton," his brother-in-law, a publisher of popular literature, such as the *Athenian Mercury*. Emily (no date) explains the phenomena as the revenge for her father's recent sermons "against consulting those that are called cunning men, which our people are given to, and *it had a particular spite at my father*".

The disturbances by no means ended in the beginning of January, nor at other dates when a brief cessation made the Westleys hope that Jeffrey had returned to his own place. Thus on 27th March, Sukey writes to Sam, remarking that as Hetty and Emily are also writing "so particularly," she need not say much. "One thing I believe you do not know, that is, last Sunday, to my father's no small amazement, his trencher danced upon the table a pretty while, without anybody's stirring the table. . . . Send me some news for we are excluded from the sight or hearing of any versal thing, except Jeffery."

The last mention of the affair, at this time, is in a letter from Emily, of 1st April, to a Mr. Berry.

"Tell my brother the sprite was with us last night, and heard by many of our family." There are no other contemporary letters preserved, but we may note Mrs. Wesley's opinion (25th January) that it was "beyond the power of any human being to make such strange and various noises".

The next evidence is ten years after date, the statements taken down by Jack Wesley in 1726 (1720?). Mrs. Wesley adds to her former account that she "earnestly desired it might not disturb her" (at her devotions) "between five and six in the evening," and it did not rout in her room at that time. Emily added that a screen was knocked at on each side as she went round to the other. Sukey mentioned the noise as, on one occasion, coming gradually from the garret stairs, outside the nursery door, up to Hetty's bed, "who trembled strongly in her sleep. It then removed to the room overhead, where it knocked my father's knock on the ground, as if it would beat the house down." Nancy said that the noise used to follow her, or precede her, and once a bed, on which she sat playing cards, was lifted up under her several times to a considerable height. Robin, the servant, gave evidence that he was greatly plagued with all manner of noises and movements of objects.

John Wesley, in his account published many years after date in his *Arminian Magazine*, attributed the affair of 1716 to his father's broken vow of deserting his mother till she recognised the Prince of Orange as king! He adds that the mastiff "used to tremble and creep away before the noise began".

Some other peculiarities may be noted. All persons did not always hear the noises. It was three weeks before Mr. Wesley heard anything. "John and Kitty Maw, who lived over against us, listened several nights in the time of the disturbance, but could never hear anything." Again, "The first time my mother ever heard any unusual noise at Epworth was long before the disturbance of old Jeffrey . . . the door and windows jarred very loud, and presently several distinct strokes, three by three, were struck. From that night it never failed to give notice in much the same manner, against any signal misfortune or illness of any belonging to the family," writes Jack.

Once more, on 10th February, 1750, Emily (now Mrs. Harper) wrote to her brother John, "that wonderful thing called by us Jeffery, how certainly it calls on me against any extraordinary new affliction".

This is practically all the story of Old Jeffrey. The explanations have been, trickery by servants (Priestley), contagious hallucinations (Coleridge), devilry (Southey), and trickery by Hetty Wesley (Dr. Salmon, of Trinity College, Dublin). Dr. Salmon points out that there is no evidence from Hetty; that she was a lively, humorous girl, and he conceives that she began to frighten the maids, and only reluctantly exhibited before her father against whom, however, Jeffrey developed "a particular spite ". He adds that certain circumstances were peculiar to Hetty, which, in fact, is not the case. The present editor has examined Dr. Salmon's arguments in *The Contemporary Review*, and shown reason, in the evidence, for acquitting Hetty Wesley, who was never suspected by her family.

Trickery from without, by "the cunning men," is an explanation which, at least, provides a motive, but how the thing could be managed from without remains a mystery. Sam Wesley, the friend of Pope, and Atterbury, and Lord Oxford, not unjustly said : "Wit, I fancy, might find many interpretations, but wisdom none ".[1]

As the Wesley tale is a very typical instance of a very large class, our study of it may exempt us from printing the well-known parallel case of "The Drummer of Tedworth". Briefly, the house of Mr. Mompesson, near Ludgarshal, in Wilts, was disturbed in the usual way, for at least two years, from April, 1661, to April, 1663, or later. The noises, and copious phenomena of moving objects apparently untouched, were attributed to the unholy powers of a wandering drummer, deprived by Mr. Mompesson of his drum. A grand jury presented the drummer for trial, on a charge of witchcraft, but the petty jury would not convict, there being a want of evidence to prove threats, *malum minatum*, by the drummer. In 1662 the Rev. Joseph Glanvil, F.R.S., visited the house, and, in the bedroom of Mr. Mompesson's little girls, the chief sufferers, heard and saw much the same phenomena as the elder Wesley describes in his own nursery. The

[1] 30th January, 1717.

"little modest girls" were aged about seven and eight. Charles II. sent some gentlemen to the house for one night, when nothing occurred, the disturbances being intermittent. Glanvil published his narrative at the time, and Mr. Pepys found it "not very convincing". Glanvil, in consequence of his book, was so vexed by correspondents "that I have been haunted almost as bad as Mr. Mompesson's house". A report that imposture had been discovered, and confessed by Mr. Mompesson, was set afloat, by John Webster, in a well-known work, and may still be found in modern books. Glanvil denied it till he was "quite tired," and Mompesson gave a formal denial in a letter dated Tedworth, 8th November, 1672. He also, with many others, swore to the facts on oath, in court, at the drummer's trial.[1]

In the Tedworth case, as at Epworth, and in the curious Cideville case of 1851, a quarrel with "cunning men" preceded the disturbances. In Lord St. Vincent's case, which follows, nothing of the kind is reported. As an almost universal rule children, especially girls of about twelve, are centres of the trouble; in the St. Vincent story, the children alone were exempt from annoyance.

LORD ST. VINCENT'S GHOST STORY.

Sir Walter Scott, writing about the disturbances in the house occupied by Mrs. Ricketts, sister of the great admiral, Lord St. Vincent, asks: "Who has

---

[1] Glanvil's *Sadducismus Triumphatus*, 1726. Preface to part ii., Mompesson's letters.

seen Lord St. Vincent's letters?" He adds that
the gallant admiral, after all, was a sailor, and im-
plies that "what the sailor said" (if he said anything)
"is not evidence".

The fact of unaccountable disturbances which
finally drove Mrs. Ricketts out of Hinton Ampner,
is absolutely indisputable, though the cause of the
annoyances may remain as mysterious as ever. The
contemporary correspondence (including that of Lord
St. Vincent, then Captain Jervis) exists, and has been
edited by Mrs. Henley Jervis, grand-daughter of Mrs.
Ricketts.[1]

There is only the very vaguest evidence for hauntings at Lady Hillsborough's old house of Hinton
Ampner, near Alresford, before Mr. Ricketts took it
in January, 1765. He and his wife were then disturbed by footsteps, and sounds of doors opening and
shutting. They put new locks on the doors lest the
villagers had procured keys, but this proved of no
avail. The servants talked of seeing appearances of
a gentleman in drab and of a lady in silk, which Mrs.
Ricketts disregarded. Her husband went to Jamaica
in the autumn of 1769, and in 1771 she was so disturbed that her brother, Captain Jervis, a witness of
the phenomena, insisted on her leaving the house in
August. He and Mrs. Ricketts then wrote to Mr.
Ricketts about the affair. In July, 1772, Mrs.
Ricketts wrote a long and solemn description of her
sufferings, to be given to her children.

We shall slightly abridge her statement, in which
she mentions that when she left Hinton she had not

[1] *Gentleman's Magazine*, November, December, 1872.

one of the servants who came thither in her family,
which "evinces the impossibility of a confederacy".
Her new, like her former servants, were satisfactory ;
Camis, her new coachman, was of a yeoman house
of 400 years' standing. It will be observed
that Mrs. Ricketts was a good deal annoyed even
before 2nd April, 1771, the day when she dates the
beginning of the worst disturbances. She believed
that the agency was human—a robber or a practical
joker—and but slowly and reluctantly became convinced that the "exploded" notion of an abnormal
force might be correct. We learn that while Captain
Jervis was not informed of the sounds he never heard
them, and whereas Mrs. Ricketts heard violent noises
after he went to bed on the night of his vigil, he heard
nothing. "Several instances occurred where very
loud noises were heard by one or two persons, when
those equally near and in the same direction were
not sensible of the least impression." [1]

With this preface, Mrs. Ricketts may be allowed
to tell her own tale.

"Sometime after Mr. Ricketts left me (autumn,
1769) I—then lying in the bedroom over the kitchen—
heard frequently the noise of some one walking in the
room within, and the rustling as of silk clothes against
the door that opened into my room, sometimes so
loud, and of such continuance as to break my rest.
Instant search being often made, we never could

[1] This happened, to a less degree, in the Wesley case, and is not
uncommon in modern instances. The inference seems to be that the
noises, like the sights occasionally seen, are hallucinatory, not real.
Gentleman's Magazine, Dec., 1872, p. 666.

discover any appearance of human or brute being. Repeatedly disturbed in the same manner, I made it my constant practice to search the room and closets within, and to secure the only door on the inside. . . . Yet this precaution did not preclude the disturbance, which continued with little interruption."

Nobody, in short, could enter this room, except by passing through that of Mrs. Ricketts, the door of which "was always made fast by a drawn bolt". Yet somebody kept rustling and walking in the inner room, which somebody could never be found when sought for.

In summer, 1770, Mrs. Ricketts heard someone walk to the foot of her bed in her own room, "the footsteps as distinct as ever I heard, myself perfectly awake and collected". Nobody could be discovered in the chamber. Mrs. Ricketts boldly clung to her room, and was only now and then disturbed by "sounds of harmony," and heavy thumps, down stairs. After this, and early in 1771, she was "frequently sensible of a hollow murmuring that seemed to possess the whole house: it was independent of wind, being equally heard on the calmest nights, and it was a sound I had never been accustomed to hear".

On 27th February, 1771, a maid was alarmed by "groans and fluttering round her bed": she was "the sister of an eminent grocer in Alresford". On 2nd April, Mrs. Ricketts heard people walking in the lobby, hunted for burglars, traced the sounds to a room whence their was no outlet, and found nobody. This kind of thing went on till Mrs. Ricketts despaired of any natural explanation. After mid-

summer, 1771, the trouble increased, in broad daylight, and a shrill female voice, answered by two male
voices was added to the afflictions. Captain Jervis
came on a visit, but was told of nothing, and never
heard anything. After he went to Portsmouth, "the
most deep, loud tremendous noise seemed to rush
and fall with infinite velocity and force on the lobby
floor adjoining my room," accompanied by a shrill
and dreadful shriek, seeming to proceed from under
the spot where the rushing noise fell, and repeated
three or four times.

Mrs. Ricketts' "resolution remained firm," but
her health was impaired; she tried changing her
room, without results. The disturbances pursued
her. Her brother now returned. She told him
nothing, and he heard nothing, but next day she
unbosomed herself. Captain Jervis therefore sat
up with Captain Luttrell and his own man. He
was rewarded by noises which he in vain tried to
pursue. "I should do great injustice to my sister"
(he writes to Mr. Ricketts on 9th August, 1771), "if I
did not acknowledge to have heard what I could not,
after the most diligent search and serious reflection,
any way account for." Captain Jervis during a whole
week slept by day, and watched, armed, by night.
Even by day he was disturbed by a sound as of
immense weights falling from the ceiling to the floor
of his room. He finally obliged his sister to leave
the house.

What occurred after Mrs. Ricketts abandoned
Hinton is not very distinct. Apparently Captain
Jervis's second stay of a week, when he did hear

the noises, was from 1st August to 8th August. From a statement by Mrs. Ricketts it appears that, when her brother joined his ship, the *Alarm* (9th August), she retired to Dame Camis's house, that of her coachman's mother. Thence she went, and made another attempt to live at Hinton, but was "soon after assailed by a noise I never before heard, very near me, and the terror I felt not to be described". She therefore went to the Newbolts, and thence to the old Palace at Winton; later, on Mr. Ricketts' return, to the Parsonage, and then to Longwood (to the *old* house there) near Alresford.

Meanwhile, on 18th September, Lady Hillsborough's agent lay with armed men at Hinton, and, making no discovery, offered £50 (increased by Mr. Ricketts to £100) for the apprehension of the persons who caused the noises. The reward was never claimed. On 8th March, 1772, Camis wrote: "I am very sorry that we cannot find out the reason of the noise"; at other dates he mentions sporadic noises heard by his mother and another woman, including "the murmur". A year after Mrs. Ricketts left a family named Lawrence took the house, and, according to old Lucy Camis, in 1818, Mr. Lawrence very properly threatened to dismiss any servant who spoke of the disturbances. The result of this sensible course was that the Lawrences left suddenly, at the end of the year—and the house was pulled down. Some old political papers of the Great Rebellion, and a monkey's skull, not exhibited to any anatomist, are said to have been discovered under the floor of the lobby, or of one of the rooms. Mrs. Ricketts adds sadly, "The unbelief of Chancellor Hoadley went nearest my heart," as he had previously a high opinion of her veracity. The Bishop of St. Asaph was incredulous, "on the ground that such means were unworthy of the Deity to employ".

Probably a modern bishop would say that there were no noises at all, that every one who heard the sounds was under the influence of "suggestion," caused first in Mrs. Ricketts' own mind by vague tales of a gentleman in drab seen by the servants.

The contagion, to be sure, also reached two distinguished captains in the navy, but not till one of them was told about disturbances which had not previously disturbed him. If this explanation be true, it casts an unusual light on the human imagination. Physical science has lately invented a new theory. Disturbances of this kind are perhaps "seismic,"—caused by earthquakes! (See Professor Milne, in *The Times*, 21st June, 1897.)

CHAPTER XI.

MORE HAUNTED HOUSES.

A PHYSICIAN, as we have seen, got the better of the demon in Mrs. Shchapoff's case, at least while the lady was under his care. Really these disturbances appear to demand the attention of medical men. If the whole phenomena are caused by imposture, the actors, or actresses, display a wonderful similarity of symptoms and an alarming taste for fire-raising. Professor William James, the well-known psychologist, mentions ten cases whose resemblances "suggest a natural type," and we ask, is it a type of hysterical disease?[1] He chooses, among others, an instance in Dr. Nevius's book on *Demon Possession in China*, and there is another in Peru. He also mentions *The Great Amherst Mystery*, which we give, and the Rerrick case in Scotland (1696), related by Telfer, who prints, on his margins, the names of the attesting witnesses of each event, lairds, clergymen, and farmers. At Rerrick, as in Russia, the *little hand* was seen by Telfer himself, and the fire-raising was endless. At Amherst too, as in a pair of recent Russian cases and others, there was plenty of fire-raising. By a lucky chance an English case occurred at Wem, in Shropshire, in November, 1883. It began at a farm called the Woods, some ten miles from Shrewsbury. First a saucepan full of eggs "jumped" off the fire in the kitchen, and the tea-things, leaping from the table, were broken. Cinders "were thrown out of the fire," and set some clothes in a blaze. A globe leaped off a lamp. A farmer, Mr. Lea, saw all the windows of the upper story "as it were on fire," but it was no such matter. The nurse-maid ran out in a fright, to a neighbour's, and her dress spontaneously combusted as she ran. The people attributed these and similar events, to something in the coal, or in the air, or to electricity. When the nurse-girl, Emma Davies, sat on the lap of the school mistress, Miss Maddox, her boots kept flying off, like the boot laces in *The Daemon of Spraiton*.

All this was printed in the London papers, and, on 15th November, *The Daily Telegraph* and *Daily News*

[1] *S.P.R. Proceedings*, vol. xii., p. 7.

published Emma's confession that she wrought by sleight of hand and foot. On 17th November, Mr. Hughes went from Cambridge to investigate. For some reason investigation never begins till the fun is over. On the 9th the girl, now in a very nervous state (no wonder!) had been put under the care of a Dr. Mackey. This gentleman and Miss Turner said that things had occurred since Emma came, for which they could not account. On 13th November, however, Miss Turner, looking out of a window, spotted Emma throwing a brick, and pretending that the flight of the brick was automatic. Next day Emma confessed to her tricks, but steadfastly denied that she had cheated at Woods Farm, and Weston Lullingfield, where she had also been. Her evidence to this effect was so far confirmed by Mrs. Hampson of Woods Farm, and her servant, Priscilla Evans, when examined by Mr. Hughes. Both were " quite certain " that they saw crockery rise by itself into air off the kitchen table, when Emma was at a neighbouring farm, Mr. Lea's. Priscilla also saw crockery come out of a cupboard, in detachments, and fly between her and Emma, usually in a slanting direction, while Emma stood by with her arms folded. Yet Priscilla was not on good terms with Emma. Unless, then, Mrs. Hampson and Priscilla fabled, it is difficult to see how Emma could move objects when she was "standing at some considerable distance, standing, in fact, in quite another farm ".

Similar evidence was given and signed by Miss Maddox, the schoolmistress, and Mr. and Mrs. Lea. On the other hand Mrs. Hampson and Priscilla believed that Emma managed the fire-raising herself. The flames were "very high and white, and the articles were very little singed". This occurred also at Rerrick, in 1696, but Mr. Hughes attributes it to Emma's use of paraffin, which does not apply to the Rerrick case. Paraffin smells a good deal—nothing is said about a smell of paraffin.

Only one thing is certain: Emma was at last caught in a cheat. This discredits her, but a man who cheats at cards *may* hold a good hand by accident. In the same way, if such wonders can happen (as so much world-wide evidence declares), they *may* have happened at Woods Farm, and Emma, "in a very nervous state," *may* have feigned then, or rather did feign them later.

The question for the medical faculty is: Does a decided taste for wilful fire-raising often accompany exhibitions of dancing furniture and crockery, gratuitously given by patients of hysterical temperament? This is quite a normal inquiry. Is there a nervous malady of which the symptoms are domestic arson, and amateur *leger-de-main?* The complaint, if it exists, is of very old standing and wide prevalence, including Russia, Scotland, New England, France, Iceland, Germany, China and Peru.

As a proof of the identity of symptoms in this malady, we give a Chinese case. The Chinese, as to diabolical possession, are precisely of the same opinion as the inspired authors of the Gospels. People are "possessed," and, like the woman having a spirit of divination in the Acts of the Apostles, make a good thing out of it. Thus Mrs. Ku was approached by a native Christian. She became rigid and her demon, speaking through her, acknowledged the Catholic verity, and said that if Mrs. Ku were converted he would have to leave. On recovering her everyday consciousness, Mrs. Ku asked what Tsehwa, her demon, had said. The Christian told her, and perhaps she would have deserted her erroneous courses, but her fellow-villagers implored her to pay homage to the demon. They were in the habit of resorting to it for medical advice (as people do to Mrs. Piper's demon in the United States), so Mrs. Ku decided to remain in the business.[1] The parallel to the case in the Acts is interesting.

HAUNTED MRS. CHANG.

Mr. Chang, of that ilk (Chang Chang Tien-ts), was a man of fifty-seven, and a graduate in letters. The ladies of his family having accommodated a demon with a shrine in his house, Mr. Chang said he " would have none of that nonsense ". The spirit then entered into Mrs. Chang, and the usual fire-raising began all over the place. The furniture and crockery danced in the familiar way, and objects took to disappearing mysteriously, even when secured under lock and key. Mr. Chang was as unlucky as Mr. Chin. At *his* house "doors would open of their own accord, footfalls were heard, as of persons walking in the house, although no one could be seen. Plates, bowls and the tea-

---

[1] *Demon Possession in China*, p. 399. By the Rev. John L. Nevius, D.D. Forty years a missionary in China. Revel, New York, 1894.

pot would suddenly rise from the table into the air." [1]

Mrs. Chang now tried the off chance of there being something in Christianity, stayed with a native Christian (the narrator), and felt much better. She could enjoy her meals, and was quite a new woman. As her friend could not go home with her, Mrs. Fung, a native Christian, resided for a while at Mr. Chang's; "comparative quiet was restored," and Mrs. Fung retired to her family.

The symptoms returned; the native Christian was sent for, and found Mr. Chang's establishment full of buckets of water for extinguishing the sudden fires. Mrs. Chang's daughter-in-law was now possessed, and "drank wine in large quantities, though ordinarily she would not touch it". She was staring and tossing her arms wildly; a service was held, and she soon became her usual self.

In the afternoon, when the devils went out of the ladies, the fowls flew into a state of wild excitement, while the swine rushed furiously about and tried to climb a wall.

The family have become Christians, the fires have ceased; Mr. Chang is an earnest inquirer, but opposed, for obvious reasons, to any public profession of our religion. [2]

In Mr. Niu's case "strange noises and rappings were frequently heard about the house. The buildings were also set on fire in different places in some mysterious way." The Christians tried to convert

[1] Translated from report of Hsu Chung-ki, Nevius, p. 61.

[2] Nevius, pp. 403-406.

Mr. Niu, but as the devil now possessed his female slave, whose success in fortune-telling was extremely lucrative, Mr. Niu said that he preferred to leave well alone, and remained wedded to his idols.[1]

We next offer a recent colonial case, in which the symptoms, as Mr. Pecksniff said, were "chronic".

THE GREAT AMHERST MYSTERY.

On 13th February, 1888, Mr. Walter Hubbell, an actor by profession, "being duly sworn" before a Notary Public in New York, testified to the following story:—

In 1879 he was acting with a strolling company, and came to Amherst, in Nova Scotia. Here he heard of a haunted house, known to the local newspapers as "The Great Amherst Mystery". Having previously succeeded in exposing the frauds of spiritualism Mr. Hubbell determined to investigate the affair of Amherst. The haunted house was inhabited by Daniel Teed, the respected foreman in a large shoe factory. Under his roof were Mrs. Teed, "as good a woman as ever lived"; little Willie, a baby boy; and Mrs. Teed's two sisters, Jennie, a very pretty girl, and Esther, remarkable for large grey eyes, pretty little hands and feet, and candour of expression. A brother of Teed's and a brother of Mrs. Cox made up the family. They were well off, and lived comfortably in a detached cottage of two storys.

It began when Jennie and Esther were in bed one

[1] *Op. cit.*, p. 415. There are other cases in Mr. Denny's *Folklore of China.*

night. Esther jumped up, saying that there was a mouse in the bed. Next night, a green band-box began to make a rustling noise, and then rose a foot in the air, several times. On the following night Esther felt unwell, and "was a swelling wisibly before the werry eyes" of her alarmed family. Reports like thunder peeled through her chamber, under a serene sky. Next day Esther could only eat "a small piece of bread and butter, and a large green pickle". She recovered slightly, in spite of the pickle, but, four nights later, all her and her sister's bed-clothes flew off, and settled down in a remote corner. At Jennie's screams, the family rushed in, and found Esther "fearfully swollen". Mrs. Teed replaced the bed-clothes, which flew off again, the pillow striking John Teed in the face. Mr. Teed then left the room, observing, in a somewhat unscientific spirit, that "he had had enough of it". The others, with a kindness which did them credit, sat on the edges of the bed, and repressed the desire of the sheets and blankets to fly away. The bed, however, sent forth peels like thunder, when Esther suddenly fell into a peaceful sleep.

Next evening Dr. Carritte arrived, and the bolster flew at his head, *and then went back again under Esther's*. While paralysed by this phenomenon, unprecedented in his practice, the doctor heard a metal point scribbling on the wall. Examining the place whence the sound proceeded, he discovered this inscription :—

> Esther Cox ! You are
> mine to kill.

Mr. Hubbell has verified the inscription, and often, later, recognised the hand, in writings which "came out of the air and fell at our feet". Bits of plaster now gyrated in the room, accompanied by peels of local thunder. The doctor admitted that his diagnosis was at fault. Next day he visited his patient when potatoes flew at him. He exhibited a powerful sedative, but pounding noises began on the roofs and were audible at a distance of 200 yards, as the doctor himself told Mr. Hubbell.

The clergy now investigated the circumstances, which they attributed to electricity. "Even the most exclusive class" frequented Mr. Teed's house, till December, when Esther had an attack of diphtheria. On recovering she went on to visit friends in Sackville, New Brunswick, where nothing unusual occurred. On her return the phenomena broke forth afresh, and Esther heard a voice proclaim that the house would be set on fire. Lighted matches then fell from the ceiling, but the family extinguished them. The ghost then set a dress on fire, apparently as by spontaneous combustion, and this kind of thing continued. The heads of the local fire-brigade suspected Esther of these attempts at arson, and Dr. Nathan Tupper suggested that she should be flogged. So Mr. Teed removed Esther to the house of a Mr. White.

In about a month "all," as Mrs. Nickleby's lover said, "was gas and gaiters". The furniture either flew about, or broke into flames. Worse, certain pieces of iron placed as an experiment on Esther's lap "became too hot to be handled with comfort," and then flew away.

Mr. Hubbell himself now came on the scene, and, not detecting imposture, thought that "there was money in it". He determined to "run" Esther as a powerful attraction, he lecturing, and Esther sitting on the platform.

It did not pay. The audience hurled things at Mr. Hubbell, and these were the only volatile objects. Mr. Hubbell therefore brought Esther back to her family at Amherst, where, in Esther's absence, his umbrella and a large carving knife flew at him with every appearance of malevolence. A great arm-chair next charged at him like a bull, and to say that Mr. Hubbell was awed "would indeed seem an inadequate expression of my feelings". The ghosts then thrice undressed little Willie in public, in derision of his tears and outcries. Fire-raising followed, and that would be a hard heart which could read the tale unmoved. Here it is, in the simple eloquence of Mr. Hubbell :—

"This was my first experience with Bob, the demon, as a fire-fiend; and I say, candidly, that until I had had that experience I never fully realised what an awful calamity it was to have an invisible monster, somewhere within the atmosphere, going from place to place about the house, gathering up old newspapers into a bundle and hiding it in the basket of soiled linen or in a closet, then go and steal matches out of the match-box in the kitchen or somebody's pocket, as he did out of mine, and after kindling a fire in the bundle, tell Esther that he had started a fire, but would not tell where; or perhaps not tell her at all, in which case the first intimation we would have was the smell of the smoke pouring through the house, and then the most intense excitement, everybody running with buckets of water. I say it was the most truly awful calamity that could possible befall any family, infidel or Christian, that could be conceived in the mind of man or ghost.

"And how much more terrible did it seem in this little cottage, where all were strict members of church, prayed, sang hymns and read the Bible. Poor Mrs. Teed!"

On Mr. Hubbell's remarking that the cat was not tormented, "she was instantly lifted from the floor to a height of five feet, and then dropped on Esther's back. . . . I never saw any cat more frightened; she ran out into the front yard, where she remained for the balance (rest) of the day." On 27th June "a trumpet was heard in the house all day".

The Rev. R. A. Temple now prayed with Esther, and tried a little amateur exorcism, including the use of slips of paper, inscribed with Habakkuk ii. 3. The ghosts cared no more than Voltaire for *ce coquin d'Habacuc.*

Things came to such a pass, matches simply raining all round, that Mr. Teed's landlord, a Mr. Bliss, evicted Esther. She went to a Mr. Van Amburgh's, and Mr. Teed's cottage was in peace.

Some weeks later Esther was arrested for incendiarism in a barn, was sentenced to four months' imprisonment, but was soon released in deference to public opinion. She married, had a family; and ceased to be a mystery.

This story is narrated with an amiable simplicity,

and is backed, more or less, by extracts from Amherst and other local newspapers. On making inquiries, I found that opinion was divided. Some held that Esther was a mere impostor and fire-raiser; from other sources I obtained curious tales of the eccentric flight of objects in her neighbourhood. It is only certain that Esther's case is identical with Madame Shchapoff's, and experts in hysteria may tell us whether that malady ever takes the form of setting fire to the patient's wardrobe, and to things in general.[1]

After these modern cases of disturbances, we may look at a few old, or even ancient examples. It will be observed that the symptoms are always of the same type, whatever the date or country. The first is Gaelic, of last century.

DONALD BAN AND THE BOCAN.[2]

It is fully a hundred years ago since there died in Lochaber a man named Donald Ban, sometimes called "the son of Angus," but more frequently

[1] *The Great Amherst Mystery*, by Walter Hubbell. Brentano, New York, 1882. I obtained some additional evidence at first hand published in *Longman's Magazine*.

[2] The sources for this tale are two Gaelic accounts, one of which is printed in the *Gael*, vol. vi., p. 142, and the other in the *Glenbard Collection of Gaelic Poetry*, by the Rev. A. Maclean Sinclair, p. 297 ff. The former was communicated by Mr. D. C. Macpherson from local tradition; the latter was obtained from a tailor, a native of Lochaber, who emigrated to Canada when about thirty years of age. When the story was taken down from his lips in 1885, he was over eighty years old, and died only a few months later.

known as Donald Ban of the Bocan. This surname was derived from the troubles caused to him by a bocan—a goblin—many of whose doings are preserved in tradition.

Donald drew his origin from the honourable house of Keppoch, and was the last of the hunters of Mac-vic-Ronald. His home was at Mounessee, and later at Inverlaire in Glenspean, and his wife belonged to the MacGregors of Rannoch. He went out with the Prince, and was present at the battle of Culloden. He fled from the field, and took refuge in a mountain shieling, having two guns with him, but only one of them was loaded. A company of soldiers came upon him there, and although Donald escaped by a back window, taking the empty gun with him by mistake, he was wounded in the leg by a shot from his pursuers. The soldiers took him then, and conveyed him to Inverness, where he was thrown into prison to await his trial. While he was in prison he had a dream; he saw himself sitting and drinking with Alastair MacCholla, and Donald MacRonald Vor. The latter was the man of whom it was said that he had two hearts; he was taken prisoner at Falkirk and executed at Carlisle. Donald was more fortunate than his friend, and was finally set free.

It was after this that the bocan began to trouble him; and although Donald never revealed to any man the secret of who the bocan was (if indeed he knew it himself), yet there were some who professed to know that it was a "gillie" of Donald's who was killed at Culloden. Their reason for believing this was that on one occasion the man in question had given away more to a poor neighbour than Donald was pleased to spare. Donald found fault with him, and in the quarrel that followed the man said, " I will be avenged for this, alive or dead ".

It was on the hill that Donald first met with the bocan, but he soon came to closer quarters, and haunted the house in a most annoying fashion. He injured the members of the household, and destroyed all the food, being especially given to dirtying the butter (a thing quite superfluous, according to Captain Burt's description of Highland butter). On one occasion a certain Ronald of Aberardair was a guest in Donald's house, and Donald's wife said, "Though I put butter on the table for you to-night, it will just be dirtied ". " I will go with you to the butter-keg," said Ronald, " with my dirk in my hand, and hold my bonnet over the keg, and he will not dirty it this night." So the two went together to fetch the butter, but it was dirtied just as usual.

Things were worse during the night and they could get no sleep for the stones and clods that came flying about the house. " The bocan was throwing things out of the walls, and they would hear them rattling at the head of Donald's bed." The minister came (Mr. John Mor MacDougall was his name) and slept a night or two in the house, but the bocan kept away so long as he was there. Another visitor, Angus MacAlister Ban, whose grandson told the tale, had more experience of the bocan's reality. "Something seized his two big toes, and he could not get free any more than if he had been caught by the smith's tongs. It was the bocan, but he did

nothing more to him." Some of the clergy, too, as
well as laymen of every rank, were witnesses to the
pranks which the spirit carried on, but not even
Donald himself ever saw him in any shape whatever. So famous did the affair become that Donald
was nearly ruined by entertaining all the curious
strangers who came to see the facts for themselves.

In the end Donald resolved to change his abode,
to see whether he could in that way escape from the
visitations. He took all his possessions with him
except a harrow, which was left beside the wall of
the house, but before the party had gone far on the
road the harrow was seen coming after them. "Stop,
stop," said Donald; "if the harrow is coming after
us, we may just as well go back again." The
mystery of the harrow is not explained, but Donald
did return to his home, and made no further attempt
to escape from his troubles in this way.

If the bocan had a spite at Donald, he was still
worse disposed towards his wife, the MacGregor
woman. On the night on which he last made his
presence felt, he went on the roof of the house and
cried, "Are you asleep, Donald Ban?" "Not just
now," said Donald. "Put out that long grey tether,
the MacGregor wife," said he. "I don't think I'll
do that to-night," said Donald. "Come out yourself,
then," said the bocan, "and leave your bonnet."
The good-wife, thinking that the bocan was outside
and would not hear her, whispered in Donald's ear
as he was rising, "Won't you ask him when the
Prince will come?" The words, however, were
hardly out of her mouth when the bocan answered

her with, " Didn't you get enough of him before, you grey tether ? "

Another account says that at this last visit of the bocan, he was saying that various other spirits were along with him. Donald's wife said to her husband : " I should think that if they were along with him they would speak to us "; but the bocan answered, " They are no more able to speak than the sole of your foot ". He then summoned Donald outside as above. " I will come," said Donald, " and thanks be to the Good Being that you have asked me." Donald was taking his dirk with him as he went out, but the bocan said, " leave your dirk inside, Donald, and your knife as well ".

Donald then went outside, and the bocan led him on through rivers and a birch-wood for about three miles, till they came to the river Fert. There the bocan pointed out to Donald a hole in which he had hidden some plough-irons while he was alive. Donald proceeded to take them out, and while doing so the two eyes of the bocan were causing him greater fear than anything else he ever heard or saw. When he had got the irons out of the hole, they went back to Mounessie together, and parted that night at the house of Donald Ban.

Donald, whether naturally or by reason of his ghostly visitant, was a religious man, and commemorated his troubles in some verses which bear the name of " The Hymn of Donald Ban of the Bocan ". In these he speaks of the common belief that he had done something to deserve all this annoyance, and makes mention of the " stones and clods " which flew about his house in the night time. Otherwise the hymn is mainly composed of religious sentiments, but its connection with the story makes it interesting, and the following is a literal translation of it.

THE HYMN OF DONALD BAN.

O God that created me so helpless,
Strengthen my belief and make it firm.
Command an angel to come from Paradise,
And take up his abode in my dwelling,
To protect me from every trouble
That wicked folks are putting in my way;
Jesus, that did'st suffer Thy crucifixion,
Restrain their doings, and be with me Thyself.

Little wonder though I am thoughtful—
Always at the time when I go to bed
The stones and the clods will arise—
How could a saint get sleep there?
I am without peace or rest,
Without repose or sleep till the morning;
O Thou that art in the throne of grace,
Behold my treatment and be a guard to me.

Little wonder though I am troubled,
So many stories about me in every place.
Some that are unjust will be saying,
" It is all owing to himself, that affair ".
Judge not except as you know,
Though the Son of God were awaking you;
No one knows if I have deserved more
Than a rich man that is without care.

Although I am in trouble at this time,
Verily, I shall be doubly repaid;
When the call comes to me from my Saviour,
I shall receive mercy and new grace;
I fear no more vexation,
When I ascend to be with Thy saints;
O Thou that sittest on the throne,
Assist my speaking and accept my prayer.

O God, make me mindful
Night and day to be praying,
Seeking pardon richly
For what I have done, on my knees.
Stir with the spirit of Truth
True repentance in my bosom,
That when Thou sendest death to seek me,
Christ may take care of me.

The bocan was not the only inhabitant of the spirit-world that Donald Ban encountered during his lifetime. A cousin of his mother was said to have been carried off by the fairies, and one night Donald saw him among them, dancing away with all his might. Donald was also out hunting in the year of the great snow, and at nightfall he saw a man mounted on the back of a deer ascending a great rock. He heard the man saying, " Home, Donald Ban," and fortunately he took the advice, for that night there fell eleven feet of snow in the very spot where he had intended to stay.

We now take two modern Icelandic cases, for the purpose of leading up to the famous Icelandic legend of Grettir and Glam the Vampire, from the Grettis Saga. It is plain that such incidents as those in the two modern Icelandic cases (however the effects were produced) might easily be swollen into the prodigious tale of Glam in the course of two or three centuries, between Grettir's time and the complete formation of his Saga.

THE DEVIL OF HJALTA-STAD.[1]

The sheriff writes: "The Devil at Hjalta-stad was outspoken enough this past winter, although no one saw him. I, along with others, had the dishonour to hear him talking for nearly two days, during which he addressed myself and the minister, Sir Grim, with words the like of which 'eye hath not seen nor ear heard'. As soon as we reached the front of the house there was heard in the door an iron voice saying: 'So Hans from Eyrar is come now, and wishes to talk with me, the —— idiot'. Compared with other names that he gave me this might be considered as flattering. When I inquired who it was that addressed me with such words, he answered in a fierce voice, 'I was called Lucifer at first, but now I am called Devil and Enemy'. He threw at us both stones and pieces of wood, as well as other things, and broke two windows in the minister's room. He spoke so close to us that he seemed to be just at our side. There was an old woman there of the name of Opia, whom he called his wife, and a 'heavenly blessed soul,' and asked Sir Grim to marry them, with various other remarks of this kind, which I will not recount.

"I have little liking to write about his ongoings, which were all disgraceful and shameful, in accordance with the nature of the actor. He repeated the

---

[1] John Arnason, in his *Icelandic Folklore and Fairy Tales* (vol. i., p. 309), gives the account of this as written by the Sheriff Hans Wium in a letter to Bishop Haldorr Brynjolfsson in the autumn of 1750.

'Pater Noster' three times, answered questions from the Catechism and the Bible, said that the devils held service in hell, and told what texts and psalms they had for various occasions. He asked us to give him some of the food we had, and a drink of tea, etc. I asked the fellow whether God was good. He said, 'Yes'. Whether he was truthful. He answered, 'Not one of his words can be doubted'. Sir Grim asked him whether the devil was good-looking. He answered: 'He is far better-looking than you, you —— ugly snout!' I asked him whether the devils agreed well with each other. He answered in a kind of sobbing voice: 'It is pain-ful to know that they never have peace'. I bade him say something to me in German, and said to him *Lass uns Teusc redre* (sic), but he answered as if he had misunderstood me.

"When we went to bed in the evening he shouted fiercely in the middle of the floor, 'On this night I shall snatch you off to hell, and you shall not rise up out of bed as you lay down'. During the evening he wished the minister's wife good-night. The minister and I continued to talk with him during the night; among other things we asked him what kind of weather it was outside. He answered: 'It is cold, with a north wind'. We asked if he was cold. He answered: 'I think I am both hot and cold'. I asked him how loud he could shout. He said, 'So loud that the roof would go off the house, and you would all fall into a dead faint'. I told him to try it. He answered: 'Do you think I am come to amuse you, you —— idiot?' I asked him to show us a little specimen. He said he would do so, and gave three shouts, the last of which was so fearful that I have never heard anything worse, and doubt whether I ever shall. Towards daybreak, after he had parted from us with the usual compliments, we fell asleep.

"Next morning he came in again, and began to waken up people; he named each one by name, not forgetting to add some nickname, and asking whether so-and-so was awake. When he saw they were all awake, he said he was going to play with the door now, and with that he threw the door off its hinges with a sudden jerk, and sent it far in upon the floor. The strangest thing was that when he threw anything it went down at once, and then went back to its place again, so it was evident that he either went inside it or moved about with it.

"The previous evening he challenged me twice to come out into the darkness to him, and this in an angry voice, saying that he would tear me limb from limb. I went out and told him to come on, but nothing happened. When I went back to my place and asked him why he had not fulfilled his promise, he said, 'I had no orders for it from my master'. He asked us whether we had ever heard the like before, and when we said 'Yes,' he answered, 'That is not true: the like has never been heard at any time'. He had sung 'The memory of Jesus' after I arrived there, and talked frequently while the word of God was being read. He said that he did not mind this, but that he did not like the 'Cross-school Psalms,' and said it must have been a great idiot who composed them. This enemy came like a devil, departed as such, and behaved himself as such while he was present, nor would it befit any one but the devil to declare all that he said. At the same time it must be added that I am not quite convinced that it was a spirit, but my opinions on this I cannot give here for lack of time."

In another work[1] where the sheriff's letter is given with some variations and additions, an attempt is made to explain the story. The phenomena were said to have been caused by a young man who had learned ventriloquism abroad. Even if this art could have been practised so successfully as to puzzle the sheriff and others, it could hardly have taken the door off its hinges and thrown it into the room. It is curious that while Jon Espolin in his *Annals* entirely discredits the sheriff's letter, he yet gives a very similar account of the spirit's proceedings.

A later story of the same kind, also printed by Jon Arnason (i., 311), is that of the ghost at Garpsdal as related by the minister there, Sir Saemund, and written down by another minister on 7th June, 1808. The narrative is as follows:—

THE GHOST AT GARPSDAL.

In Autumn, 1807, there was a disturbance by night in the outer room at Garpsdal, the door being smashed. There slept in this room the minister's men-servants, Thorsteinn Gudmundsson, Magnus

[1] *Huld*, part 3, p. 25, Keykjavik, 1893.

Jonsson, and a child named Thorstein. Later, on
16th November, a boat which the minister had lying
at the sea-side was broken in broad daylight, and
although the blows were heard at the homestead yet
no human form was visible that could have done this.
All the folks at Garpsdal were at home, and the
young fellow Magnus Jonsson was engaged either at
the sheep-houses or about the homestead; the spirit
often appeared to him in the likeness of a woman.
On the 18th of the same month four doors of the
sheep-houses were broken in broad daylight, while
the minister was marrying a couple in the church;
most of his people were present in the church,
Magnus being among them. That same day in the
evening this woman was noticed in the sheep-houses;
she said that she wished to get a ewe to roast, but
as soon as an old woman who lived at Garpsdal and
was both skilled and wise (Gudrun Jons-dottir by
name) had handled the ewe, its struggles ceased and
it recovered again. While Gudrun was handling the
ewe, Magnus was standing in the door of the house;
with that one of the rafters was broken, and the
pieces were thrown in his face. He said that the
woman went away just then. The minister's horses
were close by, and at that moment became so scared
that they ran straight over smooth ice as though it
had been earth, and suffered no harm.

On the evening of the 20th there were great disturbances, panelling and doors being broken down in
various rooms. The minister was standing in the
house door along with Magnus and two or three girls
when Magnus said to him that the spirit had gone

into the sitting-room. The minister went and stood at the door of the room, and after he had been there a little while, talking to the others, a pane of glass in one of the room windows was broken. Magnus was standing beside the minister talking to him, and when the pane broke he said that the spirit had gone out by that. The minister went to the window, and saw that the pane was all broken into little pieces. The following evening, the 21st, the spirit also made its presence known by bangings, thumpings, and loud noises.

On the 28th the on-goings of the spirit surpassed themselves. In the evening a great blow was given on the roof of the sitting-room. The minister was inside at the time, but Magnus with two girls was out in the barn. At the same moment the partition between the weaving-shop and the sitting-room was broken down, and then three windows of the room itself—one above the minister's bed, another above his writing-table, and the third in front of the closet door. A piece of a table was thrown in at one of these, and a spade at another. At this the household ran out of that room into the loft, but the minister sprang downstairs and out ; the old woman Gudrun who was named before went with him, and there also came Magnus and some of the others. Just then a vessel of wash, which had been standing in the kitchen, was thrown at Gudrun's head. The minister then ran in, along with Magnus and the girls, and now everything that was loose was flying about, both doors and splinters of wood. The minister opened a room near the outer door intending to go in there, but just then a sledge hammer which lay at the door was thrown at him, but it only touched him on the side and hip, and did him no harm. From there the minister and the others went back to the sitting-room, where everything was dancing about, and where they were met with a perfect volley of splinters of deal from the partitions. The minister then fled, and took his wife and child to Muli, the next farm, and left them there, as she was frightened to death with all this. He himself returned next day.

On the 8th of December, the woman again made her appearance in broad daylight. On this occasion she broke the shelves and panelling in the pantry, in presence of the minister, Magnus, and others. According to Magnus, the spirit then went out through the wall at the minister's words, and made its way to the byre-lane. Magnus and Gudrun went after it, but were received with throwings of mud and dirt. A stone was also hurled at Magnus, as large as any man could lift, while Gudrun received a blow on the arm that confined her to her bed for three weeks.

On the 26th of the month the shepherd, Einar Jonsson, a hardy and resolute fellow, commanded the spirit to show itself to him. Thereupon there came over him such a madness and frenzy, that he had to be closely guarded to prevent him from doing harm to himself. He was taken to the house, and kept in his bed, a watch being held over him. When he recovered his wits, he said that this girl had come above his head and assailed him. When he had completely got over this, he went away from Garpsdal altogether.

Later than this the minister's horse was found dead in the stable at Muli, and the folks there said that it was all black and swollen.

These are the most remarkable doings of the ghost at Garpsdal, according to the evidence of Sir Saemund, Magnus, Gudrun, and all the household at Garpsdal, all of whom will confirm their witness with an oath, and aver that no human being could have been so invisible there by day and night, but rather that it was some kind of spirit that did the mischief. From the story itself it may be seen that neither Magnus nor any other person could have accomplished the like, and all the folk will confirm this, and clear all persons in the matter, so far as they know. In this form the story was told to me, the subscriber, to Samuel Egilsson and Bjarni Oddsson, by the minister himself and his household, at Garpsdal, 28th May, 1808. That this is correctly set down, after what the minister Sir Saemund related to me, I witness here at Stad on Reykjanes, 7th June, 1808.

GISLI OLAFSSON.

Notwithstanding this declaration, the troubles at Garpsdal were attributed by others to Magnus, and the name of the "Garpsdale Ghost" stuck to him throughout his life. He was alive in 1862, when Jon Arnason's volume was published.

These modern instances lead up to "the best story in the world," the old Icelandic tale of Glam.

CHAPTER XII.

The Story of Glam. The Foul Fords.

THE STORY OF GLAM.

THERE was a man named Thorhall, who lived at Thorhall-stead in Forsaela-dala, which lies in the north of Iceland. He was a fairly wealthy man, especially in cattle, so that no one round about had so much live-stock as he had. He was not a chief, however, but an honest and worthy yeoman.

"Now this man's place was greatly haunted, so that he could scarcely get a shepherd to stay with him, and although he asked the opinion of many as to what he ought to do, he could find none to give him advice of any worth.

"One summer at the Althing, or yearly assembly of the people, Thorhall went to the booth of Skafti, the law man, who was the wisest of men and gave good counsel when his opinion was asked. He received Thorhall in a friendly way, because he knew he was a man of means, and asked him what news he had.

"'I would have some good advice from you,' said Thorhall.

"'I am little able to give that,' said Skafti; 'but what is the matter?'

"'This is the way of it,' said Thorhall, 'I have had very bad luck with my shepherds of late. Some of them get injured, and others will not serve out their time ; and now no one that knows how the case stands will take the place at all.'

" ' Then there must be some evil spirit there,' said Skafti, ' when men are less willing to herd your sheep, than those of others. Now since you have asked my advice, I will get a shepherd for you. Glam is his name, he belongs to Sweden, and came out here last summer. He is big and strong, but not very well liked by most people.'

" Thorhall said that he did not mind that, if he looked well after the sheep. Skafti answered that there was no hope of other men doing it, if Glam could not, seeing he was so strong and stout-hearted. Their talk ended there, and Thorhall left the booth.

" This took place just at the breaking up of the assembly. Thorhall missed two of his horses, and went to look for them in person, from which it may be seen that he was no proud man. He went up to the mountain ridge, and south along the fell that is called Armann's fell. There he saw a man coming down from the wood, leading a horse laden with bundles of brushwood. They soon met each other and Thorhall asked his name. He said he was called Glam. He was tall of body, and of strange appearance ; his eyes were blue and staring, and his hair wolf-grey in colour. Thorhall was a little startled when he saw him, and was certain that this was the man he had been told about.

" ' What work are you best fitted for ? ' he asked. Glam said that he was good at keeping sheep in winter.

" ' Will you look after *my* sheep ? ' said Thorhall. ' Skafti has put you into my hands.'

" ' On this condition only will I take service with you,' said Glam, ' that I have my own free will, for I am ill-tempered if anything does not please me.'

" ' That will not harm me,' said Thorhall, ' and I should like you to come to me.'

" ' I will do so,' said Glam ; ' but is there any trouble at your place.'

" ' It is believed to be haunted,' said Thorhall.

" ' I am not afraid of such bug-bears,' said Glam, ' and think that it will be all the livelier for that.'

" ' You will need all your boldness,' said Thorhall, ' It is best not to be too frightened for one's self there.'

" After this they made a bargain between them, and Glam was to come when the winter nights began. Then they parted, and Thorhall found his horses where he had just newly looked for them, and rode home, after thanking Skafti for his kindness.

" The summer passed, and Thorhall heard nothing of the shepherd, nor did any one know the least about him, but at the time appointed he came to Thorhall-stead. The yeoman received him well, but the others did not like him, and the good-wife least of all. He began his work among the sheep which gave him little trouble, for he had a loud, hoarse voice, and the flock all ran together whenever he shouted. There was a church at Thorhall-stead, but Glam would never go to it nor join in the service. He was unbelieving, surly, and difficult to deal with, and ever one felt a dislike towards him.

"So time went on till it came to Christmas eve. On that morning Glam rose early and called for his food. The good-wife answered: 'It is not the custom of Christain people to eat on this day, for to-morrow is the first day of Christmas, and we ought to fast to-day'. Glam replied: 'You have many foolish fashions that I see no good in. I cannot see that men are any better off now than they were when they never troubled themselves about such things. I think it was a far better life when men were heathens; and now I want my food, and no nonsense.' The good-wife answered: 'I am sure you will come to sorrow to-day if you act thus perversely'.

"Glam bade her bring his food at once, or it would be the worse for her. She was afraid to refuse, and after he had eaten he went out in a great rage.

"The weather was very bad. It was dark and gloomy all round; snowflakes fluttered about; loud noises were heard in the air, and it grew worse and worse as the day wore on. They heard the shepherd's voice during the forenoon, but less of him as the day passed. Then the snow began to drift, and by evening there was a violent storm. People came to the service in church, and the day wore on to evening, but still Glam did not come home. There was some talk among them of going to look for him, but no search was made on account of the storm and the darkness.

"All Christmas eve Glam did not return, and in the morning men went to look for him. They found the sheep scattered in the fens, beaten down by the

storm, or up on the hills.   Thereafter they came
to a place in the valley where the snow was all
trampled, as if there had been a terrible struggle
there, for stones and frozen earth were torn up all
round about.   They looked carefully round the place,
and found Glam lying a short distance off, quite
dead.   He was black in colour, and swollen up as
big as an ox.   They were horrified at the sight, and
shuddered in their hearts.   However, they tried to
carry him to the church, but could get him no further
than to the edge of a cleft, a little lower down; so
they left him there and went home and told their
master what had happened.

"Thorhall asked them what had been the cause of
Glam's death.   They said that they had traced foot-
prints as large as though the bottom of a cask had
been set down in the snow leading from where the
trampled place was up to the cliffs at the head of
the valley, and all along the track there were huge
blood-stains.   From this they guessed that the evil
spirit which lived there must have killed Glam, but
had received so much hurt that it had died, for
nothing was ever seen of it after.

"The second day of Christmas they tried again to
bring Glam to the church.   They yoked horses to
him, but after they had come down the slope and
reached level ground they could drag him no further,
and he had to be left there.

"On the third day a priest went with them, but
Glam was not be found, although they searched for
him all day.   The priest refused to go a second time,
and the shepherd was found at once when the priest

was not present. So they gave over their attempts to take him to the church, and buried him on the spot.

"Soon after this they became aware that Glam was not lying quiet, and great damage was done by him, for many that saw him fell into a swoon, or lost their reason. Immediately after Yule men believed that they saw him about the farm itself, and grew terribly frightened, so that many of them ran away. After this Glam began to ride on the house-top by night,[1] and nearly shook it to pieces, and then he walked about almost night and day. Men hardly dared to go up into the valley, even although they had urgent business there, and every one in the district thought great harm of the matter.

"In spring, Thorhall got new men, and started the farm again, while Glam's walkings began to grow less frequent as the days grew longer. So time went on, until it was mid-summer. That summer a ship from Norway came into Huna-water (a firth to the north of Thorhall-stead), and had on board a man called Thorgaut. He was foreign by birth, big of body, and as strong as any two men. He was un-hired and unmarried, and was looking for some employment, as he was penniless. Thorhall rode to the ship, and found Thorgaut there. He asked him whether he would enter his service. Thorgaut answered that he might well do so, and that he did not care much what work he did.

"'You must know, however,' said Thorhall, 'that it is not good for any faint-hearted man to live at

[1] As at Amherst!

my place, on account of the hauntings that have been of late, and I do not wish to deceive you in any way.'

" ' I do not think myself utterly lost although I see some wretched ghosts,' said Thorgaut. ' It will be no light matter for others if *I* am scared, and I will not throw up the place on that account.'

" Their bargain was quickly made, and Thorgaut was to have charge of the sheep during the winter. The summer went past, and Thorgaut began his duties with the winter nights, and was well liked by every one. Glam began to come again, and rode on the house-top, which Thorgaut thought great sport, and said that the thrall would have to come to close quarters before he would be afraid of him. Thorhall bade him not say too much about it. ' It will be better for you,' said he, ' if you have no trial of each other.'

" ' Your courage has indeed been shaken out of you,' said Thorgaut, ' but I am not going to fall dead for such talk.'

" The winter went on till Christmas came again, and on Christmas eve the shepherd went out to his sheep. ' I trust,' said the good-wife, ' that things will not go after the old fashion.'

" ' Have no fear of that, good-wife,' said Thorgaut; ' there will be something worth talking about if I don't come back.'

" The weather was very cold, and a heavy drift blowing. Thorgaut was in the habit of coming home when it was half-dark, but on this occasion he did not return at his usual time. People came to church, and they now began to think that things were not unlikely to fall out as they had done before. Thorhall wished to make search for the shepherd, but the church-goers refused, saying that they would not risk themselves in the hands of evil demons by night, and so no search was made.

"After their morning meal on Christmas day they went out to look for the shepherd. They first made their way to Glam's cairn, guessing that he was the cause of the man's disappearance. On coming near to this they saw great tidings, for there they found the shepherd with his neck broken and every bone in his body smashed in pieces. They carried him to the church, and he did no harm to any man thereafter. But Glam began to gather strength anew, and now went so far in his mischief that every one fled from Thorhall-stead, except the yeoman and his wife.

"The same cattleman, however, had been there for a long time, and Thorhall would not let him leave, because he was so faithful and so careful. He was very old, and did not want to go away either, for he saw that everything his master had would go to wreck and ruin, if there was no one to look after it.

"One morning after the middle of winter the good-wife went out to the byre to milk the cows. It was broad daylight by this time, for no one ventured to be outside earlier than that, except the cattleman, who always went out when it began to grow clear. She heard a great noise and fearful bellowing in the byre, and ran into the house again, crying out and saying that some awful thing was going on there.

Thorhall went out to the cattle and found them goring each other with their horns. To get out of their way, he went through into the barn, and in doing this he saw the cattleman lying on his back with his head in one stall and his feet in another. He went up to him and felt him and soon found that he was dead, with his back broken over the upright stone between two of the stalls.

"The yeoman thought it high time to leave the place now, and fled from his farm with all that he could remove. All the live-stock that he left behind was killed by Glam, who then went through the whole glen and laid waste all the farms up from Tongue.

"Thorhall spent the rest of the winter with various friends. No one could go up into the glen with horse or dog, for these were killed at once; but when spring came again and the days began to lengthen, Glam's walkings grew less frequent, and Thorhall determined to return to his homestead. He had difficulty in getting servants, but managed to set up his home again at Thorhall-stead. Things went just as before. When autumn came, the hauntings began again, and now it was the yeoman's daughter who was most assailed, till in the end she died of fright. Many plans were tried, but all to no effect, and it seemed as if all Water-dale would be laid waste unless some remedy could be found.

"All this befell in the days of Grettir, the son of Asmund, who was the strongest man of his day in Iceland. He had been abroad at this time, outlawed for three years, and was only eighteen years of age when he returned. He had been at home all through the autumn, but when the winter nights were well advanced, he rode north to Water-dale, and came to Tongue, where lived his uncle Jökull. His uncle received him heartily, and he stayed there for three nights. At this time there was so much talk about Glam's walkings, that nothing was so largely spoken of as these. Grettir inquired closely about all that had happened, and Jökull said that the stories told no more than had indeed taken place; 'but are you intending to go there, kinsman?' said he. Grettir answered that he was. Jökull bade him not do so, 'for it is a dangerous undertaking, and a great risk for your friends to lose you, for in our opinion there is not another like you among the young men, and "ill will come of ill" where Glam is. Far better it is to deal with mortal men than with such evil spirits.'

"Grettir, however, said that he had a mind to fare to Thorhall-stead, and see how things had been going on there. Jökull replied: 'I see now that it is of no use to hold you back, but the saying is true that "good luck and good heart are not the same"'. Grettir answered: '"Woe stands at one man's door when it has entered another's house". Think how it may go with yourself before the end.'

"'It may be,' said Jökull, 'that both of us see some way into the future, and yet neither of us can do anything to prevent it.'

"After this they parted, and neither liked the other's forebodings.

"Grettir rode to Thorhall-stead, and the yeoman

received him heartily. He asked Grettir where he
was going, who said that he wished to stay there
all night if he would allow him. Thorhall said
that he would be very glad if he would stay, 'but
few men count it a gain to be guests here for long.
You must have heard how matters stand, and I shall
be very unwilling for you to come to any harm on
my account. And even although you yourself escape
safe and sound, I know for certain that you will
lose your horse, for no man that comes here can
keep that uninjured.'

"Grettir answered that there were horses enough to
be got, whatever might happen to this one. Thorhall was delighted that he was willing to stay, and
gave him the heartiest reception. The horse was
strongly secured in an out-house; then they went to
sleep, and that night passed without Glam appearing.

"'Your coming here,' said Thorhall, 'has made a
happy change, for Glam is in the habit of riding the
house every night, or breaking up the doors, as you
may see for yourself.'

"'Then one of two things will happen,' said Grettir; 'either he will not restrain himself for long, or
the hauntings will cease for more than one night. I
shall stay for another night, and see how things go.'

"After this they went to look at Grettir's horse, and
found that he had not been meddled with, so the
yeoman thought that everything was going on well.
Grettir stayed another night, and still the thrall did
not come about them. Thorhall thought that things
were looking brighter, but when he went to look to
Grettir's horse he found the out-house broken up,

the horse dragged outside, and every bone in it broken. He told Grettir what had happened, and advised him to secure his own safety, 'for your death is certain if you wait for Glam'.

"Grettir answered: 'The least I can get for my horse is to see the thrall'. Thorhall replied that it would do him no good to see him, 'for he is unlike anything in human shape; but I am fain of every hour that you are willing to stay here'.

"The day wore on, and when it was bed-time Grettir would not take off his clothes, but lay down on the floor over against Thorhall's bed-closet. He put a thick cloak above himself, buttoning one end beneath his feet, and doubling the other under his head, while he looked out at the hole for the neck. There was a strong plank in front of the floored space, and against this he pressed his feet. The door-fittings were all broken off from the outer door, but there was a hurdle set up instead, and roughly secured. The wainscot that had once stretched across the hall was all broken down, both above and below the cross-beam. The beds were all pulled out of their places, and everything was in confusion.

"A light was left burning in the hall, and when the third part of the night was past Grettir heard loud noises outside. Then something went up on top of the house, and rode above the hall, beating the roof with its heels till every beam cracked. This went on for a long time; then it came down off the house and went to the door. When this was opened Grettir saw the thrall thrust in his head; ghastly big he seemed, and wonderfully huge of feature.

Glam came in slowly, and raised himself up when he was inside the doorway, till he loomed up against the roof. Then he turned his face down the hall, laid his arms on the cross-beam, and glared all over the place. Thorhall gave no sign during all this, for he thought it bad enough to hear what was going on outside.

" Grettir lay still and never moved. Glam saw that there was a bundle lying on the floor, and moved further up the hall and grasped the cloak firmly. Grettir placed his feet against the plank, and yielded not the least. Glam tugged a second time, much harder than before, but still the cloak did not move. A third time he pulled with both his hands, so hard that he raised Grettir up from the floor, and now they wrenched the cloak asunder between them. Glam stood staring at the piece which he held in his hands, and wondering greatly who could have pulled so hard against him. At that moment Grettir sprang in under the monster's hands, and threw his arms around his waist, intending to make him fall backwards. Glam, however, bore down upon him so strongly that Grettir was forced to give way before him. He then tried to stay himself against the seat-boards, but these gave way with him, and everything that came in their path was broken.

" Glam wanted to get him outside, and although Grettir set his feet against everything that he could, yet Glam succeeded in dragging him out into the porch. There they had a fierce struggle, for the thrall meant to have him out of doors, while Grettir saw that bad as it was to deal with Glam inside the house it would be worse outside, and therefore strove with all his might against being carried out. When they came into the porch Glam put forth all his strength, and pulled Grettir close to him. When Grettir saw that he could not stay himself he suddenly changed his plan, and threw himself as hard as he could against the monster's breast, setting both his feet against an earth-fast stone that lay in the doorway. Glam was not prepared for this, being then in the act of pulling Grettir towards him, so he fell backwards and went crashing out through the door, his shoulders catching the lintel as he fell. The roof of the porch was wrenched in two, both rafters and frozen thatch, and backwards out of the house went Glam, with Grettir above him.

" Outside there was bright moonshine and broken clouds, which sometimes drifted over the moon and sometimes left it clear. At the moment when Glam fell the cloud passed off the moon, and he cast up his eyes sharply towards it; and Grettir himself said that this was the only sight he ever saw that terrified him. Then Grettir grew so helpless, both by reason of his weariness and at seeing Glam roll his eyes so horribly, that he was unable to draw his dagger, and lay well-nigh between life and death.

" But in this was Glam's might more fiendish than that of most other ghosts, that he spoke in this fashion: 'Great eagerness have you shown to meet me, Grettir, and little wonder will it be though you get no great good fortune from me; but this I may tell you, that you have now received only half of the strength and vigour that was destined for you if you

had not met with me. I cannot now take from
you the strength you have already gained, but this
I can see to, that you will never be stronger than
you are now, and yet you are strong enough, as
many a man shall feel. Hitherto you have been
famous for your deeds, but henceforth you shall be a
manslayer and an outlaw, and most of your deeds
will turn to your own hurt and misfortune. Outlawed
you shall be, and ever have a solitary life for your
lot; and this, too, I lay upon you, ever to see these
eyes of mine before your own, and then you will think
it hard to be alone, and that will bring you to your
death.'

"When Glam had said this the faintness passed off
Grettir, and he then drew his dagger, cut off Glam's
head, and laid it beside his thigh. Thorhall then
came out, having put on his clothes while Glam was
talking, but never venturing to come near until he
had fallen. He praised God, and thanked Grettir
for overcoming the unclean spirit. Then they set to
work, and burned Glam to ashes, which they placed
in a sack, and buried where cattle were least likely
to pasture or men to tread. When this was done
they went home again, and it was now near daybreak.

"Thorhall sent to the next farm for the men there,
and told them what had taken place. All thought
highly of the exploit that heard of it, and it was the
common talk that in all Iceland there was no man
like Grettir Asnundarson for strength and courage
and all kinds of bodily feats. Thorhall gave him a
good horse when he went away, as well as a fine

suit of clothes, for the ones he had been wearing were all torn to pieces. The two then parted with the utmost friendship.

" Thence Grettir rode to the Ridge in Water-dale, where his kinsman Thorvald received him heartily, and asked closely concerning his encounter with Glam. Grettir told him how he had fared, and said that his strength was never put to harder proof, so long did the struggle between them last. Thorvald bade him be quiet and gentle in his conduct, and things would go well with him, otherwise his troubles would be many. Grettir answered that his temper was not improved ; he was more easily roused than ever, and less able to bear opposition. In this, too, he felt a great change, that he had become so much afraid of the dark that he dared not go anywhere alone after night began to fall, for then he saw phantoms and monsters of every kind. So it has become a saying ever since then, when folk see things very different from what they are, that Glam lends them his eyes, or gives them glam-sight.

" This fear of solitude brought Grettir, at last, to his end."

Ghosts being seldom dangerous to human life, we follow up the homicidal Glam with a Scottish traditional story of malevolent and murderous sprites.

'THE FOUL FORDS' OR THE LONGFORMACUS FARRIER.

" About 1820 there lived a Farrier of the name of Keane in the village of Longformacus in Lammermoor. He was a rough, passionate man, much addicted to swearing. For many years he was farrier to the Eagle or Spottiswood troop of Yeomanry. One day he went to Greenlaw to attend the funeral of his sister, intending to be home early in the afternoon. His wife and family were surprised when he did not appear as they expected and they sat up watching for him. About two o'clock in the morning a heavy weight was heard to fall against the door of the house, and on opening it to see what was the matter, old Keane was discovered lying in a fainting fit on the threshold. He was put to bed and means used for his recovery, but when he came out of the fit he was raving mad and talked of such frightful things that his family were quite terrified. He continued till next day in the same state, but at length his senses returned and he desired to see the minister alone.

"After a long conversation with him he called all his family round his bed, and required from each of his children and his wife a solemn promise that they would none of them ever pass over a particular spot in the moor between Longformacus and Greenlaw, known by the name of 'The Foul Ferds' (it is the ford over a little water-course just east of Castle Shields). He assigned no reason to them for this demand, but the promise was given and he spoke no more, and died that evening.

"About ten years after his death, his eldest son Henry Keane had to go to Greenlaw on business, and in the afternoon he prepared to return home. The last person who saw him as he was leaving the town was the blacksmith of Spottiswood, John Michie. He tried to persuade Michie to accompany him home, which he refused to do as it would take him several miles out of his way. Keane begged him most earnestly to go with him as he said he *must* pass the Foul Fords that night, and he would rather go through hell-fire than do so. Michie asked him why he said he *must* pass the Foul Fords, as by going a few yards on either side of them he might avoid them entirely. He persisted that he *must* pass them and Michie at last left him, a good deal surprised that he should talk of going over the Foul Fords when every one knew that he and his whole family were bound, by a promise to their dead father, never to go by the place.

"Next morning a labouring man from Castle Shields, by name Adam Redpath, was going to his work (digging sheep-drains on the moor), when on the Foul Fords he met Henry Keane lying stone dead and with no mark of violence on his body. His hat, coat, waistcoat, shoes and stockings were lying at about 100 yards distance from him on the Greenlaw side of the Fords, and while his flannel drawers were off and lying with the rest of his clothes, his trousers were on. Mr. Ord, the minister of Longformacus, told one or two persons what John Keane (the father) had said to him on his deathbed, and by degrees the story got abroad. It was this. Keane said that he was returning home slowly after his sister's funeral, looking on the ground, when he was suddenly roused by hearing the tramping of horses, and on looking up he saw a large troop of riders coming towards him two and two. What was his horror when he saw that one of the two foremost was the sister whom he had that day seen buried at Greenlaw! On looking further he saw many relations and friends long before dead; but when the two last horses came up to him he saw that one was mounted by a dark man whose face he had never seen before. He led the other horse, which, though saddled and bridled, was riderless, and on this horse the whole company wanted to compel Keane to get. He struggled violently, he said, for some time, and at last got off by promising that one of his family should go instead of him.

" There still lives at Longformacus his remaining son Robert; he has the same horror of the Foul Fords that his brother had, and will not speak, nor allow any one to speak to him on the subject.

" Three or four years ago a herd of the name of Burton was found dead within a short distance of the spot, without any apparent cause for his death."[1]

[1] Written out from tradition on 24th May, 1852. The name of the afflicted family is here represented by a pseudonym.

CHAPTER XIII.

The Marvels at Fróðá.

THE following tale has all the direct simplicity and truth to human nature which mark the ancient literature of Iceland. Defoe might have envied the profusion of detail; "The large chest with a lock, and the small box," and so on. Some of the minor portents, such as the disturbances among inanimate objects, and the appearance of a glow of mysterious light, "the Fate Moon," recur in modern tales of haunted houses. The combination of Christian exorcism, then a novelty in Iceland, with legal proceedings against the ghosts, is especially characteristic.

THE MARVELS AT FRÓÐÁ.[1]

During that summer in which Christianity was adopted by law in Iceland (1000 A.D.), it happened that a ship came to land at Snowfell Ness. It was a Dublin vessel, manned by Irish and Hebrideans, with few Norsemen on board. They lay there for a long time during the summer, waiting for a favourable wind to sail into the firth, and many people from the

---

[1] From *Eyrbyggja Saga*, chaps. l.-lv. Fróðá is the name of a farm on the north side of Snæfell Ness, the great headland which divides the west coast of Iceland.

Ness went down to trade with them. There was on board a Hebridean woman named Thorgunna, of whom her shipmates said that she owned some costly things, the like of which would be difficult to find in Iceland. When Thurid, the housewife at Fródá, heard of this she was very curious to see the articles, for she was a woman that was fond of show and finery. She went to the ship and asked Thorgunna whether she had any woman's apparel that was finer than the common. Thorgunna said that she had nothing of the kind to sell, but had some good things of her own, that she might not be affronted at feasts or other gatherings. Thurid begged a sight of these, and Thorgunna showed her treasures. Thurid was much pleased with them, and thought them very becoming, though not of high value. She offered to buy them, but Thorgunna would not sell. Thurid then invited her to come and stay with her, because she knew that Thorgunna was well provided, and thought that she would get the things from her in course of time.

Thorgunna answered, " I am well pleased to go to stay with you, but you must know that I have little mind to pay for myself, because I am well able to work, and have no dislike to it, though I will not do any dirty work. I must be allowed to settle what I shall pay for myself out of such property as I have."

Although Thorgunna spoke in this fashion, yet Thurid would have her to go with her, and her things were taken out of the ship; these were in a large chest with a lock and a small box, and both were taken home to Fródá. When Thorgunna arrived there she asked for her bed to be shown her, and was given one in the inner part of the hall. Then she opened up the chest, and took bed-clothes out of it : they were all very beautiful, and over the bed she spread English coverlets and a silken quilt. Out of the chest she also brought a bed-curtain and all the hangings that belonged to it, and the whole outfit was so fine that folk thought they had never seen the like of it.

Then said Thurid the housewife : "Name the price of all your bed-clothes and hangings ".

Thorgunna answered, "I will not lie among straw for you, although you are so stately, and bear yourself so proudly".

Thurid was ill pleased at this, and offered no more to buy the things.

Thorgunna worked at cloth-making every day when there was no hay-making, but when the weather was dry she worked among the dry hay in the home field, and had a rake made for herself which she alone was to use. Thorgunna was a big woman, both broad and tall, and very stout; she had dark eyebrows, and her eyes were close set ; her hair brown and in great abundance. She was well-mannered in her daily life, and went to church every day before beginning her work, but she was not of a light disposition nor of many words. Most people thought that Thorgunna must be in the sixties, yet she was a very active woman.

At this time one Thorir "wooden-leg" and his wife Thorgrima "charm-cheek" were being maintained at Fródá, and there was little love between them and

Thorgunna. The person that she had most ado with was Kjartan, the son of the house; him she loved much, but he was rather cold towards her, and this often vexed her. Kjartan was then fifteen years old and was both big of body and manly in appearance.

The summer that year was very wet, but in the autumn there came dry days. By this time the hay-work at Fródá was so far advanced that all the home field was mown, and nearly the half of it was quite dry. There came then a fine dry day, clear and bright, with not a cloud to be seen in all the sky. Thorodd, the yeoman, rose early in the morning and arranged the work of each one; some began to cart off the hay, and some to put it into stalks, while the women were set to toss and dry it. Thorgunna also had her share assigned to her, and the work went on well during the day. When it drew near to three in the afternoon, a mass of dark clouds was seen rising in the north which came rapidly across the sky and took its course right above the farm. They thought it certain that there was rain in the cloud and Thorodd bade his people rake the hay together; but Thorgunna continued to scatter hers, in spite of the orders that were given. The clouds came on quickly, and when they were above the homestead at Fródá there came such darkness with them that the people could see nothing beyond the home field; indeed, they could scarcely distinguish their own hands. Out of the cloud came so much rain that all the hay which was lying flat was quite soaked. When the cloud had passed over and the sky cleared again, it was seen that blood had fallen amid the rain. In the evening there was a good draught, and the blood soon dried off all the hay except that which Thorgunna had been working at ; it did not dry, nor did the rake that she had been using.

Thurid asked Thorgunna what she supposed this marvel might portend. She said that she did not know, "but it seems to me most likely that it is an evil omen for some person who is present here". In the evening Thorgunna went home and took off her clothes, which had been stained with the blood ; then she lay down in her bed and breathed heavily, and it was found that she was taken with sickness. The shower had not fallen anywhere else than at Fródá.

All that evening Thorgunna would taste no food. In the morning Thorodd came to her and asked about her sickness, and what end she thought it would have. She answered that she did not expect to have any more illnesses. Then she said : "I consider you the wisest person in the homestead here, and so I shall tell you what arrangements I wish to make about the property that I leave behind me, and about myself, for things will go as I tell you, though you think there is nothing very remarkable about me. It will do you little good to depart from my instructions, for this affair has so begun that it will not pass smoothly off, unless strong measures are taken in dealing with it."

Thorodd answered : "There seems to me great likelihood that your forebodings will come true ; and therefore," said he, "I shall promise to you not to depart from your instructions".

"'These are my arrangements," said Thorgunna, "that I will have myself taken to Skálholt if I die of this sickness, for my mind forbodes me that that place will some time or other be the most glorious spot in this land. I know also that by now there are priests there to sing the funeral service over me. So I ask you to have me carried thither, and for that you shall take so much of my property that you suffer no loss in the matter. Of my other effects, Thurid shall have the scarlet cloak that I own, and I give it her so that she may readily consent to my disposing of all the rest as I please. I have a gold ring, and it shall go to the church with me; but as for my bed and bed-hangings, I will have them burned with fire, because they will be of service to no one. I do not say this because I grudge that any one should possess these treasures, if I knew that they would be of use to them; rather am I so earnest in the matter, because I should be sorry for folk to fall into such trouble for me, as I know will be the case if my words are not heeded."

Thorodd promised to do as she asked him, and after this Thorgunna's sickness increased, so that she lay but few days before she died. The body was first taken to the church, and Thorodd had a coffin made for it. On the following day Thorodd had all the bed-clothes carried out into the open air, and made a pile of wood beside them. Then Thurid the housewife came up, and asked what he was going to do with the bed-clothes. He answered that he was to burn them with fire, as Thorgunna had directed him. "I will not have such treasures burned," said Thurid.

Thorodd answered: "She declared strongly that it would not do to depart from what she said". "That was mere jealousy," said Thurid; "she grudged any other person the use of them, and that was why she gave these orders; but nothing terrible will happen though her words are set aside." "I doubt," said he, "whether it will be well to do otherwise than as she charged me."

Then Thurid laid her arms round his neck, and besought him not to burn the furnishings of the bed, and so much did she press him in this that his heart gave way to her, and she managed it so that Thorodd burned the mattresses and pillows, while she took for herself the quilt and coverlets and all the hangings. Yet neither of them was well pleased.

After this the funeral was made ready; trustworthy men were sent with the body, and good horses which Thorodd owned. The body was wrapped in linen, but not sewed up in it, and then laid in the coffin. After this they held south over the heath as the paths go, and went on until they came to a farm called Lower Ness, which lies in the Tongues of Staf-holt. There they asked leave to stay over night, but the farmer would give them no hospitality. However, as it was close on nightfall, they did not see how they could go on, for they thought it would be dangerous to deal with the White River by night. They therefore unloaded their horses, and carried the body into an out-house, after which they went into the sitting-room and took off their outer clothes, intending to stay there over night without food.

The people of the house were going to bed by day-light, and after they were in bed a great noise was heard in the kitchen. Some went to see whether thieves had not broken in, and when they reached the kitchen they saw there a tall woman. She was quite naked, with no clothes whatever upon her, and was busy preparing food. Those who saw her were so terrified that they dared not go near her at all. When the funeral party heard of this they went thither, and saw what the matter was—Thorgunna had come there, and it seemed advisable to them all not to meddle with her. When she had done all that she wanted, she brought the food into the room, set the tables and laid the food upon them. Then the funeral party said to the farmer: " It may happen in the end, before we part, that you will think it dearly bought that you would show us no hospitality". Both the farmer and the housewife answered: " We will willingly give you food, and do you all other services that you require ".

As soon as the farmer had offered them this, Thorgunna passed out of the room into the kitchen, and then went outside, nor did she show herself again. Then a light was kindled in the room, and the wet clothes of the guests were taken off, and dry ones given them in their place. After this they sat down at table, and blessed their food, while the farmer had holy water sprinkled over all the house. The guests ate their food, and it harmed no man, although Thorgunna had prepared it. They slept there that night, and were treated with great hospitality.

In the morning they continued their journey, and

things went very smoothly with them; wherever this affair was heard of, most people thought it best to do them all the service that they required, and of their journey no more is to be told. When they came to Skál-holt, they handed over the precious things which Thorgunna had sent thither: the ring and other articles, all of which the priests gladly received. Thorgunna was buried there, while the funeral party returned home, which they all reached in safety.

At Fródá there was a large hall with a fireplace in the midde, and a bed-closet at the inner end of it, as was then the custom. At the outer end were two store-closets, one on each side; dried fish were piled in one of these, and there was meal in the other. In this hall fires were kindled every evening, as was the custom, and folk sat round these fires for a long while before they went to supper. On that evening on which the funeral party came home, while the folk at Fródá were sitting round the fires, they saw a half-moon appear on the panelling of the hall, and it was visible to all those who were present. It went round the room backwards and against the sun's course, nor did it disappear so long as they sat by the fires. Thorodd asked Thorir Wooden-leg what this might portend. "It is the Moon of Fate," said Thorir, "and deaths will come after it." This went on all that week that the Fate-Moon came in every evening.

The next tidings that happened at Fródá were that the shepherd came in and was very silent; he spoke little, and that in a frenzied manner. Folk were most inclined to believe that he had been bewitched, because he went about by himself, and talked to himself. This went on for some time, but one evening, when two weeks of winter had passed, the shepherd came home, went to his bed, and lay down there. When they went to him in the morning he was dead, and was buried at the church.

Soon after this there began great hauntings. One night Thorir Wooden-leg went outside and was at some distance from the door. When he was about to go in again, he saw that the shepherd had come between him and the door. Thorir tried to get in, but the shepherd would not allow him. Then Thorir tried to get away from him, but the shepherd followed him, caught hold of him, and threw him down at the door. He received great hurt from this, but was able to reach his bed; there he turned black as coal, took sickness and died. He was also buried at the church there, and after this both the shepherd and Thorir were seen in company, at which all the folk became full of fear, as was to be expected.

This also followed upon the burial of Thorir, that one of Thorodd's men grew ill, and lay three nights before he died; then one died after another, until six of them were gone. By this time the Christmas fast had come, although the fast was not then kept in Iceland. The store-closet, in which the dried fish were kept, was packed so full that the door could not be opened; the pile reached nigh up to the rafters, and a ladder was required to get the fish off the top of it. One evening while the folk were sitting round the fires, the fish were torn, but when search was made no living thing could be found there.

During the winter, a little before Christmas, Thorodd went out to Ness for the fish he had there; there were six men in all in a ten-oared boat, and they stayed out there all night. The same evening that Thorodd went from home, it happened at Fródá, when folk went to sit by the fires that had been made, that they saw a seal's head rise up out of the fireplace. A maid-servant was the first who came forward and saw this marvel; she took a washing-bat which lay beside the door, and struck the seal's head with this, but it rose up at the blow and gazed at Thorgunna's bed-hangings. Then one of the men went up and beat the seal, but it rose higher at every blow until it had come up above the fins; then the man fell into a swoon, and all those who were present were filled with fear. Then the lad Kjartan sprang forward, took up a large iron sledge-hammer and struck at the seal's head; it was a heavy blow, but it only shook its head, and looked round. Then Kjartan gave it stroke after stroke, and the seal went down as though he were driving in a stake. Kjartan hammered away till the seal went down so far that he beat the floor close again above its head, and during the rest of the winter all the portents were most afraid of Kjartan.

Next morning, while Thorodd and the others were coming in from Ness with the fish, they were all lost out from Enni; the boat and the fish drove on shore there, but the bodies were never found. When the news of this reached Fródá, Kjartan and Thurid invited their neighbours to the funeral banquet, and the ale prepared for Christmas was used for this purpose. The first evening of the feast, however, after the folk had taken their seats, there came into the hall Thorodd and his companions, all dripping wet. The folk greeted Thorodd well, thinking this a good omen, for at that time it was firmly believed that drowned men, who came to their own funeral feast, were well received by Rán, the sea-goddess; and the old beliefs had as yet suffered little, though folk were baptised and called Christians.

Thorodd and his fellows went right along the hall where the folk sat, and passed into the one where the fires were, answering no man's greeting. Those of the household who were in the hall ran out, and Thorodd and his men sat down beside the fires, where they remained till they had fallen into ashes; then they went away again. This befel every evening while the banquet lasted, and there was much talk about it among those who were present. Some thought that it would stop when the feast was ended. When the banquet was over the guests went home, leaving the place very dull and dismal.

On the evening after they had gone, the fires were kindled as usual, and after they had burned up, there came in Thorodd with his company, all of them wet. They sat down by the fire and began to wring their clothes; and after they had sat down there came in Thorir Wooden-leg and his five companions, all covered with earth. They shook their clothes and scattered the earth on Thorodd and his fellows. The folk of the household rushed out of the hall, as might be expected, and all that evening they had no light nor any warmth from the fire.

Next evening the fires were made in the other hall, as the dead men would be less likely to come there ; but this was not so, for everything happened just as it had done on the previous evening, and both parties came to sit by the fires.

On the third evening Kjartan advised that a large fire should be made in the hall, and a little fire in another and smaller room. This was done, and things then went on in this fashion, that Thorodd and the others sat beside the big fire, while the household contented themselves with the little one, and this lasted right through Christmas-tide.

By this time there was more and more noise in the pile of fish, and the sound of them being torn was heard both by night and day. Some time after this it was necessary to take down some of the fish, and the man who went up on the pile saw this strange thing, that up out of the pile there came a tail, in appearance like a singed ox-tail. It was black and covered with hair like a seal. The man laid hold of it and pulled, and called on the others to come and help him. Others then got up on the heap, both men and women, and pulled at the tail, but all to no purpose. It seemed to them that the tail was dead, but while they tugged at it, it flew out of their hands taking the skin off the palms of those who had been holding it hardest, and no more was ever seen of the tail. The fish were then taken up and every one was found to be torn out of the skin, yet no living thing was to be found in the pile.

Following upon this, Thorgrima Charm-cheek, the wife of Thorir Wooden-leg, fell ill, and lay only a little while before she died, and the same evening that she was buried she was seen in company with her husband Thorir. The sickness then began a second time after the tail had been seen, and now the women died more than the men. Another six persons died in this attack, and some fled away on account of the ghosts and the hauntings. In the autumn there had been thirty in the household, of whom eighteen were dead, and five had run away, leaving only seven behind in the spring.

When these marvels had reached this pitch, it happened one day that Kjartan went to Helga-fell to see his uncle Snorri, and asked his advice as to what should be done. There had then come to Helga-fell a priest whom Gizurr the white had sent to Snorri, and this priest Snorri sent to Fródá along with Kjartan, his son Thord, and six other men. He also gave them this advice, that they should burn all Thorgunna's bed-hangings and hold a law court at the door, and there prosecute all those men who were walking after death. He also bade the priest hold service there, consecrate water, and confess the people. They summoned men from the nearest farms to accompany them, and arrived at Fródá on the evening before Candlemas, just at the time when the fires were being kindled. Thurid the housewife had then taken the sickness after the same fashion as those who had died. Kjartan went in at once, and saw that Thorodd and the others were sitting by the fire as usual. He took down Thorgunna's bed-hangings, went into the hall, and carried out a live coal from the fire: then all the bed-gear that Thorgunna had owned was burned.

After this Kjartan summoned Thorir Wooden-leg, and Thord summoned Thorodd, on the charge of going about the homestead without leave, and depriving men of both health and life; all those who sat beside the fire were summoned in the same way. Then a court was held at the door, in which the charges were declared, and everything done as in a regular law court; opinions were given, the case summed up, and judgment passed. After sentence had been pronounced on Thorir Wooden-leg, he rose up and said: "Now we have sat as long as we can bear". After this he went out by the other door from that at which the court was held. Then sentence was passed on the shepherd, and when he heard it he stood up and said: "Now I shall go, and I think it would have been better before". When Thorgrima heard sentence pronounced on her, she rose up and said: "Now we have stayed while it could be borne". Then one after another was summoned, and each stood up as judgment was given upon him; all of them said something as they went out, and showed that they were loath to part. Finally sentence was passed on Thorodd himself, and when he heard it, he rose and said: "Little peace I find here, and let us all flee now," and went out after that. Then Kjartan and the others entered and the priest carried holy water and sacred relics over all the house. Later on in the day he held solemn service, and after this all the hauntings and ghost-walkings at Fródá ceased, while Thurid recovered from her sickness and became well again.

CHAPTER XIV.

*Spiritualistic Floating Hands.   Hands in Haunted
    Houses.   Jerome Cardan's Tale.   "The Cold
    Hand."   The Beach-comber's Tale.   "The Black
    Dogs and the Thumbless Hand."   The Pakeha
    Maori and "The Leprous Hand".   "The Hand of
    the Ghost that Bit."*

HANDS ALL ROUND.

NOTHING was more common, in the *séances* of Home,
the "Medium," than the appearance of "Spirit
hands". If these were made of white kid gloves,
stuffed, the idea, at least, was borrowed from ghost
stories, in which ghostly hands, with no visible
bodies, are not unusual. We see them in the
Shchapoff case, at Rerrick, and in other haunted
houses. Here are some tales of Hands, old or new.

THE COLD HAND.

[Jerome Cardan, the famous physician, tells the
following anecdote in his *De Rerum Varietate*, lib. x.,
93. Jerome only once heard a rapping himself, at
the time of the death of a friend at a distance. He
was in a terrible fright, and dared not leave his room
all day.]

A story which my father used often to tell: " I was
brought up," he said, "in the house of Joannes

Resta, and therein taught Latin to his three sons; when I left them I supported myself on my own means. It chanced that one of these lads, while I was studying medicine, fell deadly sick, he being now a young man grown, and I was called in to be with the youth, partly for my knowledge of medicine, partly for old friendship's sake. The master of the house happened to be absent; the patient slept in an upper chamber, one of his brothers and I in a lower room, the third brother, Isidore, was not at home. Each of the rooms was next to a turret; turrets being common in that city. When we went to bed on the first night of my visit, I heard a constant knocking on the wall of the room.

"'What is that?' I said.

"'Don't be afraid, it is only a familiar spirit,' said my companion. 'They call them *follets*; it is harmless enough, and seldom so troublesome as it is now: I don't know what can be the matter with it.'

"The young fellow went to sleep, but I was kept awake for a while, wondering and observing. After half an hour of stillness I felt a thumb press on my head, and a sense of cold. I kept watching; the fore-finger, the middle finger, and the rest of the hand were next laid on, the little finger nearly reaching my forehead. The hand was like that of a boy of ten, to guess by the size, and so cold that it was extremely unpleasant. Meantime I was chuckling over my luck in such an opportunity of witnessing a wonder, and I listened eagerly.

"The hand stole with the ring finger foremost

over my face and down my nose, it was slipping into my mouth, and two finger-tips had entered, when I threw it off with my right hand, thinking it was uncanny, and not relishing it inside my body. Silence followed and I lay awake, distrusting the spectre more or less. In about half an hour it returned and repeated its former conduct, touching me very lightly, yet very chilly. When it reached my mouth I again drove it away. Though my lips were tightly closed, I felt an extreme icy cold in my teeth. I now got out of bed, thinking this might be a friendly visit from the ghost of the sick lad upstairs, who must have died.

"As I went to the door, the thing passed before me, rapping on the walls. When I was got to the door it knocked outside; when I opened the door, it began to knock on the turret. The moon was shining; I went on to see what would happen, but it beat on the other sides of the tower, and, as it always evaded me, I went up to see how my patient was. He was alive, but very weak.

"As I was speaking to those who stood about his bed, we heard a noise as if the house was falling. In rushed my bedfellow, the brother of the sick lad, half dead with terror.

"'When you got up,' he said, 'I felt a cold hand on my back. I thought it was you who wanted to waken me and take me to see my brother, so I pretended to be asleep and lay quiet, supposing that you would go alone when you found me so sound asleep. But when I did not feel you get up, and the cold hand grew to be more than I could bear, I hit out to push your hand away, and felt your place empty—but warm. Then I remembered the *follet*, and ran upstairs as hard as I could put my feet to the ground : never was I in such a fright ! '

" The sick lad died on the following night."

Here Carden the elder stopped, and Jerome, his son, philosophised on the subject.

Miss Dendy, on the authority of Mr. Elijah Cope, an itinerant preacher, gives this anecdote of similar familiarity with a *follet* in Staffordshire.

" Fairies ! I went into a farmhouse to stay a night, and in the evening there came a knocking in the room as if some one had struck the table. I jumped up. My hostess got up and ' Good-night,' says she, ' I'm off '. ' But what was it ? ' says I. ' Just a poor old fairy,' says she ; ' Old Nancy. She's a poor old thing ; been here ever so long ; lost her husband and her children ; it's bad to be left like that, all alone. I leave a bit o' cake on the table for her, and sometimes she fetches it, and sometimes she don't."

THE BLACK DOG AND THE THUMBLESS HAND.

[Some years ago I published in a volume of tales called *The Wrong Paradise*, a paper styled " My Friend the Beach-comber ". This contained genuine adventures of a kinsman, my oldest and most intimate friend, who has passed much of his life in the Pacific, mainly in a foreign colony, and in the wild New Hebrides. My friend is a man of education, an artist, and a student of anthropology and ethnology. Engaged on a work of scientific research, he has not committed any of his innumerable adventures, warlike or wandering, to print. The following "yarn" he sent to me lately, in a letter on some points of native customs. Of course the description of the Beach-comber, in the book referred to, is purely fictitious. The yarn of "The Thumbless Hand" is here cast in a dialogue, but the whole of the strange experience described is given in the words of the narrator. It should be added that, though my friend was present at some amateur *séances*, in a remote isle of the sea, he is not a spiritualist, never was one, and has no theory to account for what occurred, and no belief in "spooks" of any description. His faith is plighted to the theories of Mr. Darwin, and that is his only superstition. The name of the principal character in the yarn is, of course, fictitious. The real name is an old but not a noble one in England.]

" Have the natives the custom of walking through fire ? " said my friend the Beach-comber, in answer to a question of mine. "Not that I know of. In fact the soles of their feet are so thick-skinned that they would think nothing of it."

"Then have they any spiritualistic games, like the Burmans and Maories? I have a lot of yarns about them."

" They are too jolly well frightened of bush spirits to invite them to tea," said the Beach-comber. "I knew a fellow who got a bit of land merely by whistling up and down in it at nightfall.[1] They think

---

[1] Fact.

spirits whistle. No, I don't fancy they go in for *séances*. But we once had some, we white men, in one of the islands. Not the Oui-ouis " (native name for the French), " real white men. And that led to Bolter's row with me."

" What about ? "

" Oh, about his young woman. I told her the story; it was thoughtless, and yet I don't know that I was wrong. After all, Bolter could not have been a comfortable fellow to marry."

In this opinion readers of the Beach-comber's narrative will probably agree, I fancy.

" Bad moral character ? "

" Not that I know of. Queer fish; kept queer company. Even if she was ever so fond of dogs, I don't think a girl would have cared for Bolter's kennel. Not in her bedroom anyway."

" But she could surely have got him to keep them outside, however doggy he was ? "

" He was not doggy a bit. I don't know that Bolter ever saw the black dogs himself. He certainly never told me so. It is that beastly Thumbless Hand, no woman could have stood it, not to mention the chance of catching cold when it pulled the blankets off."

" What on earth are you talking about ? I can understand a man attended by black dogs that nobody sees but himself. The Catholics tell it of John Knox, and of another Reformer, a fellow called Smeaton. Moreover, it is common in delirium tremens. But you say Bolter didn't see the dogs ? "

" No, not so far as he told me, but I did, and other

fellows, when with Bolter. Bolter was asleep; he didn't see anything. Also the Hand, which was a good deal worse. I don't know if he ever saw it. But he was jolly nervous, and he had heard of it."

The habits of the Beach-comber are absolutely temperate, otherwise my astonishment would have been less, and I should have regarded all these phenomena as subjective.

"Tell me about it all, old cock," I said.

"I'm sure I told you last time I was at home."

"Never; my memory for yarns is only too good. I hate a chestnut."

"Well, here goes! Mind you I don't profess to explain the thing; only I don't think I did wrong in telling the young woman, for, however you account for it, it was not nice."

"A good many years ago there came to the island, as a clerk, *un nommé* Bolter, English or Jew."

"His name is not Jewish."

"No, and I really don't know about his breed. The most curious thing about his appearance was his eyes: they were large, black, and had a peculiar dull dead lustre."

"Did they shine in the dark? I knew a fellow at Oxford whose eyes did. Chairs ran after him."

"I never noticed; I don't remember. 'Psychically,' as you superstitious muffs call it, Bolter was still more queer. At that time we were all gone on spirit-rapping. Bolter turned out a great acquisition, 'medium,' or what not. Mind you, I'm not saying Bolter was straight. In the dark he'd tell you what you had in your hand, exact time of your watch, and so on. I didn't take stock in this, and one night brought some photographs with me, and asked for a description of them. This he gave correctly, winding up by saying, 'The one nearest your body is that of ———.'"

Here my friend named a person well known to both of us, whose name I prefer not to introduce here. This person, I may add, had never been in or near the island, and was totally unknown to Bolter.

"Of course," my friend went on, "the photographs were all the time inside my pocket. Now, really, Bolter had some mystic power of seeing in the dark."

"Hyperæsthesia!" said I.

"Hypercriticism!" said the Beach-comber.

"What happened next *might* be hyperæsthesia—I suppose you mean abnormal intensity of the senses —but how could hyperæsthesia see through a tweed coat and lining?"

"Well, what happened next?"

"Bolter's firm used to get sheep by every mail from ———, and send them regularly to their station, six miles off. One time they landed late in the afternoon, and yet were foolishly sent off, Bolter in charge. I said at the time he would lose half the lot, as it would be dark long before he could reach the station. He didn't lose them!

"Next day I met one of the niggers who was sent to lend him a hand, and asked results.

"'Master,' said the nigger, 'Bolter is a devil! He sees at night. When the sheep ran away to right or left in the dark, he told us where to follow.'"

"He *heard* them, I suppose," said I.

"Maybe, but you must be sharp to have sharper senses than these niggers. Anyhow, that was not Bolter's account of it. When I saw him and spoke to him he said simply, 'Yes, that when excited or interested to seek or find anything in obscurity the object became covered with a dim glow of light, which rendered it visible'. 'But things in a pocket.' 'That also,' said he. 'Curious isn't it? Probably the Röntgen rays are implicated therein, eh?'"

"Did you ever read Dr. Gregory's *Letters on Animal Magnetism?*"

"The cove that invented Gregory's Mixture?"

"Yes."

"Beast he must have been. No, I never read him."

"He says that Major Buckley's hypnotised subjects saw hidden objects in a blue light—mottoes inside a nut, for example."

"Röntgen rays, for a fiver! But Bolter said nothing about seeing *blue* light. Well, after three or four *séances* Bolter used to be very nervous and unwilling to sleep alone, so I once went with him to his one-roomed hut. We turned into the same bed. I was awakened later by a noise and movement in the room. Found the door open; the full moon streaming in, making light like day, and the place full of great big black dogs—well, anyhow there were four or five! They were romping about, seemingly playing. One jumped on the bed, another rubbed his muzzle on mine! (the bed was low, and I slept outside). Now I never had anything but love for dogs of any kind, and as—*n'est-ce pas?*—love casts out fear, I simply got up, turned them all out, shut the door, and turned in again myself. Of course my idea was that they were flesh and blood, and I allude to physical fear.

"I slept, but was anew awakened by a ghastly feeling that the blanket was being dragged and creeping off the bed. I pulled it up again, but anew began the slow movement of descent.

"Rather surprised, I pulled it up afresh and held it, and must have dozed off, as I suppose. Awoke, to feel it being pulled again ; it was slipping, slipping, and then with a sudden, violent jerk it was thrown on the floor. *Il faut dire* that during all this I had glanced several times at Bolter, who seemed profoundly asleep. But now alarmed I tried to wake him. In vain, he slept like the dead; his face, always a pasty white, now like marble in the moonlight. After some hesitation I put the blanket back on the bed and held it fast. The pulling at once began and increased in strength, and I, by this time thoroughly alarmed, put all my strength against it, and hung on like grim death.

"To get a better hold I had taken a turn over my head (or perhaps simply to hide), when suddenly I felt a pressure outside on my body, and a movement like fingers—they gradually approached my head. Mad with fear I chucked off the blanket, grasped a Hand, gazed on it for one moment in silent horror, and threw it away! No wonder, it was attached to no arm or body, it was hairy and dark coloured, the fingers were short, blunt, with long, claw-like nails, and it was minus a thumb! Too frightened to get up

I had to stop in bed, and, I suppose, fell to sleep again, after fresh vain attempts to awaken Bolter. Next morning I told him about it. He said several men who had thus passed the night with him had seen this hand. 'But,' added he, 'it's lucky you didn't have the big black dogs also.' *Tableau!*

"I was to have slept again with him next night to look further into the matter, but a friend of his came from —— that day, so I could not renew the experiment, as I had fully determined to do. By-the-bye, I was troubled for months after by the same feeling that the clothes were being pulled off the bed.

"And that's the yarn of the Black Dogs and the Thumbless Hand."

"I think," said I, "that you did no harm in telling Bolter's young woman,"

"I never thought of it when I told her, or of her interest in the kennel; but, by George, she soon broke off her engagement."

"Did you know Manning, the Pakeha Maori, the fellow who wrote *Old New Zealand?*"

"No, what about him?"

"He did not put it in his book, but he told the same yarn, without the dogs, as having happened to himself. He saw the whole arm, and *the hand was leprous.*"

"Ugh!" said the Beach-comber.

"Next morning he was obliged to view the body of an old Maori, who had been murdered in his garden the night before. That old man's hand was the hand he saw. I know a room in an old house in England where plucking off the bed-clothes goes on, every now and then, and has gone on as long as the present occupants have been there. But I only heard lately, and *they* only heard from me, that the same thing used to occur, in the same room and no other, in the last generation, when another family lived there."

"Anybody see anything?"

"No, only footsteps are heard creeping up, before the twitches come off."

"And what do the people do?"

"Nothing! We set a camera once to photograph the spook. He did not sit."

"It's rum!" said the Beach-comber. "But mind you, as to spooks, I don't believe a word of it."[1]

THE GHOST THAT BIT.

The idiot Scotch laird in the story would not let the dentist put his fingers into his mouth, "for I'm feared ye'll bite me". The following anecdote proves that a ghost may entertain a better founded alarm on this score. A correspondent of *Notes and Queries* (3rd Sept., 1864) is responsible for the narrative, given "almost *verbatim* from the lips of the lady herself," a person of tried veracity.

"Emma S——, one of seven children, was sleeping alone, with her face towards the west, at a large house near C——, in the Staffordshire moorlands. As she had given orders to her maid to call her at an early hour, she was not surprised at being awakened between three and four on a fine August morning in 1840 by a sharp tapping at her door, when in spite of a "thank you, I hear," to the first and second raps, with the third came a rush of wind, which caused the curtains to be drawn up in the centre of the bed. She became annoyed, and sitting up called out, " Marie, what are you about ? "

Instead, however, of her servant, she was astonished to see the face of an aunt by marriage peering above and between the curtains, and at the same moment— whether unconsciously she threw forward her arms, or whether they were drawn forward, as it were, in a vortex of air, she cannot be sure—one of her thumbs was sensibly pressed between the teeth of the apparition, though no mark afterwards remained on it. All this notwithstanding, she remained collected and unalarmed; but instantly arose, dressed, and went downstairs, where she found not a creature stirring.

Her father, on coming down shortly afterwards, naturally asked what had made her rise so early; rallied her on the cause, and soon afterwards went on to his sister-in-law's house, where he found that she had just unexpectedly died. Coming back again, and not noticing his daughter's presence in the room, in consequence of her being behind a screen near the fire, he suddenly announced the event to his wife, as being of so remarkable a character that he could in no way account for it. As may be anticipated, Emma, over-hearing this unlooked-for *dénouement* of her dream, at once fell to the ground in a fainting condition.

On one of the thumbs of the corpse was found a mark as if it had been bitten in the death agony.[1]

---

[1] This story should come under the head of " Common Deathbed Wraiths," but, it is such an uncommon one !

We have now followed the "ghostly" from its germs in dreams, and momentary hallucinations of eye or ear, up to the most prodigious narratives which popular invention has built on bases probably very slight. Where facts and experience, whether real or hallucinatory experience, end, where the mythopœic fancy comes in, readers may decide for themselves.